The Biography Famous

The Biography Famous

An Intellectual Autobiography within a Biography

ALFRED G. MEYER

ARRANGED AND EDITED
BY STEFAN G. MEYER

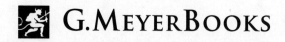 G.MEYERBOOKS

When I read the book, the biography famous
And is this, then, (said I,) what the author calls a man's life?
And so will some one, when I am dead and gone, write my life
(As if any man really knew aught of my life;
Why, even I myself, I often think, know little or nothing of my real life;
Only a few hints—a few diffused, faint clues and indirections,
I seek, for my own use, to trace out here.)

— Walt Whitman, *Leaves of Grass*

CONTENTS

PREFACE

TOWARD THE END of a distinguished writing and teaching career in the field of political science, my father wrote two books that were never published. The first was a biography of Friedrich Engels, and the second was a memoir that looked back on his life and career. The reaction of prospective publishers to the Engels biography was that it was not rigorous enough from a scholarly point of view, yet too academic to appeal to a general readership. The memoir suffered from a similar problem. What my father produced was a lively and entertaining document, full of sharply drawn and humorous observations of the people he met during his life, yet overall dominated by his intellectual curiosity rather than his feelings. In short, he had written an intellectual autobiography-in-brief, which was illuminating to his friends and associates, but did not give a full account of the true stirrings that animated his nature.

In going over my father's papers some months after my mother's death, and several years after his, I came upon the Engels manuscript and noticed the quotation from Whitman's *Leaves of Grass* that he had intended for the frontispiece. The fragment of poetry not only suggested the honor that he intended to do Engels in the writing of his biography ("And so will someone when I am dead and gone write my life"), but also the similar tribute that he might wish to enjoy at the hands of a future writer who happened to stumble upon the records of his own life and find them worth exploring. The poem fragment also captured the sense of frustration that he obviously felt in attempting to write about himself ("When I myself often think I know little or nothing of my real life"). Finally, it suggested a way that a prospective editor might approach the retrospective task of helping him to sum up his life after his death, by making use of the "few hints" and "diffused faint clews and indirections" that he himself had left behind.

So I conceived a plan to merge the two manuscripts, by taking the chapters of his memoir that focused on his career as a political scientist and teacher, and juxtaposing them with the Engels manuscript. The idea was to add greater fullness and depth to his own intellectual self-portrait through the biography, for whatever the limitations of the latter as an example of scholarship it clearly was a document that illuminated my father's interests and passions. My father saw a great deal of himself in Engels, and also much of what he wished he could be, or could have been. He was in love with Engels's intellectual curiosity, with his brashness and nerve, and perhaps most of all with the luck or intuitive perception that allowed him to place himself at the very center of quickening historical developments.

The biography of Engels, in turn, cannot be fully appreciated without understanding the context in which it was written. My father's deep sympathy with the student counterculture of the 60s, his wrangles with the bureaucracy of academia, and even his view of himself as a feminist are mirrored in the Romantic underpinnings of Engels's political philosophy.

Missing from this assembled work are the early chapters of my father's memoir that dealt with his childhood in Nazi Germany, his emigration to the United States, and his enlistment and service in the U.S. Army during World War II, as well as the final chapters that dealt with his home and family life, recreation, and prolonged illness, all of which raise personal issues that are outside the scope of this project.

His autobiographical narrative therefore picks up in the fall of 1945, after he had returned to the U.S. from the Western Front and received his honorable discharge. This is the point at which he embarked on his academic career, and it is therefore the appropriate position at which to place the starting strokes of his intellectual portrait. His introduction to the Engels biography has been inverted, and now serves as the conclusion. Finally, I have written a brief postscript in which I attempt to tie some of the threads between the two pieces of writing together. I hope that this arrangement of two texts answers in some oblique way the question posed by Whitman: "And is this then (said I) what the author calls a man's life?"

Stefan G. Meyer
Ann Arbor, Michigan
March 2006

Chapter 1

Graduate Studies

FOR ME, NOW discharged from the service, the time had come to make some decisions of my own. I had no doubt that I wanted to go to college. As for a field of study, I took the line of least resistance. My knowledge of Russian, acquired during the war, still made me somewhat of a rare bird in the United States, and so I decided to study Slavic languages and literature—but where? Still in my uniform, I paid a visit to Samuel H. Cross, the chair and only tenured professor of the Slavic Department at Harvard. He received me in his office in Widener Library, a room lined with books and journals from floor to ceiling. I asked him whether he remembered me from the Army Specialized Training Program (ASTP), and he said he did.

I then told him I would like to enter Harvard College and asked how I might go about that. I was still a recent immigrant and very green, especially concerning the American system of higher education. "One fills in an application form," he said dryly, whereupon I hemmed and hawed and timidly asked whether in view of my good performance in the ASTP Harvard might accept me as a sophomore or even as a junior. He looked at me, dialed a phone number—it was that of Payson Wilde, the Dean of the Graduate School. "Payson," he said, "I have a young man here who wants to enter Graduate School. I want you to give him most favorable consideration." With that, he sent me over to 24 Quincy Street, the office of the Graduate School. I filled in an application blank and two weeks later received a letter of acceptance.

Why was I accepted so readily? My academic credentials were unorthodox, to put it mildly, but they may have looked good to the graduate admissions committee. I had received outstanding grades in the

5

ASTP and a seemingly solid German *Gymnasium* education, even though truncated by a year. Four-and-a-half years of army service may have added to my learning experience, or so they may have thought. Like many other veterans, I was a few years older than ordinary college graduates, hence likely to be a bit more mature, more eager to learn, and equally eager to finish the degree program. I would not be a financial burden to Harvard because under the GI Bill of Rights, the government would pay my tuition plus a monthly stipend and a book allowance. It was a very generous law. Some of my fellow students abused it by buying not only assigned textbooks but also books that were merely recommended. For them, the GI Bill of Rights laid the foundation for their professional library. In later years, I had cause to wonder why the veterans of World War II were treated so lavishly, those of the Korean conflict much less generously, and those of the Vietnam War with disgusting shabbiness.

I began my graduate studies in February 1946 and finished my course work in August 1947, after I had passed my oral exam for the doctorate. In short, I took courses in five semesters, including two summer terms. In summer term courses, professors as well as students tended to take it rather easy because of the heat. I enrolled in the Slavic Department, taking third-year Russian, Russian history, and a seminar on problems in contemporary world politics. Russian history was taught very well, and the seminar on world politics allowed me to pursue a stimulating topic largely on my own. The instructor in the Russian language course was an interesting and eccentric man, but a poor teacher. The students in the seminar were a lively group with a wide range of political opinions, which generated much good discussion. I also took an independent reading course, but really had little idea what to read and where to start. The professor left me to my own devices, trusting that I would make good use of my time, but I did not. At the end of the first semester I realized that I was not interested in Slavic languages, literature or linguistics, but rather in history and politics, and without any difficulty transferred to a doctoral program in the Government Department. There, I took courses for another twelve months.

In retrospect, I learned little in these courses. What I did learn came not primarily from courses and seminars but from discussions with fellow students outside of class. They included some very bright people from many different countries and backgrounds. Some of them made illustrious careers in public life. The faculty advisor to whom I was assigned was very kind and hospitable. The parties he gave for his graduate students in his spacious Belmont home were delightful. William Yandell Elliott—that was his name—was a Southern Democrat of a type that predominated in American politics at the time. Born and raised in Eastern Tennessee, he had attended Vanderbilt University and then gone to Oxford as a Rhodes scholar. An early supporter of the New Deal, he had broken with Franklin Roosevelt over his attempt to pack the Supreme Court, but still had lots of good friends in Washington.

I remember a heated discussion he had with a graduate student during a seminar session. The student had suggested that the race problem in the United States would be solved through intermarriage, and Elliott passionately declared 'miscegenation' to be abominable. All his life he had had some cause that he pursued with vigor and tenacity. In the 1920's, it had been his realization that fascism presented a clear and present danger. In the 1930's, it had been his conviction that there were flaws in the U.S. constitution, which might be remedied by our adopting some elements of British government. Now, in the 1940's, his preoccupation was with the perils posed by Marxism and communism, and this fear caused him to drift further to the Right politically.

Professor Elliott welcomed me as his student and encouraged me to write a doctoral dissertation about the founding father of communism, V. I. Lenin. Unfortunately, my thesis did not turn into the anti-Communist indictment he obviously had expected, and he therefore did not promote my career any further. I found that academia in the U.S. functioned very much like an old boys' network in which senior people make the crucial decisions affecting their disciples' careers. In the end, Bill Elliott found a student who was much more in tune with him politically, and whom he had spotted when the student was still an undergraduate. I once met this young man when Elliott called me into his office, saying, "Al, I want you to meet Henry. He is very bright and will be going places." Henry Kissinger indeed owed the rocket-like start of his career to this professor.

When at the end of three terms in the Government Department, I declared myself ready for the dreaded oral exam my adviser should have told me that I was out of my mind. This was especially true in view of the fact that I offered myself for examination in a field in which I had done no coursework whatever. Instead, he scheduled the exam, and I passed by the skin of my teeth. If I were to sum up my experience as a graduate student, I would be tempted to say that I started to learn something mostly after obtaining my Ph.D., and what forced me to learn was the need to prepare courses. There is a Latin saying that I have adopted as my own motto: *Docendo discimus*—we learn by teaching.

My introduction to teaching came soon. When I transferred to the Government Department, I was offered a Teaching Fellowship. Recipients of such fellowships either assisted various professors in courses with large enrollment, or they served as tutors—academic advisors to undergraduate students in the Honors program. Advising them meant seeing each 'tutee' fairly regularly, discussing their course work with them, trying to stimulate their interest in related courses or subjects, and supervising their work on a Senior Honors thesis.

Even before the new academic year had started, one Senior Honors student to whom I had been assigned as a tutor came to me for advice. He was a brilliant student, and socially successful as well. He had managed to enter a prestigious club—not one of the most exclusive ones, but a distinguished one, nonetheless. His dormitory was Eliot House, which at that time was the dorm preferred by the social elite. He was also the commanding officer of the Naval ROTC unit at Harvard. In the summer prior to his last year in college, he had participated in a summer cruise on a U.S. Navy vessel. While on that cruise, he had been invited by one of the sailors to a homosexual encounter. The invitation had been a trap. When he entered the designated room, he was greeted by a group of jeering sailors. The matter became a scandal, which, of course, was reported to the Dean at Harvard. Now, Harvard was going to throw him out unceremoniously.

I considered it my duty as his tutor to come to his defense, and I made an appointment with the Dean of the College of Arts and Sciences. He received me politely, heard my plea on behalf of the student, and then remarked that he would not even consider retaining him. Harvard, he said in so many words, already had a reputation as a place for wimps. Given such a reputation, it could not afford to keep a student who had even the slightest brush with homosexuality. I often wondered what became of this young man. This incident reminded me of another young man I once met. In early 1942, I was doing guard duty at the Presidio of Monterey—guard duty of an unusual kind. A soldier had been tried for homosexual activity. He was convicted and sentenced to life imprisonment. He was now in the post guardhouse awaiting shipment to the military prison in Fort Leavenworth, and, because he was believed to be suicidal, had to be guarded around the clock. He was a gaunt young man with an intelligent face who talked pleasantly with those who guarded him. During the night, while he slept peacefully, I found it difficult to stay awake and alert, sitting by his bunk with my rifle at the ready.

When I entered graduate school, Russian studies hardly existed in the United States. At Berkeley, Columbia, Harvard, and the University of Chicago, perhaps in other places as well, there were a few individual professors who taught courses on Russian history, literature, or geography. The Slavic Department at Harvard had only one tenured member, however. Once one moved into the field of Soviet studies—the post-revolutionary era—the pickings got even slimmer. There were professors at Columbia and Harvard who had studied law or administration in the USSR, but at Harvard, the professor teaching Russian history stopped when he came to the revolution of 1917. At that point, he said, Russian history had come to an end, and politics had begun.

For anyone interested in theory and ideology, the situation was even bleaker. I doubt whether a student could have taken a course in Marxism at any American university. Philosophers claimed that Marx was not a philosopher. Most economists argued that he had not been an economist, or at least not an economist whom one needed to take seriously, and specialists in political or sociological thought said similar things. To the best of my knowledge, the course on Marxism I taught at Harvard in 1951 or 1952 was the first such course in an American institution of higher learning.

I couldn't learn the subject from anyone. My interest in the history of social thought had been awakened, however. My knowledge of Russian naturally directed that interest toward a specialization in Soviet ideology, and my advisor encouraged me to go in this direction. Since Soviet ideology supposedly was based on the writings of Engels and Marx, it seemed appropriate that my study of it should also begin with a study of Marxism. Since no one at Harvard seemed to have sufficient knowledge of it to serve as my tutor, I had to study it on my own through independent, largely unsupervised reading. A book I published in 1956 was based on this attempt to come to grips with the basic propositions of Marxism. While it contained little that I had later cause to repudiate, in retrospect I felt that it showed how inadequately I had surveyed the relevant literature. Of course, had I really taken the time to read everything I should have, I would never have managed to finish writing the book.

My academic career was largely shaped by the Cold War. Many different views could be advanced regarding when the Cold War began. For instance, one might argue that it began around 1943, when George Kennan, then an official at the U.S. Embassy in Moscow, began sending message after message to President Roosevelt warning him that, once Germany had been defeated, our next enemy would be the Soviet Union. At the very same time, the Kremlin alerted Soviet leaders to the likelihood that, once Germany was defeated, the Soviet Union would face a hostile Western alliance.

One could go farther back, to 1919, when anti-Communist sentiments were high in the United States, the Attorney General staged raids on left-wing organizations, and veterans of World War I founded the American Legion to combat all forms of left-wing ideology. One might even go back to November 1917, the time of the October revolution. Czarist Russia, in the eyes of the American public, had been the evil empire, because its government was as far removed from the ideas of American constitutional democracy as any European government could be. When czarism fell and was replaced by the Provisional Government, a wave of popular good will hailed the dawning of democracy in that country. This good will turned into deep hostility, however, when the Provisional Government was overthrown, signaling the beginning of the Soviet regime.

Instead of moving back from 1943, one could also move forward in time and suggest that the Cold War began in May 1945, when Germany surrendered, or one could point to August 1945, when President Truman twice displayed the awesome might of our atomic weaponry. One could also cite the summer of 1946, when Secretary of State Byrnes in his speech in Stuttgart hinted that U.S. policy ought to aim at the reconstruction of West Germany as a bulwark against the Communist menace.

From the point of view of American academia, the Cold War began around 1946 or 1947. This beginning was signified by the attention that, for the first time, American universities were paying to things Russian and Soviet. At Columbia University, a Russian Institute was founded, and a year later Harvard followed suit with the creation of its Russian Research Center. The Rockefeller Foundation sponsored research fellowship in Russian studies at the Hoover Institution on the campus of Stanford University. I received one of these fellowships and, in early September of 1947, my wife Eva and I were off to California, a trip we made by car.

We had thought of buying a used hearse to get us there. That would have been quite reasonable. Hearses usually were sturdy cars, such as Cadillacs or Chryslers. They rarely if ever were driven at top speed, which meant that their motors had not been abused. They were also roomy, and on a long trip coast to coast, two young vagabonds could easily stow all their belongings, including two sleeping bags and a camping stove, in them to save on motel and restaurant bills. We actually looked at one or two such vehicles, but my mother-in-law was horrified by the idea of her daughter traveling in a hearse, and we then bought another used car—a real lemon, as it turned out. It got us there, however. For the first few days or weeks, we lived in a rented room, but then found a charming little house a few miles away from the campus, where we spent the remainder of the academic year.

Stanford University is located on a peninsula that stretches from San Jose in the South to San Francisco and the Golden Gate in the North. Today that peninsula is densely settled almost up to the crest of the picturesque mountain chain that runs along its middle. In 1947, however, it was still primarily orchard country, its apricot, peach, and almond groves a miracle of fragrant pink and white blossoms in the spring. Along the crest of the mountain ridge, one could drive through stands of redwood trees, and on the Western shore, where artichokes were the principal cash crop there were beaches with wild surf and very few visitors. The Stanford campus was pretty, with eucalyptus and palm groves and its own little lake. Right next to the Hoover Institution there was an outdoor swimming pool, for men only, where it was customary to swim and sunbathe in the nude. Most of the time the weather was mild and sunny. The fog that often enveloped San Francisco came down to Stanford only rarely if at all.

The Hoover Institution was located in a phallus-shaped tower jokingly referred to as "Hoover's last erection." It housed the thousands of books, pamphlets, and documents that Herbert Hoover's employees had amassed in the years immediately following World War I, when Hoover was sent to Europe on famine and refugee relief missions. Since then, much more material on wars and revolutions had been added, including many crates of documents recently obtained in China. The curator of these documents, Mary Wright, was a splendid scholar, outgoing, energetic, and warm-hearted, exceedingly bright, and politically to the left of center. She later taught modern Chinese history at Yale University but died very young.

The top floor of the Hoover tower contained the former President's own offices, where he worked, assisted by Mr. Wilbur, his former Secretary of the Interior. One day in the spring of 1948, the entire staff of the institute gathered in the lobby of the building to greet Herbert Hoover on his birthday. He was sitting in a wheelchair when he came out of the elevator. Someone made a speech in his honor, and while the speaker droned on, Hoover sat sunk in his chair, looking old and tired. When it came time for him to reply, however, he rose, straightened up, immediately looked twenty years younger, and gave an off-the-cuff thank-you speech. He had obviously learned to conserve his energies in very effective fashion. It was an impressive performance.

The Hoover Institution today is a bastion of political conservatism, or at least it has that reputation. That is not, however, what it was in 1947. To be sure, the curator of the Russian collection may have been conservative, but the Director of the Institution was not. And the Rockefeller fellows who were there together with me ranged all over the political spectrum and included at least one man whose ideas were close to those of the Communist Party. Nobody seemed to mind. There was little interaction between the several fellows. Each one did his or her research undisturbed by the others. I was given an office and access to the stacks of the library, and I spent my days reading the collected works of V. I. Lenin, trying to find out what that man was about, how his ideas cohered, and what kind of sense one could make of them. I did not know of any work that had tried to explain Lenin's political thought systematically.

To write a book about a political leader's ideas, however, one does not merely read his writings and speeches, even if they are as richly annotated as they were in the second Russian edition of his collected works— twenty or thirty thick volumes in small print. Ideas arise and are developed in several contexts, and to understand what a politician is talking about one has to know this context well. This includes the issues and problems that his speeches, pamphlets and books address, the political culture that has shaped the language, the habits, and the priorities of the man and his party. It also includes the subculture within which he grew up and against which he may be rebelling, as well as the leader's personal background and previous experiences that may have shaped his or her character and view of the world. Of course, having studied Russian history, I was familiar with some of this context, but by no` means sufficiently. If the book that came out of this study turned out to be a pioneering work, that was, in retrospect, somewhat of a miracle.

Reading all those many thick tomes of Lenin's work from cover to cover, in Russian, was not only stupid, but also unpleasant. Lenin's writing style was that of a radical orator—angry, repetitive, and dogmatic. It was full of invective for anyone not agreeing with him, and ultimately very boring. In time, I did get bored, and boredom gave me intellectual indigestion. I had mountains of notes on his ideas and pronouncements, but I did not know how to organize them into anything coherent. That got to be so bothersome that in the end I laid all of it aside and began to read unrelated material, just to give my mind a vacation. One day I was reading a book by George Sorel, when I made myself some notes that turned out to fill an entire page. When I looked over what I had written, it became apparent that I had written an outline for my book—not the outline that I ultimately used, but at least something to start with. The ice had been broken.

Eva was not very happy at Stanford. She had never been away from Cambridge for as much as an entire year and she was homesick. She may also have been bored, with no job of her own, and only a tiny house to keep. Sometime during the year, she got herself a dog, but that was not enough to keep her busy and happy. Eventually, she found work as a research assistant on an interesting project conceived and run by a famous political scientist, Harold Lasswell, and two young political sociologists that oversaw the actual management of the project. It was a comparative study of political culture in different nations based on so-called 'content analysis' of newspaper editorials—an example of the application of 'behavioral studies' or 'positivism' to political science.

For many decades, students of human behavior and human interaction—economists, sociologists, and historians—had looked with envy and admiration at the natural sciences, especially physics. There they saw branches of learning that were rigorously objective and the results of this scientific objectivity were spectacular. On the basis of discoveries made in physics, chemistry, geology and biology, the human species had been able to harness incredible amounts of energy and erect a technology that routinely performed miracles every day. Instant communication over the entire globe was commonplace, as was travel at supersonic speed, wonder drugs, and synthetic materials built to specification. Science had made many people believe that there are no limits to the human potential for reshaping the world in our image and doing away with material want.

It was generally accepted that this science, which had given us almost god-like powers, depended on certain rigorous methods of inquiry that had been recognized and refined over the centuries. Central to this scientific method was the importance of measurement, hence of expressing all reality in terms of measurable quantities and of making all reality fit into mathematical formulas. A second element of scientific method was that of laboratory research, which isolated the phenomena to be measured from outside influences. Still another trend in the development of scientific method was that of breaking reality down to its smallest possible components, referred to as miniaturization.

Positivism in the social science disciplines was based on the conviction that these methods of rigorous scientific inquiry could and must be applied to the study of human behavior and human interaction—to economics, politics, history, social relations, and psychology. Harold Lasswell and Daniel Lerner were pioneers of this kind of positivism. In the decades after World War II, it dominated most American social science, and the development of computers and other data-processing techniques gave it a tremendous boost, for now researchers were able to handle volumes of quantified data that earlier would have totally overwhelmed them. For the cause of its popularity, I borrowed a term (in altered form) from the vocabulary of Sigmund Freud: 'physics envy,' by which I meant envy of the rigorous method of the 'hard' sciences. I became convinced that the emphasis on these methods was significantly impoverishing the social sciences.

I was first introduced to the behavioral mode in social science when I was a graduate student at Harvard. There the core of the doctoral program was the history of political theory: a survey of philosophic systems from the ancient Greeks to the 19th century, with certain key contributors singled out: Plato, Aristotle, St. Augustine, St. Thomas Aquinas, Machiavelli, Hobbes, Locke and Rousseau. They were the Great Teachers, those who had asked the eternally important questions about the purposes of government, the duties of citizenship, the bases of authority and legitimacy, human rights, and the advantages or disadvantages of different government institutions and styles. The history of political thought was thus supposed to be a study of the great ideas that had supposedly shaped our civilization.

This approach, of course, ignored the extent to which civilizations, including ours, had been shaped by human passions, most of them combative and destructive, backed up by bad ideas about human failings and differences, but enveloped in a halo of 'noble' principles. This would turn the history of political thought into a history of fraud, deception, illusion, and self-deception. It would turn the history of political ideas into a history of political ideologies.

Other courses at Harvard analyzed political institutions and their functioning—state, city, town, and county government, the interplay between various government organizations, the presidency, various federal departments and agencies, and the Congress. Similar institutional analysis was provided for various government systems in Europe and for international politics and international law. Political thought, taught this way, could stimulate fruitful reflection about citizenship, leadership, authority and obedience, rights and duties. It could also, however, turn into an antiquarian concern with issues that had little relevance to contemporary problems. Indeed, it could be a deliberate flight into an intellectual ivory tower. Then all political theory turned into a self-seeking and ultimately futile concern to make the world safe for intellectuals.

The institutional-legal approach also appeared arid as soon as one realized that actual behavior deviates from formal rules. Why study international law when the great powers consistently disregarded it? Why learn about the President's authority over the federal bureaucracy when the U.S. Army Corps of Engineers, with the help of its friends in Congress, could repeatedly defy his will? Why should one be interested in the role of the French *Préfet*, or the precise relationship between the British Labour Party and the trade union leadership, if these various political institutions were studied purely in terms of their formal arrangements?

In the 1930's, some students of politics had rebelled against the traditional ways of studying the subject. Their pioneers, teaching at the University of Chicago, called themselves behaviorists. They wanted to make the study of politics scientific. Their model was not actually physics, but classical economics, which they thought had scientific validity, and the ability to predict economic trends.

Economics does deal with quantifiable data—volumes of production and consumption, prices for goods, money and labor, turnover and depreciation. It studies the relationship between these, and is able to express these relations in mathematical terms. On the basis of experience, hunch, bias, and other motives, economists also generate theories about the grand interrelation of all these things, and, guided by theory, formulate hypotheses that can then be tested. In micro-economic research, discrete economic events are isolated and tested as if under laboratory conditions. While some of the hypotheses may try to identify cause-and-effect relationships, most—a bit more modestly—seek to find recurrent correlation between different variables, and probability theory determines whether a correlation is significant or random.

When I was a graduate student, the first beginnings of the behavioral revolution in political science were felt at Harvard. Some of my fellow graduate students began to dismiss the Department's preoccupation with political theory as unscientific. They were interested in 'facts,' not in 'values,' they said. I myself found some of their arguments plausible, although I had not thought about the problem sufficiently to have mature views.

Harold D. Lasswell had studied at Chicago and had become one of the most ardent advocates of behavioral science. If the study of politics could be pursued with scientific rigor, we would be able to predict toward what forms of society the major powers were moving. The scientific method was based on quantification. Instead of gathering impressions, we needed hard and fast evidence, and while impressions were subjective, data had to be objective and replicable. Since the world of politics was complex and the amount of data infinitely great, we had to employ sampling techniques.

Lasswell was no mere methodological faddist. He was a man deeply committed to a democratic and egalitarian ethic. He distinguished between progressive and reactionary trends in politics, seeking to promote the former and to prevent the latter. One of the first people to warn against totalitarian trends in American politics, he was politically on the Left. That is easily forgotten because most of his disciples wound up more in the mainstream of American politics and ideology. In contrast to them, Lasswell had absorbed the writings of Marx as well as of Freud and sought to synthesize them. He seems to have believed that liberation from oppression and exploitation should be combined with sexual liberation. At the same time, his appraisal of the real world of politics seems to have been somewhat cynical. He was convinced that all government, even the most democratic type, was ruled by elite groups, and he stressed the seductive and deceptive power of words, the importance of propaganda in all politics, and the irrationality and gullibility of the masses. He was fascinated by the power of language. In the sermon, the lawyer's argument, and the rhetoric of the politician, words became tools to sway minds and attitudes. Hence, he was interested in symbols, their manipulation and their effect.

During his entire career as a student of politics, Lasswell had been interested in propaganda and its use in political life, and he was convinced that by studying propaganda we would be able to predict political behavior. The choice of propaganda 'symbols', he apparently believed, not only revealed the intentions of those that emitted the messages, but determined the actions or inclinations of those that received them. What distinguished Lasswell's study of propaganda from other such studies was the quantitative approach. He broke propaganda messages down into their smallest component parts, words that he called 'symbols'. Symbols were categorized according to the message they carried—democratic or authoritarian, critical or laudatory, referring to specific 'values' like wealth, prestige, or security. He then counted the changing frequency with which key symbols were used, placed the resultant numbers into statistical tables, and these tables supposedly revealed trends of developing political attitudes. When extrapolated to the future, the statistical curves suggested where the countries under study were headed. The entire procedure was called content analysis, although the content of communications was precisely what this method of word counting neglected.

Content analysis had been applied to the slogan issued each year by the Soviet Communist Party for its May Day celebrations. It had also been used on the propaganda statements of the Communist International. These were ritualistic statements made on regularly recurrent occasions, and therefore they were ideally suited as material for tracing shifts in the Kremlin's priorities between 1918 and 1943. This research, therefore, did no more than provide 'scientific' confirmation of trends long recognized by careful observers of Soviet and *Comintern* politics—that the Soviet Union had become conservative and isolationist, and that the Communist International was a total failure, and its programmatic statements had become increasingly unrealistic. Content analysis of this material not only proved the obvious, but it was wasted effort, because these obvious insights were unpopular among the political, academic, and journalistic elite of the United States, to say nothing about the general reading public. Therefore this type of work had no influence.

The project set up by Lasswell at the Hoover Institution, and for which Eva did some research work, was called RADIR, meaning Revolution and the Development of International Relations. It was an exercise in content analysis. What was to be investigated was the changing frequency of democratic words ('symbols') appearing in the editorials of establishment ('elite') newspapers in different countries between 1890 and 1950. Democratic symbols were words symbolizing shared power, mutual respect, equality of wealth, acquisition of skills, or the common good. When the study appeared in print, its conclusions were disturbing. They suggested a growing polarization of the world and trends toward militarization and totalitarianism everywhere. Could that, however, not have been predicted on evidence other than a mechanical sampling of words?

When Eva discussed her work with me, we both agreed that what she was asked to record was indeed mechanical and mindless—key words or phrases that fitted into any of the categories Lasswell had established. If the word 'war' occurred, that was taken to be an indication of belligerence on the part of the editorial writer. Words, however, are never used standing alone. Instead, it is the context that gives the word positive, negative, ambivalent, or valueless connotation. Content analysis as practiced in this study neglected context and therefore overlooked the evaluation behind the words. In this way, the 'content' of the editorials being studied was disregarded. What was being studied was empty form. There were many other things wrong with this project, such as the choice of newspapers deemed to be representative, the exclusion from the study of any attempt to show the effect of these symbols on the reader, and the neglect of the style in which the editorials were written. When I communicated my reservations to one of the two men whom Lasswell had left in charge of the project, he asked me to put my criticism in writing. He even paid me a few dollars for it. Some years later, I was pleased to discover that Lasswell himself seemed to agree with much of my criticism.

Lasswell had many young disciples who took from him his quantification methods and his elitist view of politics. They did not, however, adopt his breadth of vision, his humanist attitudes and radical critique of trends in American society, and certainly not his habit of questioning his own views and methods. Behaviorism in general, with its emphasis on quantification and mathematical modeling became the dominant mode of studying politics. Its preoccupation with rigorous methods of inquiry induced many of its advocates to spend much effort and money on irrelevant, trivial stuff just because it lent itself to measurement. In particular, there was a tremendous growth in the study of electoral behavior which, given the basic similarity of the two major parties in the United States, and the practical lack of any meaningful alternative, represented a preoccupation with political shadow-boxing.

Mathematical precision in the study of politics was misplaced not only because what was quantifiable often was much less interesting than what did not lend itself to quantification, but also because to concentrate on what was measurable often meant asking the wrong questions. More generally, no terms in the study of human relations were well defined. Words such as democracy, equality, legitimacy, welfare, and the like, had multiple meanings. Further, in human relations context was everything. Finally, all social science had to begin with some theories that were not provable, such as the rational actor theory, the theory of human depravity—or, conversely, of innate human goodness—or the theory of development or progress. The assumptions behind these theories colored all our studies, including those done with rigorous behavioral methods.

My life's work—the study of the Soviet Union and of communist regimes in general—made me sensitive to the issue about the validity of the positivist approach. The reasons for my sensitivity were several. First, the Soviet Union until the late 1950's was absolutely inaccessible, and even after that, access to it was severely limited. Western scholars could not travel everywhere, could not freely talk to Soviet citizens, and did not have access to governmental records. Simply because of this, some of my colleagues seriously advised doctoral students not to study Soviet or communist political systems. Since they could not freely gather quantifiable data there, they would be able to produce only worthless impressionistic studies.

The general assumption among political scientists in the United States, and indeed in the Western world, was that the Soviet Union and its client states were unique and that therefore one could not, or should not, apply to it social science models or concepts used to study other political systems. Those of us who tried to integrate Sovietology with general social science by using its language were accused of equating communist states with Western societies. Totalitarianism, we were told, was a unique and novel phenomenon, and to describe totalitarian societies in terms borrowed from theories about Western societies was an attempt to play down this uniqueness and novelty. Moreover, since the concepts and models specific to the study of Western societies were specific to democratic societies and therefore had moral implications, their use in the study of communist systems implied a shameful betrayal of democratic values. Some critics of Sovietology called this alleged betrayal the theory of moral equivalency.

Sovietologists were trained to be aware of contexts and connections. They were alert to the inseparability of such factors as geography, economics, history, literature, religion, culture, social structure, and even language. In order to study Soviet politics properly, they had to have some knowledge from all or many of these disciplines. In the eyes of the strict methodologists, that made them appear as dilettantes. In many academic departments, 'area specialists,' devoted to studying a particular region of the world, often found themselves on the margin of their profession, not promoted to tenured rank, nor rewarded with high salaries. Later, after the collapse of the Soviet Union and its European client states, they were criticized for not predicting these events. Now that the successor states are open to any Western scholar who wishes to do research there, the positivists have begun to rush in to do their survey work. Their ignorance of the relevant languages, history, geography, and so forth, does not seem to trouble them.

A joyous event occurred just at the time I had completed my doctoral dissertation—the birth of our son, Stefan Garris. Garris was the name of a dear friend of ours, the tenor John Garris, whose career with the Metropolitan Opera had taken a promising turn until he was murdered while on tour in the South. Whenever he happened to be in Boston, he and his male companion would visit us. He would sing entire Schubert song cycles while accompanying himself on the. Shortly before Stefan's birth, the Metropolitan Opera had performed in Atlanta, and the next morning John Garris was found dead in an alley. By giving his name to our son, we set him a monument in our hearts. The initial, G, however, was also to remind me of my father, Gustav, who perished in the Holocaust.

Once Eva came home from the hospital with the baby, there were several forces that clashed in our home: the baby's, his mother's, the pediatrician's, my own humble opinion, and that of my mother-in-law, whose strong will won out over all the others. The clash of wills and opinions led to such friction between Eva and her mother that we decided to flee the field of battle, take a vacation, and let Grandma take care of the baby for a while. During that vacation, in a farmhouse near Peterboro, NH, the baby's sister was conceived. She was born a year and a week after her brother, and was named Vera.

My dissertation was finished. The formal defense seemed little more than a formality. In the summer of 1950, I got my Ph.D. The Russian Research Center kept me on as a post-doctoral fellow and assistant to the Director, and in my last year there, my title was changed to Assistant Director. That was a purely cosmetic change; my duties were no different from what they had been before. I taught a couple of courses at Harvard. One was on Marxism and the other was on totalitarian governments, both fascist and communist. Some of the students I had in these classes had interesting careers, subsequently; having studied with me did not seem to have permanently handicapped them. I enjoyed this work, and I was pleased to be a member of the faculty in so distinguished a university.

Whenever I had lunch at the Harvard faculty club, I would order the specialty of the house—horse steak with mushroom sauce. It had been introduced into the menu during the war and turned out to be so popular that the chef continued to serve it. In the lobby of the club one could see a large lithograph by Daumier showing two men dining at a horsemeat restaurant. One of them seemed barely able to choke his meal down. Women were allowed into the faculty club, but had to use a back entrance.

Clyde Kluckhohn was then working, together with Alfred Kroeber, on a book in which these two cultural anthropologists sought to survey all the meanings and connotations that the term 'culture' had assumed.

Because I was fluent in German and Russian, he asked me to do some research assistant work for him. I was to survey the many uses of the term in German, Russian, and Soviet writings. I did as told and, after some weeks or months, handed him two lengthy reports on the matter. Kluckhohn and Kroeber liked these reports so much that, without any alteration, they printed them as appendices to their book.

I learned about this only after the book came out. It was the first time that I had seen my name in print as the author of anything, and was therefore something of a milestone. Years later, an anthropology professor asked me whether I was THE Alfred G. Meyer. I knew exactly what he meant, because in those years the book on culture was must reading for all cultural anthropologists.

The 1947-8 academic year ended. It was summer, and by the end of August, my fellowship at the Hoover Institution was coming to its end, and with it the monthly stipend and library privileges. I do not remember having made any effort to find employment for the next year; if I did, I was unsuccessful; if I didn't, it was because I knew nothing about the academic job market, and nobody had found it necessary to enlighten me about it. By the beginning of August, however, I must have started to worry about it.

Then, in the middle of the month, I received a job offer for an instructorship at a distinguished liberal arts college in New England. The offer came from the chairman of its political science department, who had been a guest professor at Harvard, and I had taken some course work from him. The salary he offered me was $2700 a year. I immediately sat down to type a letter of acceptance when I received a wire or phone message offering me a job as Graduate Student Fellow with the newly created Russian Research Center at Harvard University. The pay was slightly higher. My duties would be to complete my doctoral dissertation and to participate in the Center's discussions and seminars. It seemed a good deal, and I accepted it.

In subsequent years, I often wondered whether that had not been a mistake. Had I accepted the teaching position, I would have received tenure within a few years, and that would have meant lifetime security at a very fine school. My job worries would have been over forever, unless I was an academic entrepreneur who used his current position merely as a jumping-off point for a more attractive one. I was never such an entrepreneur and paid a price for this. Thus, job worries stayed with me for another decade.

To Eva's delight, we moved back to Cambridge. Just at that moment, her parents moved to Vermont because her father had taken a job as a professor of economics at Middlebury College. We therefore could move into their old apartment and did not have to hunt for housing. At the Russian Research Center, then located in an old frame house on Quincy Street, I was given a desk in an office that I shared with another student fellow, and then I concentrated on writing my dissertation.

The Russian Research Center had been created in early 1948 on the basis of a generous grant from the Carnegie Corporation, whose President, John Gardner, took a personal interest in it and made his weight felt in its management. When Gustav Hilger came to the Center to look for a co-author, Gardner insisted on interviewing every candidate for this job himself.

Hilger, born in Moscow, the son of a German industrialist, had spent virtually all his life, except for a few years as an engineering student, in Russia. He knew the country and its culture well and actually spoke German with a slight Russian accent. When, in 1919, the German republic resumed diplomatic relations with Soviet Russia, the German embassy in Moscow hired him as someone familiar with the country. Except for a very brief interlude, he stayed at the Embassy until the time of the German invasion in June 1941, rising to the rank of Embassy Counselor. Although many of his views on international politics, and on politics in general, were naive and unsophisticated, his reputation among the members of the Moscow diplomatic corps was high. He had, after all, dealt personally with virtually every major communist leader— Lenin, Trotsky, Stalin, Bukharin, Radek, Chicherin, Rakovski, and many others. He could be a fascinating *raconteur* about his experiences with these fabled people. Of course, he also had been associated with interesting personalities in the German Foreign Service in the Weimar republic, as well as in the Third Reich.

After the war, when the Soviet Union wanted to try him as a war criminal, he went into hiding and his friends from their Moscow days, George Kennan and Charles ("Chip") Bohlen, secretly spirited him to the United States. They set him up in an apartment in Washington and hired him as a consultant to the Department of State, where he wrote position papers on past and present issues. They also urged him to write his memoirs, but he correctly argued that he did not have the talent to write a book and needed an academic person to do it for him or with him. Kennan then went to the Carnegie Corporation to get funding for such a project, and John Gardner referred him to the Russian Research Center. Thus, Hilger came to Cambridge to pick a co-author for his memoirs. I was one of the graduate students he interviewed, and he and I liked each other, even though (or, perhaps, because) I identified myself to him, from the very beginning, as being to the left of center politically. When John Gardner interviewed me and asked for my opinion of Hilger, I voiced some opinions that he thought disrespectful, and he strongly opposed my appointment as Hilger's co-author. The Director of the Center, Clyde K. M. Kluckhohn, managed to make him acquiesce in my appointment, however.

Kluckhohn, a cultural anthropologist, had done important fieldwork among the Navajos of New Mexico. During the war, he, together with Ruth Benedict, had studied Japanese culture for the OSS. Several of the senior fellows at the Center had had similar connections. Barrington Moore, perhaps the sharpest mind I have ever met, had worked there, and so, if I am not mistaken, had Alex Inkeles. One of the non-academic godfathers of the Center, known as "General" Osborne, had been with the Psychological Warfare branch of the War Department. When "the General" came to inspect the Center, we were warned to be on our best behavior.

From the very beginning, the hidden connections to the Federal government were felt in the form of ideological screening. One of the graduate student fellows, a historian, turned out to have had left-wing associations, and quickly lost his appointment. The Assistant Director, a brilliant historian, was removed from his job because during the 1948 election he supported Henry Wallace and his Progressive party. He got an appointment at Stanford, but ultimately returned to Harvard.

In 1952, when I was serving as Assistant Director of the Russian Research Center, Clyde Kluckhohn once called me into his office for a confidential chat. "Once in a while," he said, "I send a memo to all the members of the Center in which I suggest that we discuss a specific problem." Of course, I had seen such memos and responded to them. "Well," he continued, "such suggestions of mine usually come from the local field office of the CIA, who phone me. 'Our uncle in Washington,' they say, 'would like to know what you people think about such and such a problem.'" Kluckhohn told me that during the next semester he was going to be on leave, and the CIA agents wanted someone appointed to be their contact person. "Would you mind serving in that function?" he asked.

"Not at all," I said, "but I guarantee you that I will flunk clearance."

He did nominate me, and came to me weeks later in considerable embarrassment to tell me that I had indeed flunked clearance. He then nominated a senior professor of impeccable ideological credentials, who also flunked clearance and was furious about it. The third nominee finally passed muster.

In the earlier decades of the post-war era, many Americans regarded people engaged in Russian and Soviet studies with suspicion. In 1949, I was chatting with a neighbor-an officer on leave from the Navy to pursue graduate studies at MIT. He asked me what I was doing, and I told him I was writing my doctoral dissertation. He asked on what topic I was writing, and I told him it was on Lenin. Whereupon he looked at me with a cold stare and said, "Well, I guess I disagree with you a hundred percent." A year or two earlier, I had given a talk on some aspect of Russian history or Soviet government at the International Student Center in Cambridge. During the discussion after my presentation, a student asked me whether I would like to live in Russia. When I said that I would not, she asked, "Then why do you talk about it so much?" Similarly, in the 1950's, students in my courses on Marxism or Soviet politics made it clear that they did not want their parents to know that they were taking such courses.

At the same time, those engaged in these studies believed that they were serving an important national intelligence function. So, obviously, thought those that had created and financed institutes like the Russian Research Center. So also thought the students who nicknamed my courses the 'Know thy enemy' courses. Indeed, in the 1950's, many of my students were politically conservative, conventional in dress and appearance, and often came to class in their ROTC uniforms. Ten or fifteen years later, the radical students of the counter-culture would replace them.

At the Russian Research Center, we took it for granted that our scholarly work was in the national interest. That was made even clearer a few years after the Center had been founded. In the early 1950's, it launched an ambitious project that sought to apply up-to-date social science survey methods to large numbers of former Soviet citizens then living in the Western world, primarily in Germany and the United States. That project was 'target research' financed and sponsored by the U.S. Air Force. They, quite understandably, were interested in our exploring the strengths and weaknesses of Soviet society. Simultaneously, the U.S. Navy was financing a similar project headed by Margaret Mead. They wanted her and her colleagues to apply psychological and anthropological techniques to predict Soviet behavior under stress. A typical question they wanted answered was how Soviet submarine crews might be expected to react when bombarded by depth charges.

Opponents of the cold war have often assumed that research sponsored under such auspices would be politically tainted, and that its results would therefore be invalid. Anyone familiar with the studies produced by the Air Force project, however, will know that these studies in fact went against the grain of generally accepted cold-war images about the Soviet Union. The works produced on the basis of thousands of interviews with former Soviet citizens actually dispelled much ideological nonsense about the nature of Soviet totalitarianism. The totalitarian 'model' of the USSR had been sketched out by George

Kennan's famous article, in which he suggested the heavy fist of dictatorship had so atomized the society that the social structure had virtually been destroyed.

Kennan further suggested that no significant groups in the society had benefited or were benefiting from Soviet rule, and that the Party would therefore be able to maintain itself in power only if it engaged in foreign adventures. According to Kennan, the compulsion to expand into other lands was built into the Soviet system. Ideas of this kind were supplemented by books like those of Nathan Leites, who argued that the leaders of the Soviet Union were, in essence, suffering from collective paranoia and were therefore likely to respond only to force, not to reason.

The survey research done by the Russian Research Center for the U.S. Air Force demonstrated the falsity of these and other images linked to the totalitarian model. It discovered widespread resistance to party policy, evasion of party rules, and a variety of informal arrangements that people made under the cover of formal rules and regulations. It showed that this 'informal' behavior often looked like inefficiency, but just as often allowed the entire system to function. It discovered groups of the population who had benefited from Soviet rule, and found out, rather to the scholars' surprise, that even some of the sharpest critics of the regime had some good things to say about it, and felt they had shared some of its benefits. In short, the interview project had discovered an actual society beneath the hard crust of the party dictatorship.

Just how unpopular some of the findings of the project were with the American public, saturated as it was with cold-war propaganda, is illustrated by a response that Clyde Kluckhohn received when he reported some of the results of the survey in a lecture at a Harvard alumni club. He told the alumni that many of the former Soviet citizens had been interviewed twice, the first time in a German displaced persons camp, the second time after immigrating to the United States. Among those interviewed twice, the trend had been to voice disappointment in the United States, after being here for a while. Kluckhohn was booed for giving this information and was unable to continue his lecture.

Just because the government sponsored research did not mean the results were flawed. The military, after all, was interested in facts, not ideology. As they used to tell us at Camp Ritchie: "Your Commanding General is not interested in the enemy's intentions, but only in his capabilities." The honesty of the work done by the Air Force project should have been compared to the dishonesty of some of the work done at the other end of Massachusetts Avenue. Sometime around 1950, a Center for International Studies had been set up at MIT. Some of its leading scholars, as well as the financing of the Center, came from the CIA. One of its projects was to produce a book on the nature of the Soviet system. Its chief author, possessing no specialized knowledge of that subject, hired a couple of young historians to do the basic research and, in effect, draft the book for him. Most of these drafts were done by a good friend of mine, a solid scholar and, today, a widely acknowledged authority on the history of communist revolutions and their regimes. To his dismay, my friend discovered that the principal author was rewriting his drafts in such a fashion as to give all the material a Cold War twist, thus systematically transforming his scholarship into ideology. Although a listing as a principal contributor to the book would have given my friend's academic career a tremendous boost, he did not wish to be identified with such intellectual dishonesty, and therefore asked that his name not be mentioned in it.

A board of directors who were senior professors at Harvard governed the Russian Research Center. Most of them, however, were not specialists in Russian or Soviet studies. Besides Kluckhohn, the most influential member of this board seems to have been the then eminent sociologist, Talcott Parsons. Members of this board reviewed all book manuscripts produced by Center staff personnel. The Center had an agreement with Harvard University Press, according to which the Press would publish any book produced at the Center as long as the board of directors gave it their imprimatur. In the case of my books, Professor Parsons seems to have written the decisive positive opinions, although in his recommendations, he made judgments about them that made very little sense to me.

The working staff of the Center included a number of senior fellows who also held professorial appointments in various departments of the university—Merle Fainsod in the Department of Government, Alexander Gerschenkron in Economics, Harold J. Berman in the Law School, and others. They may also have held membership on the board of directors at one time or another. Most of the graduate student fellows, all of them working on their dissertations, and graduate student assistants who were not yet at that stage also did genuine pioneer work in Soviet (and related) studies and became leading scholars in their fields. They included Gregory Grossman, Franklyn Holzman, and Joe Berliner in economics, and Robert V. Daniels, Hans Rogger, M. Kamil Dziewanowski, Mimi Haskell Berlin, and Richard Pipes in history. Others included Marc Field and H. Kent Geiger in sociology, Adam Ulam and Zbigniew K. Brzezinski in political science, and Raymond A. Bauer in social psychology. When I took a seminar in 19th-century Russian history with Professor Michael Karpovich, the class included Don Treadgold and Nicholas Ryazanovsky, Marc Raeff, Leopold Haimson, Richard Pipes, Robert MacMaster, and Stephen Fischer-Galati—a stellar group of people, all of whom became important in their field.

All people in the Center—from the Director to the clerical employees—were on a first-name basis, which made me feel uneasy, because I had been reared in the spirit of strict Prussian rules of politeness. I don't think I ever managed to call Merle Fainsod or Talcott Parsons by their first names, but that was my hang-up, not theirs. Altogether, the Center was a remarkable community of very bright people, most of whom earned great distinction in various areas of Russian, Soviet, or Chinese studies (for some years, Chinese Studies, not yet having its own center, was an appendage of the Russian Research Center). After the Center moved to a larger building, that had once been a dormitory for the wealthiest Harvard undergraduates—a so-called gold coast dorm—each of us had his or her own spacious office and a typewriter. Lunch was served every day at the Center, so that we could meet informally to share ideas and information.

The Center had its own library with a growing accumulation of microfilms. Whenever any of us among the senior faculty members or graduate students wished to present some of his or her work to the whole group, a seminar would be held. Similar seminars frequently featured interesting people from the outside, whether scholars from other universities or people who had inside information, such as former Soviet citizens or former activists in communist parties. There was plenty of stimulation, discussion, and disagreement. We all learned a lot from each other and, since Russian and Soviet studies were so new to the American academic scene, we thought ourselves intellectual pioneers mapping out hitherto unknown territory. (Many of us were unfamiliar with the mapping that had earlier been done by German scholarship, both in the Weimar period and under Hitler, and by Trotskyite, Bukharinist, and Menshevik critics of the USSR.)

Former communist leaders or functionaries who had turned to the far right politically frequently gave presentations at the Center. Ruth Fischer, for instance, was a former General Secretary of the German Communist Party, now collaborating with the House Committee on Un-American Activities, before which she testified against various people, including her two brothers, Gerhart and Hanns Eisler. She would talk to us about her own experiences as the leader of German communism, and how the bosses in Moscow manipulated her party. She also kept herself informed about current developments in the communist world, and since she was a former insider, her judgment carried weight. This was less true of Franz Borkenau, a former functionary in the German communist student movement, whose interpretations of current developments within international communism at times seemed far-fetched. When asked where he got his information, he would tell us that he had special intellectual antennas or intuition (he used the German term, *Fingerspitzengefuhl* (literally, that means, special sensitivity at the tip of his fingers) that enabled him to understand these things. Another former communist activist was Karl August Wittfogel. He had served in the cabinet of the short-lived socialist and communist coalition government in Saxony in the early

1920's. After that, he had remained active in the party. I once saw a collection of flamingly revolutionary one-act plays for the proletarian stage that he had written. He had been in France, I believe, when the Germans had marched in, and an eminent scholar studying Inner Asia had saved his life. That was Owen Lattimore, of Johns Hopkins University. Lattimore had invited Wittfogel to the United States, or in some way arranged for his immigration. When, in 1950, Senator Joseph McCarthy in vicious and totally irresponsible fashion destroyed Lattimore's career, Wittfogel does not seem to have defended Lattimore and may indeed have assisted McCarthy.

In 1954 or 1955, I participated in a faculty seminar at the Center for Far Eastern and Russian Studies at the University of Washington. Wittfogel at that time had some appointment both at Columbia University and the University of Washington. He was then working on his major work on the concept of Oriental despotism, and the members of the faculty seminar had been given a draft of one of the chapters in this book. A lengthy note appeared in that chapter, in which Wittfogel denounced all those communist scholars or ideologists who had falsified Marx's and others' ideas concerning Oriental despotism. The list of these falsifiers included Lenin, Stalin, Mao Tse-tung, a few American communists and John K. Fairbank.

Professor John K. Fairbank taught Chinese history at Harvard. He was a scholar of the highest repute, incredibly erudite, a marvelous teacher and a warm friend. He was mild-mannered and courteous in a way that made him appear almost like an eminent scholarly mandarin and he was as thoroughly decent a person as I have ever met. Where he stood politically, I have no way of knowing, but I assume that he was no further to the left of center than John Kennedy's principal advisers. I have reason to assume also that John Fairbank had hated the corrupt and oppressive *Kuomintang* regime. Millions of people in China had loathed that regime so deeply that they had greeted the communist troops of Mao as liberators. Revolutions generally serve as punishment for oppression and corruption practiced by the regimes they overthrow.

When Wittfogel appeared at the seminar in Seattle, a young

colleague of mine began by asking him whether he had meant to imply that John Fairbank was a communist. Wittfogel answered evasively, whereupon I took the cue from my colleague and asked the question again, rephrasing it. Wittfogel once more refused to give a straight answer. The two of us, my colleague and I, did not give up, but tried to pin him down, until at last the Director of the Center lost patience and directed the conversation to some other point. After the seminar, Wittfogel buttonholed me and said, "I honor your loyalty to your friend John Fairbank. Of course I know he is not a communist, but I refuse to say that in print."

CHAPTER 2

FRIEDRICH ENGELS: THE FIRST TWENTY-ONE YEARS

FRIEDRICH ENGELS WAS born in Barmen on 28 November 1820. He was thus roughly contemporary with the following outstanding personalities of the Victorian Age: Victoria and Albert, Alexander II, Vittorio Emmanuele II, Ulysses S. Grant, William T. Sherman, Bismarck, Count Crispi, Frederick Douglass, Susan B. Anthony, Matthew Arnold, Walter Bagehot, Herbert Spencer, John Ruskin, George Eliot, Herman Melville, Walt Whitman, Jacques Offenbach, Cesar Franck, and Jenny Lind, as well as Gounod, Mommsen, Buckle, Turgenev, Flaubert, Baudelaire, Dostoevsky, Courbet, Pasteur, Helmholtz, Virchow, Gregor Mendel, Elias Howe, and Florence Nightingale.

Engels was the eldest among eight children of Friedrich and Elisabeth Franciska Mauritzia Engels. Friedrich, Sr., who was twenty-four years old at the time his first son was born, was a respected and prosperous member of the Barmen business community. The origins of the family are obscure, but the name and its religious affiliation make it plausible to assume that an Engels ancestor was among those Calvinist families that fled from Antwerp or its environs in the late sixteenth or early seventeenth century to escape the ravages of the Counter-Reformation. Such families found a haven in the Duchy of Berg, and seem to have contributed to its economic prosperity and its political liberalism.[1]

Friedrich's ancestors may have settled as yeoman farmers, but if they came from Antwerp it is likely that they pursued some more urban occupation having to do with the making or trading of textiles or textile fibers. By the eighteenth century, this had become the family business. Friedrich's great-grandfather, Johan Caspar Engels, began by trading in cotton yarns, traveling from village to village on foot, carrying his merchandise on his back. His ancestors may have done the same. Johan Caspar later settled in town and established the business firm that Friedrich's father owned in 1820. This firm engaged in bleaching, ribbon-weaving, lace-making, and silk trading.

The business prospered and branched out. The nineteenth century, especially the decades following the 1830s, was a period of explosive growth for the cotton industry. Within a generation, cotton turned from a luxury commodity to the staple fiber produced for mass consumption. Thus, this was a period of feverish expansion, tremendous profits, although also—in times of reverses in the market—of dramatic failures. The Engels family, however, did well. In 1837, the elder Friedrich entered into partnership with the Ermen brothers, German cotton spinners from Nassau who had settled in Manchester, and the firm Ermen & Engels was born. Four years later, a branch factory of the company was opened in Engelskirchen, across the Rhine from Cologne.

Friedrich's mother, whose maiden name, van Haar, was even more obviously Dutch than Engels, was the daughter of a school principal, or *Rektor*, in the small Westphalian town of Hamm, forty or fifty miles from Barmen and just within the borders of the former Duchy of Berg. Her father, in whose house young Friedrich must have spent many a vacation, may have furnished the child with his first intellectual impulses.

It was immediately evident that the boy, like many children, had conflicting role models in his parents. His mother not only showed him the warmth of maternal love, but also together with her father seems to have introduced him to the life of the spirit and the intellect. His father, on the other hand, sought to instill in him a practical sense, respect for hard work and efficiency, as well as parsimony, frugality, and the duty of accounting for every penny. All his life, Friedrich harbored these conflicting souls—that of the hedonist intellectual and that of the sober businessman. (This, incidentally, should not tempt us into assuming that he might not, at times, also have wished to be either a sober intellectual or a hedonistic businessman.)

While in the long run we may fix our attention on those maternal and paternal traits that he internalized, his personal development began with a sharp emphasis on repudiating his parental teachings and examples. Friedrich's attitude toward his father was highly critical. He came to reject his religion and political views, his attitude toward the family, and his ideas concerning child rearing. Most of all, he repudiated his father's work, which was that of a businessman and manufacturer. In his youth, he often referred to commerce with the contemptuous term *Schacher*, which means petty or mean bargaining and huckstering. Derived from Yiddish, it has anti-Semitic overtones when used by non-Jews. Obviously, the entire life work of Friedrich Engels, which was a critique of capitalism, represented a repudiation of his father. Yet, in significant respects, Friedrich Junior never completely broke with Friedrich Senior.

Indeed, he was a hard-working and efficient businessman, and clung with tenacity to many of the businessman's virtues. Moreover, despite their mutual disapproval of each other and the many crises in their relationship, father and son came to develop a grudging respect for each other. Their strong ambivalence toward one another, as well as their ability to maintain a working relationship, was reflected in the double life—as respectable businessman and revolutionary—that the younger Engels led almost to the end.

The Engels family in Barmen was as large as it was substantial. Friedrich grew up amid parents and grandparents, brothers and sisters, uncles, cousins, and grand uncles, as well as their servants. There were even former servants who, in semi-feudal fashion, lived on old-age support provided by their former employer. The Engels family were known as 'good employers,' which meant precisely that they cared for their workers in patriarchal fashion, assisted them in case of unforeseen disaster, and also provided schooling and social services for them.[2] The prominence of the family was certified by the fact that the street on which Engels grew up was called Engelsbruch. Behind the house was a garden, and behind that the bleaching green, which abutted a street called Engelsgang.

When Engels, late in life, would reminisce about his youth, he liked to think about his boyish escapades and the pranks that he played in and around the parental home.[3] He seems to have been a rather unruly boy, or so his father thought. Friedrich Senior, whom Engels later described as fanatical and despotic, complained on one occasion that he could not make the boy obey him unconditionally despite the most severe corporal punishment. Whatever evidence we have, however, indicates that his childhood was not altogether different from that of most German bourgeois youths in the middle of the nineteenth century, whose upbringing was generally repressive, punitive, and authoritarian. Yet, Engels's sensual and intellectual urges were awakened by exposure to a wide variety of cultural lore, with the result that mind and body, seeking free outlets, at once clashed against prevailing orthodoxies. For the boy, release from this pressure typically took the form of pranks and 'naughtiness.' After puberty, he fled into a fantasy life by reading Romantic novels.

A conservative Calvinist, his father seems to have worried a great deal about his son's virtue, especially his sexual purity. To his wife, he wrote with great alarm about the impious literature he had discovered in the room of his adolescent son. In later years, after Friedrich had turned to communism, he described his father as politically conservative, suspicious of all liberal stirrings, and prone to blame political malcontents and troublemakers for all political disorders and social difficulties. In this he did not differentiate between liberals and communists.[4] Within the family, Friedrich described his father as a tyrant on whom his mother was completely dependent. When later in life he wrote about the bourgeois family in Protestant countries, he was very likely thinking of his own parents. In everything he wrote it is obvious that he readily generalized from his own very personal experiences and impressions.

The bourgeois son, he wrote late in his life, is allowed to pick his mate from among his own class with a certain amount of freedom. Hence, a certain measure of love may exist as the basis of the marriage, and for the sake of decency such love is always taken for granted, often quite hypocritically. Because of this modicum of affection, the

Protestant husband whores around more sluggishly than the husband in Catholic countries, where parents arrange the marriages. Women, too, in Protestant countries, practice infidelity less. Still, since in every marriage the people remain what they are, and since the Protestant bourgeois are dull, limited people, the average bourgeois monogamy in Protestant countries is characterized by a certain "leaden boredom that is given the name family bliss."[5] In this description of his family Friedrich would return many times to such themes as the conflict between Romantic love and family considerations in the choice of a mate[6] or the hypocrisy of marital fidelity in the bourgeois family.[7]

All his life, Engels spoke warmly of his mother, although his feelings toward her must have been tinged with ambivalence, also. In an early letter to Marx he described her, vaguely enough, as a person with beautiful human qualities, but also criticized her for excessive dependency on his father. For a person who all his life made it clear that he admired only women who asserted their strength as equals to men, this was strong criticism. Engels also, and with obvious disdain, described his mother as skillful in manipulating her physical ailments for the purpose of keeping her children on their good behavior. "Every time she is especially angry at me, she immediately has a headache for eight days," he wrote.[8]

With his brothers he seems to have had relatively cool relations. The second Engels child, Hermann, was about two years younger than Friedrich, and in old age the two became quite close. The other brothers were perhaps too young to become Friedrich's playmates. All of them became conservative businessmen who strongly disapproved of their elder brother, his radical associates, and his political views. On a number of occasions, the brothers behaved toward Friedrich with unconcealed hostility, especially in business dealings concerning their father's estate. In a word, they tried to cheat him out of his share of the inheritance. If Friedrich did not fight very hard for what he thought to be his due, it was out of consideration for his mother, "whom I really love," as he wrote to Marx. All her life he wrote to her with kindness and patience, even when she joined the other members of his family in chiding him for the bad company into which he had fallen. In his old age, Engels described the mother as representing a unique bond between the members of a disparate family, and the only one able to tie rival siblings together. Once she was gone, the members of the younger generation would go their own ways—a natural but painful change, which made the loss of the mother all the harder to bear.[9]

There was nothing extraordinary about Engels's youth. His upbringing was restrictive, punitive, and conventional. He was subjected to a fairly wide variety of intellectual and artistic stimuli, but an attempt was made to keep these well under control. Barmen was a relatively small town contiguous to the not much larger town of Elberfeld—twin mill towns in the valley of the Wupper, which must have been quite lovely in the early nineteenth century. One did not travel much in these horse-and-buggy times, and there is no evidence that Friedrich traveled more than other middle-class boys. The few dozen miles of the journey from Barmen to Hamm kept him within the boundaries of his native duchy, and would not have provided him with exciting glimpses of the great world. For the men of the Barmen business community, the 'big city' where they went for adult fun and games was Dusseldorf. Apparently, Friedrich never went there in his youth.

Thus, his early years were spent in towns that, at least by our standards, would have to be described as relatively small, isolated, and sleepy. Applying any of these standards, however, may be misleading. The Duchy of Berg was one of the few areas in Germany at that time that had begun industrial development. Indeed, the twin towns of Elberfeld and Barmen, with their humming textile industry, were knows as the 'German Manchester.' That Engels was aware of the similarity is clear from his statement that his early book about Manchester was indirectly addressed also to the bourgeoisie of his hometown.

The period of his youth was a time of retrenchment after the traumata of the French Revolution and the Napoleonic wars. For the people of the Barmen area, this had been an exciting period. Many of them had hailed the French Revolution as the dawn of liberty. From 1806 to 1815, their territory had come under French rule, first under

Napoleon's brother-in-law, Murat, who had been appointed Grand Duke of Berg, and after 1806 under direct rule from Paris. Napoleonic rule had left two important and somewhat contradictory residues. One was the Napoleonic Code, which was a welcome innovation from the point of view of the business community. The other was Prussian rule, complete with Prussian officials, Prussian soldiers, and Prussian authoritarianism. As long as they could keep the Napoleonic property law, the businessmen of the Wupper Valley seemed quite happy with Prussian sovereignty. Thus, they lived juridically in the nineteenth century and politically in the eighteenth century.

On Sundays when they went to their churches, however, they lived in the sixteenth or seventeenth centuries, as it were, because the local clergy preached a hard-core pietism, then rampant in Germany among both Calvinists and Lutherans. This phenomenon fiercely resisted all liberal tendencies in religious philosophy, insisted on a literal acceptance of the Scriptures, and denounced modern science, the spirit of the Enlightenment, and indeed all uncomfortable questioning as Satan's work. German Protestantism had tended in this direction ever since the terrible disaster of the Thirty Years' War. Its harsh, otherworldly, and indeed death-oriented message found exquisite expression in the music of Schutz and Bach, but its consequences for German social and political development were deplorable. Pietism was a function of Germany's backwardness, and in the period in which Engels grew up it served as an ideological prop for, and was supported by, the Metternichian system. Friedrich himself went through a deeply religious phase in his adolescence, as his first poems indicate. His closest friends in the Elberfeld *Gymnasium*, which he attended for two or three years, went on to study theology.

Before transferring to this institution, Friedrich attended the *Realschule* in Barmen and graduated from it. It is not entirely clear why his parents then sent him on to the *Gymanasium*, or why they did not allow him to finish it. The Prussian *Realschule* was a secondary school providing a limited general education for middle-class boys who did not intend to go on to the university. Intellectually less demanding than the

Gymnasium, it was correspondingly endowed with less prestige. The subjects taught in it were designed to prepare the pupils for the practical world of business. Hence, the stress was on modern languages and natural science.

In contrast, the *Gymnasium* was the stepping-stone toward admission to the university. Created in the sixteenth century, it sought to impart a classical education to the sons of the upper classes, including thorough training in Latin, Greek, Old and Middle High German, together with ancient history and training in the use of the German language. The natural sciences were almost totally neglected. Some modern languages, some mathematics, and some geography were taught. Studio art and music practice were regular parts of the curriculum, as was religious instruction. The professors in Elberfeld apparently were a lot more liberal in religious matters than the hardcore Calvinists at the Barmen institution. Classes in the *Gymnasium* were small. The teachers had great authority *in loco parentum*, and among the students fairly tight bonds formed quite naturally.

Friedrich's transfer to the *Gymnasium* indicates that his parents contemplated the possibility of his going on to university study. That might have led him to a career in theology, medicine, law, teaching, or public service in the Prussian bureaucracy. While this would have precluded him from joining his father's business firm as a junior partner and principal heir-presumptive, all these were respectable callings, and many sons of the bourgeoisie who performed well in school sought to enter them. Friedrich Senior may have nursed the natural wish that his business would one day be carried on by his first-born son. Indeed, all the evidence suggests this strongly. The presence of several younger boys, however, made it easy to recognize young Friedrich's talents by sending him to a school that would prepare him for the university.

It is less clear why he was taken out of the *Gymnasium* a year short of graduation, especially since his academic performance seems to have been excellent. Obviously, his father had made up his mind that the boy should go into business, and for that, six years of secondary education were considered sufficient. Why, however, the change of heart? An earlier biographer, Gustav Mayer believed that Friedrich himself had decided he wanted to study law and become a public official,[10] implying that his father objected to such plans. That is not at all plausible. It doesn't fit in with the father's decision to send him to the *Gymnasium* in the first place, nor was it in tune with everything we know about the exuberance of Friedrich's personality and the Romantic self-image he was soon to develop.

What his sudden departure from the *Gymnasium* does suggest is that something in the boy's development had begun to alarm his parents, and it is easy to guess what this was. His classical and literary education had stirred the young man's imagination deeply, and he had become interested in the entire gamut of arts and letters. He had become, or was threatening to become, an intellectual. He himself indicated that the only teachers who inspired him in his secondary schooling were teachers of German literature and a French language instructor.[11] Trained during his adolescence in various modes of self-expression—writing, drawing, singing, composing, and translating, as well as many sports—he seems to have been eager to continue these pursuits and make them his career. To judge from his earliest efforts as a writer of prose and poetry, he saw himself as ready to embark on a life of writing.

While a career in law, theology, or medicine would have been something his father could have encouraged, the life of a professional intellectual or artist was something against which every fiber in Friedrich Senior would have reacted with utter dismay. Considered flighty and irresponsible (Friedrich's father would have used the term *unsolide*), the intellectual and the artist were seen as antitheses to everything the 'solid' bourgeois respected and as a direct repudiation of every decent value in civilized society. Witness the attitude of his teachers to that giant of intellect, Goethe, in whom even these transmitters of German cultural heritage saw only the sensuous libertine, the deist who professed to be "decidedly non-Christian," the dangerous rebel who dared flaunt all conventions of religion, morality, propriety, and good taste.

And if his educators could thus dismiss Goethe, young Friedrich must have been aware how improper his career aspirations seemed to his father. Hence, if he ever voiced his desire to opt for the intellectual's life in the presence of his father, or even if he ever merely hinted at it, the decision to take him out of school and its confusing intellectual influences and to send him into the practical world of business must have been made without much hesitation. As for the young man himself, he may have agreed to this turn in his career quite willingly. Mayer cites evidence indicating that already at the age of seventeen he was intent or willing to embark on a double life, earning his living as a businessman and devoting his personal life to learning and writing.

It is obvious that throughout the early decades of his life he craved security in addition to freedom, a respectable position with a comfortable income as well as a bohemian life. A wealth of evidence indicates that he never totally rejected his father's bourgeois way of life or his businesslike character traits, just as he never completely broke with his father or his thoroughly bourgeois brothers. Indeed, in his early years he made repeated attempts to reconcile his own romantic dreams with his family's profession. During his apprenticeship in Bremen he wrote letters in which he infused international commerce with a certain romance, a theme later pursued to perhaps excessive length in Gustav Freytag's novel *Debit and Credit*. Steven Marcus neatly shows how the first fragment of prose fiction by Engels on record, a romantic pirate story he wrote at the age of sixteen, also reflects this ambivalent appraisal of the commercial profession.[12]

The young Friedrich's desires and ambitions may thus have meshed neatly with those of his father, even though their intentions and long-range plans were totally opposed. It is also likely that at the age of seventeen Engels did not yet have any fully matured plans for his career, and that therefore he drifted into the solution his parents found for him.[13] And so, in the summer of 1838, young Engels traveled to Bremen, by coach, because no railway had yet been built in Germany except the 4_-mile link between Nürnberg and Fürth. Boarding with a minister who, luckily, was far more liberal and permissive than the preachers in Barmen, he worked as a clerk-apprentice in a large import-export house with whose owners his father was acquainted.

He must have been pleased to leave the twin towns on the Wupper and their confining atmosphere. He was now on his own for the first time, suddenly an adult among adults, no longer a child under the supervision of a strict father who, he must have felt, neither understood nor appreciated him. A few months after his departure, he anonymously published two "Letters from the Wupper Valley" in a literary journal— impudent, irreverent, and immature gossip which Steven Marcus rightly interprets as slaps in his father's face and thus as manifestations of the young man's Oedipal rebellion.[14]

These essays describe what he had left behind: the quiet, conventional, sedate, and boring routines of a small-town business community, where stolidity and petty innocence was fortified by a grim, straight-laced Calvinist orthodoxy that allowed the souls of the successful to bask in the knowledge of their predestined salvation and gave additional pleasure to these elect through the knowledge that the unbelievers would be damned. The letters described the life of the small craftsmen in the gloomiest terms, suggesting that they found consolation only in the Bible and in booze. The miserable existence of the textile workers, his father's hired hands, was sketched in even more devastating outlines, their conditions described as so intolerable that they had to succumb totally either to religious mysticism or to orgies of drunkenness.

In his description, the squalor of people's empty lives in this town was matched only by the pollution of its once lovely river. Thus, Engels, in his very first published work, addressed himself to the effects of capitalism in ruining human lives as well as the natural environment. Besides this, he described in tones of contempt the narrowness of the education imparted by the schools he had attended, scoffed at the meager cultural life of the bourgeoisie and the arid theological squabbles of the clergy.[15] In Barmen and Elberfeld, the respectable citizens read these essays with flaming indignation, but none of them seems to have guessed who was hiding behind the author's pseudonym.

In Bremen, a different world opened for Engels, and the letters he wrote to his sister Marie and to the Graeber brothers, his friends from the *Gymnasium*, show the pleasurable excitement that gripped him. He was in a world of men active in commerce that spanned the globe. His vivid descriptions let us participate in the pleasure with which his senses took in the forest of ships' masts in the harbor, the bustle of dock activities, the smells of the port, the sounds of foreign languages, the aromas and feels of many commodities from all the continents. The education he now received was a practical one. The notion in the business world at the time was that for this work "one needed three years at the copy book, a good handwriting, as bad a German style as possible, and a spectacular lack of general knowledge.[16]

In actuality, the knowledge he did acquire went far beyond this. It included knowledge of different commodities and how to assess their quality, business practices and business law, the chaos of currencies, exchange rates and weights, transportation—especially shipping schedules—accounting, as well as some technical knowledge about machinery and manufacturing processes. In his letters to Marie, we can obtain glimpses of how his knowledge of these matters expanded and how this world of commerce stimulated and interested him, even though sitting at the desk to write business letters or to do accounts appeared hopelessly dull to him. To judge by his letters, he did not always take this work very seriously but used every opportunity, when his employer's back was turned, to do other things—write his own letters, compose poems or essays, or read.

His leisure activities were varied, and his pursuit of them vigorous, as it was in everything he did all his life. Thrown in with a group of young men in the world of commerce, he engaged in various strenuous sports with them, such as fencing, swimming, and riding. He has left us a vivid description of a water-borne outing down the Weser River to Bremerhaven, in which his skill at depicting landscapes and different classes of people, as well as his fine ear for the expression of regional and class differences in the use of language, is shown nicely. He sang in a glee club and derived great pleasure from this, also. He even tried to compose music in the manner of Bach, who had just then been rediscovered. For somebody who at times complained that he had to work himself half to death in the office,[17] and indeed for a young man of eighteen or twenty who had not finished school, the number of essays in literary criticism that he managed to publish is astonishing. Superficial, impudent, and rather immature, they discuss problems of theology, literature, children's books, the Bremen theatre, and politics. They are not great works, but they show the themes that interested this young commercial clerk.

Engels in his Bremen years—from the summer of 1838 to the spring of 1841—was trying to teach himself everything he could about the fields of world literature, philosophy, and public affairs, while at the same time training himself in the writer's craft. Educated to respect people of learning and bearers of academic titles, he seems to have regretted all his life that he did not even finish secondary school. He matched this regret, however, with the fierce determination to study on his own in some of the areas of inquiry from which he had been excluded. Thus, at the age of nineteen we see him try his hand at poetry. He wrote Romantic ballads in the style of Uhland and Freiligrath, and sometimes in a manner reminiscent of Heine. It should be noted that all three were rebels against political and social conventions, highly political poets, and quite controversial in their times. Engels tried, once in a while, to echo the style of Nordic sagas—another discovery of Romanticism—and retained a predilection for Nordic poetry and Scandinavian languages for the rest of his life.

His first poems were pietistic songs of adoration for Christ, with strong erotic undertones. His later heroes were Tell, Achilles, Geoffrey de Bouillon, Don Quixote, and Siegfried, most of them characters that perished in lone rebellion against an evil society. In the fall of 1840, some weeks before his twentieth birthday, he made a pilgrimage to Seigfried's legendary hometown, Xanten, on the lower Rhine. Why, he asked, does Siegfried grip our imagination so? Because, he answered, he is the representative spokesman of Germany's youth. We, the youth of Germany, have not yet settled down into a run of respectability. We have a thirst for action and a spirit of rebelliousness, contempt for timidity and for the eternal weighing of alternatives. We want action. We want to wield the sword. Church and State are the monsters we will slay. School is our jail. The police are the century's evil goddess of vengeance.[18]

Yet another hero of the young Engels was Ulrich con Hutten, the noble poet-warrior of the German Reformation and of German Renaissance humanism. In the summer of 1841, after his return from Bremen, Engels traveled for a few months through Switzerland and northern Italy. In his old age, he would remember with a twinkle in his eye the flirtatious rebuffs that black-eyed Italian beauties gave to his erotic advances.[19] In the brief travel journal he published shortly after his return, one of the high points, however, is a visit to Hutten's grave on a small island in Lake Zürich, totally surrounded by the Swiss Alps. Oh, to fight like him for the free idea, to rest from these fights in such a glorious Alpine setting, and then to have a young poet of rebellion (he means Herwegh) lay his beautiful poems on the grave—that, wrote Engels, is better than statues and monuments.[20] Like other themes that impressed Engels in these years, this one stayed with him throughout his life. Almost fifty years after his pilgrimage to Hutten's grave, he was given a branch of ivy that a comrade had taken from the same site. He nursed it in a flower box on his balcony, and in 1891 planted it on Marx's grave, in unconscious imitation of Georg Herwegh.[21]

One other hero who emerges from the writings of the young Engels is Napoleon, whom he praised all his life for having promoted the bourgeois revolution in Germany. In an article written in Bremen, he singled out three achievements of this Napoleonic revolution in Germany—the emancipation of the Jews, trial by jury, and a sound private law.[22] With regard to this man, too, Engels never changed his mind, except that in subsequent years he admired him even more for his military genius than for his political achievements.

Other themes struck in these earliest publications, and which held his interest for the remainder of his life, included his preoccupation with the study of German dialects. Ever since his youth, he seems to have been fascinated by the dialect differences from one village to the next in the region around his hometown. He was later to attempt a book-length study of different German dialects in precisely this region. While in Bremen, he published an article on the use of Low German, in which he suggested further study of the dialect differences in the Bremen area.[23] This interest in the German language was obviously linked to his national pride, which in his Bremen period was expressed in the contempt he showed for those emigrants who forgot their German-ness once they were abroad, as well as the pride he felt for the contributions that Germans had made to American culture and politics.[24]

Already at this time, however, the young man dissociated himself from narrow and fanatic nationalists, whom he scorned in his essay of Ernst Moritz Arndt as mere negativists who fought against foreign influence merely because it was foreign, and not because of what it contained. Nationalism of this kind, he wrote, was meaningless or groundless because it assumed that the entire universe was created for the sake of the Germans, tended to glorify a rather inglorious past, and could not recognize the contributions made to humanity by other nations.[25] Already at the age of twenty, Engels was as cosmopolitan in his allegiance as he was German.

We must be careful to note the sharply delineated political drift in much of this. In particular, the attitudes toward Napoleon and Ernst Moritz Arndt were acid tests of one's political leanings in Germany at that time. German political consciousness in the first half of the nineteenth century had been formed by the War of 1813-5 against Napoleon and the very ideas of the French Revolution. This revolution and the ensuing wars had awakened or re-awakened liberal stirrings among the Germans, but the war was won by defenders of crown, church, and noble privilege, who then imposed harsh repression on their countries.

The blow struck against reformist and democratic trends was so sharp that Germany never really recovered from it until the second half of the twentieth century. Most of German politics, at least until the end of World War II, was a round repudiation of liberal ideologies. Hence, in declaring Napoleon to be his hero, and in criticizing Arndt, one of the principal spokesmen of resistance to the French Revolution, Engels from the time of his earliest adulthood identified with everything that German political reality was frustrating. There was nothing remarkably original in his writings, but to capture the essence of the conflict then raging at the age of eighteen was noteworthy indeed, especially in one who had been brought up as a strict conformist.

The portrait Engels gave of himself at this time was that of a young man exulting in his physical strength and skills, and in his budding adulthood, mockingly avuncular when writing to his beloved sister, hard at work with his self-education and self-training, and intellectually as well as emotionally in deep turmoil as he was seeking to define the aim of his life. "There is a ferment and boiling in my breast," he wrote to Wilhelm Graeber, "a glowing in my sometimes drunken head. I long to find a great idea that would clear the ferment and blow the glowing up to a bright flame."[26] He then listed the themes he was thinking about. They were the eternal themes of German Romanticism, all symbols of alienation turned into protagonists of rebelliousness and freedom of thought—the 'eternal Jew,' the 'wild hunter,' and, of course, Faust—but a new Faust, no longer self-centered, but sacrificing himself for the human race. To these symbols he added a less conventional one, Jan Hus. In the same letter, he already expressed enthusiasm for David Friedrich Strauss and the first suggestions of an admiration for Hegel.[27]

Hegelian ideas obviously were in the air that Engels breathed in his youth. In one of the first essays he published, at the age of seventeen, he confessed a belief in progress and eventual salvation that seems like an abstraction from Hegel's dialectic. History, he wrote, is an erratic spiral. It moves, sleepily at first, around an invisible point of departure until the circles become wider and the tempo more rapid. It often seems to run in its old course, until all the shortsighted say, "You see, there is nothing new under the sun, and all ideas about progress are pipedreams." It is precisely at such points, however, that the spiral aims straight to a new sun.[28] Like Hegel, he extolled reason as an essential element of progress, but he added that reason must be balanced by sentiment and emotion, and that the most creative people combine reason and emotion in a true synthesis, which, however, is genuine only when it is conscious of itself.[29]

Even at this early date, the young Engels anticipated the Marxian inversion of Feuerbach by insisting that the most essential ingredient of any self-liberation and self-empowerment for the human race was revolutionary action. In the beginning was *praxis*, he said in effect, when in his essay on Arndt he argued that the important result of the Wars of Liberation was not the liberty won in the wars, but the action itself—the fact that the German people rose without first asking their princes' permission, that for a moment the people assumed sovereignty, that they were the ones who forced the princes to act.[30]

Among the numerous themes that bubbled in this bright young head, two demand special attention—politics and religion. Until he left his hometown, young Engels gave no evidence of being shaken in his deep commitment to the Christian credo he had been taught at home, in his church, and in school. We know from his own letters that even when he was in school he was dissatisfied with the harsh and rigid orthodoxies preached in his hometown, and that he discussed his doubts with one of his teachers who, even though he upheld the prevailing dogmas, was at least willing to listen. We can assume that the questions he asked were the same that have been asked a million times by thoughtful adolescents compelled to mouth meaningless or contradictory litanies, and who were punished or threatened severely for questioning them.

Engels found no satisfaction in the few such consultations he had. The letters about Barmen and Elberfeld, which he published soon after moving to Bremen, were his first public avowal that for some time he had been dissatisfied with Wuppertal pietism and longed for a warmer, cozier, and more human religion compatible with his own belief in reason and progress, and with his Romantic sentimentality. Having been warned that his questions were Satan-inspired, the skepticism and doubts that arose out of this questioning of long-accepted orthodoxies frightened and shook him. At the age of eighteen, during his first year away from home, he went through a profound spiritual crisis in which he struggled with his faith. The school friend in whom he confided his doubts and conflicts replied with orthodox admonitions and voiced some contempt for one so weak in his faith and so easily trapped by rationalist doubts.

The reply Engels sent to one of these letters expressed both anger and anguish. It began with a moving confession of his longing for a religion at once quiet, sentimental, and rational. "I was in need of community with God," her wrote about his school years, voicing gratitude that in one of his teachers he had found a confessor who would listen to him, even though he was a predestination fanatic. Yet he had gotten no satisfaction and never felt the ecstasy he had expected to feel. At the present, he continued, he prayed daily—yes, almost the entire day—for truth, but his faith was gone, and his prayers were not answered. "The tears come to my eyes as I write this. I am moved through and through. But I feel I will not be lost. I will come to God for whom my whole heart is longing. You," he angrily told his friend, "are smug in your faith as in a warm bed and do not know the struggle we have to go through when we human beings must make the decision whether or not God is God. You do not know the pressure of the burden one feels with the first doubt, the burden of the old faith, when one has to decide for or against, to carry on or to shake off."[31]

By this time, he was lost to Christianity, having decided that he was a rationalist. Yet, he was reluctant to leave the faith. He had just then become acquainted with the enlightened, liberal Protestantism of Friedrich Schleiermacher, who had died only a few years before, in 1834. For Schleiermacher, religion had not been a cold dogma that one's reason might seek to penetrate, but an affair of the heart and sentiments, a sacred instinct concerning the interpenetration of God and men, the infinite and the finite. Engels was charmed by this Romantic religiosity and thought that a short time ago he could still have accepted it. "If only I had known Schleiermacher's writings earlier," he wrote, "then I would not have become a rationalist," and he expressed his fury at the restrictive community that kept this kind of theology from him.[32] Not many years later, however, Engels would write about the followers of Schleiermacher with unconcealed disdain, calling them preachers of commonplace generalities and pretentious phrase-makers.[33] He had become an atheist, and remained one for the remainder of his life.

Indeed, he thought himself beyond atheism. In a passage that obviously projects his personal views, he once talked about the alleged atheism of the German workers. "This purely negative word," he wrote, "is no longer applicable to them, since their opposition to any belief in God is no longer theoretical but only practical. *They are simply done with God.* They live and think in the real world and are thus materialists."[34] He went on to warn the socialist movement against all militant atheism, arguing that persecution is the best method of promoting convictions one does not like. "This is sure," he wrote. "The only service one can still today render to God is to declare atheism to be a compulsory article of faith."[35]

Thus at the age of twenty, Friedrich Engels was done with God, although he did not call himself a materialist until years later. He was done also with established religions and their spokesmen, but he was never done with Christianity. As a historian, he was to return often to the relationship between various Protestant denominations and the socio-economic and political systems within which they flourished. His contempt for Catholicism was to blind him for most of his life to a thorough understanding of the so-called Middle Ages and the rich developments in culture, science, and industry that had occurred in them.

As a revolutionary socialist, he became fascinated with the parallels between his own movement and the underground Christianity that existed before the conversion of the Emperor Constantine. This fascination makes more sense when we realize how much of the Christian theory of salvation and damnation is contained—though in secularized form—in the communist theories of the mature Engels. Even though he was done with God, Engels remained a Christian, albeit an inverted one, both in his expectation of deliverance from evil and in his recurrent vindictive glee at the prospect of seeing the reactionary evildoers of the world receive their punishment.

As a religious skeptic, Engels was in tune with the avant-garde opinion of his time, though few of his contemporaries were as forthright and consistent as he. One could say something similar about his political views at the time. Engels himself later described what an impression Germany made on a young man in the business community around

1840. The country was not yet a true nation, nor had it yet entered upon the rapid process of industrialization that would occur in the late nineteenth century. It was still a country divided into dozens of sovereignties, and this division seemed an intolerable hindrance to commerce and industry. Every few miles one encountered another code of commercial laws, differing conditions for practicing a trade, assorted petty bureaucratic regulations, tribulations, and harassment, varying licenses, and new regulations of residence and sojourn. Hence, no entrepreneur was able to mobilize and display his material and human resources in rational fashion.

The entire system shared this inability. One of the vital preconditions for industrial development would have been an all-German citizenship and Germany-wide freedom of movement, in addition to a unified commercial law, integrated craft regulations, and a well-developed railway system. German railroad building got started late, and even paved roads were scanty. As late as 1847, all of Prussia had no more than 280 miles of railroad. Of the five or six hundred steamships plying the world's waters in 1850, only two were German.[36]

Every state, every little town, seemed to have its own money, weight, and measures. Some of them had two or three systems at the same time. Forty different sovereignties in Germany were exercising the right of coinage, using eighty different denominations.[37] The country had fifteen different postal services, and postage differed according to weight and distance, so that mailing anything was a cumbersome chore. Of the different currencies, weights, and measures, none was recognized in the world market, so that everyone engaged in international business had to also use foreign systems. The confusion caused by the endless calculations from one system to another was made worse by the fact that the courses of these currencies were not always stable. An unbelievable amount of time and money was thus lost. Once he was abroad, a German businessman was without diplomatic or consular protection. The non-Prussians had no diplomats to turn to, while the Prussian diplomats were anti-business.[38]

In as cosmopolitan a town as Bremen, whose arena of activity was the world, the difficulties that Engels described in retrospect, in 1887, must have seemed especially burdensome. To Engels, who felt that he was a Prussian by compulsion (*Musspreusse*), the domination of this most authoritarian and underdeveloped kingdom over his own hometown and much of Germany was an insulting additional burden to bear. All his life, he hated Prussia and the Prussians, whom he considered barbarians, and fought to curb or break their influence in Germany. In this hatred of Prussia, too, Engels was representative of an entire contemporary generation of young rebels.

To the agony of Germany's division, and her domination by a reactionary Prussian power, one must add the lingering memory of the French Revolution, the wars of liberation, and the philosophic and literary heritages of the German Enlightenment, the *Sturm und Drang* period, and of Romanticism to the list of influences that affected Engels and his contemporaries. A vague sense of rebelliousness was in the air, with the accumulated memory of a multitude of ideas wafting in and out that whispered of greatness, progress, and freedom. Engels himself, a little more than a decade later, described the period of his stay in Bremen as the beginning of the political movement of the German bourgeoisie.

For the first time, people from the business and professional classes voiced oppositionist sentiments. A political literature began to appear, struggling valiantly against official censorship. Republican and constitutional ideas began to be voiced, as were liberal interpretations of religion. Some people were even reading the works of the French socialists. Sexual emancipation, feminism, and cosmopolitanism were additional elements in this mixture of ideas. A resolution of the Federal Diet, in December 1835, warned publishers against printing such material and urged the governments of the Confederation to enforce the laws against the dissemination of these writings. Metternich had been careful to include the false insinuation that some of the offenders were of Jewish origin.[39]

Nonetheless, this entire mixture of ideas and stirrings, voiced by a small number of young radicals, erupted into the open at the death of the Prussian king, Friedrich Wilhelm III, in 1840. His successor, Friedrich Wilhelm IV, had the image of a young Romantic who might be receptive to avant-garde ideas. What had been tolerated under the old king, wrote Engels, seemed unbearable now, and so was proclaimed.[40]

Even before the accession of the new king, Engels had become infatuated with Young-German ideas. "I am a Young German, body and soul," he wrote to his school friend. "I cannot sleep at night because of all the ideas of this century. When I go to the post office and look at the Prussian coat of arms, the spirit of freedom grabs me. In every journal I try to trace its progress. My poems mock the obscurantists in clerical and monarchial garb."[41] About this vague sense of rebelliousness, this uncoordinated irreverence toward all established orders and the directionless confidence in something called progress or freedom, Engels not much later was to write with ill-concealed disdain. Nonetheless, much of its delightfully impudent spirit, its sense of irony, and its dedicated idealism remained with him for the rest of his life.

His three years of commercial apprenticeship over, Engels bade Bremen farewell in the spring of 1841, and returned home to Barmen. He spent about six weeks in his parents' home, but there is no record of what he did during this time. It seems certain that the fragment of a melodramatic poem, possibly meant as an opera libretto, about the abortive coup d'état of Cola di Rienzi (1313-1354), dates from this period. It deals romantically with love and politics, extols the masses, and treats the Patrician power elite as oppressors, exploiters, and wastrels.[42] Knowing his ability to work hard at several jobs at the same time, we may assume that he spent a portion of these six weeks working, or pretending to work, in his father's firm. Soon, however, he was off on an extended vacation—a trip through Switzerland and Italy, "the promised land of Germany's youth," as he called it in his travel journal.[43]

This journal, which he published a few months later in a literary periodical, contains charming, fresh, Romantic descriptions of Nature in her alpine grandeur and Italian loveliness. It contains other themes, however, which we will encounter again and again in his writings—his interest in the origins of dialects and languages, his delight in tasting new kinds of wine, his gift for describing different classes and body types of the people he met. In the middle of a landscape description, he suddenly inserts a voyeurist daydream about beautiful naked maidens bathing in a mountain stream—mythical swan maidens, of course, who are visible only to the youth with his adolescent imagination.

Prominent also is the theme of scorn for the bourgeois tourist incapable of truly appreciating the beauties of the landscape, and the snobbish assertion that only the highly educated or the more sensitive deserve to enjoy this. "Where Nature opens up in all her glory, and her slumbering idea seems to be dreaming a golden dream," he wrote, "whoever, observing this, can feel no more and say no more than, 'How beautiful you are, Nature,' does not have the right to think himself any higher than the common, flat, undifferentiated mass. Only in those of more profound soul, individual pains and sufferings rise up in such moments, but only in order to melt in the glories of Nature, and to dissolve in sweet reconciliation."[44]

As a Prussian citizen, Friedrich Engels was obliged, if physically fit, to report for military service around the time he turned twenty-one. Steven Marcus claims that he could easily have avoided serving, but I believe him to be mistaken in this. I do agree with him that for Engels the necessity (or opportunity) of spending a year as a soldier may have appeared as a welcome chance to postpone the decision of what to do with his life, and to take this moratorium in thoroughly respectable fashion, the way American students in the 1960s who were unsure about their career goals opted for two years in the Peace Corps.

As a man who had had six years of secondary schooling, Friedrich was entitled to choose, within certain limits, the time, branch of service, and place for fulfilling this duty, and the period of service was reduced to one year. We have no way of knowing how deliberately Friedrich weighed the choice of the garrison and unit, or what specifically attracted him to the regiment he picked. Berlin, where he elected to serve his year, was conveniently distant from his parental town. As the capital of the country, it may have lured the young man whose political consciousness had so recently been awakened. It is safe to assume, however, that Berlin attracted him primarily as the intellectual center of Prussia, indeed of Germany. In any event, in September of 1841, he became a One-Year Volunteer—his official rank—in Company 12 of the Royal Guards Field Artillery.

Looking handsome in his uniform, which he described in loving detail to his sister, he was obviously aware of its effect on young women. He has given no evidence that he was very interested in what he learned as a recruit, though in later life he developed high competence in military affairs and a particularly keen interest in artillery. He must have been a good soldier. By the spring of the following year, he had been promoted to the rank of Bombardier, equivalent to Sergeant. As a One-Year Volunteer, he was allowed to live in private quarters near the barracks, and he seems to have had a good deal of duty-free time. For middle-class youths, even Prussian Army service in the 1840s does not seem to have been arduous.

For his intellectual development, the year in Berlin became a crucial experience, because the nearby University and some of the people he met there provided stimuli and opportunities to learn of a kind that had not existed either in his hometown or in Bremen, despite the latter city's cosmopolitanism. At the University, he was able to listen to some of the most renowned savants read their lectures, and in the beer and wine restaurants of Berlin's Friedrichstadt he could, for the first time in his life, join like-minded young rebels and discuss his ideas with people who shared and confirmed them. The group he found was a small circle of men, all of them older than he, some of them by ten to fifteen years. Most of them had earned their doctorate and were either professionals or free-lance intellectuals.

Calling themselves The Free, but also known as the Doctor's Club, they constituted the left-most wing of the followers of Hegel and saw themselves as the leaders of a radical moral, philosophic, and political awakening. For four years, Marx had been one of their members, but he had left Berlin a few months before Engels arrived there. The circle still considered Marx to be one of them. In a long satiric poem against Schelling that Engels wrote in the summer of 1842 and published a few months later, Marx together with the other members of the 'Club' rushes into combat with the forces of heaven, a wild black monster in a devilish rage. Engels describes himself in this poem as the one who was further to the left than all his friends, a Jacobin hot as pepper, and also earthier than all the others, fingering a guillotine and singing a call to arms that is the refrain of the Marseillaise.[45]

As the new King of Prussia relaxed censorship regulations somewhat, these left-wing Hegelians found outlets in new periodicals, chiefly the *Deutsche Jahrbücher*, the *Königsberg*, and the *Hartungsche Zeitung*.[46] He read voraciously. No book seems to have made as deep an impression on him during this year as Ludwig Feuerbach's critique of Christianity, which he read in the spring of 1842. Later in life he was to assert that this book had a liberating effect on a whole generation.[47] When he was not getting drunk on wine, beer, or words in the company of his newly found friends, Engels attended lectures at the University of Berlin, apparently on a variety of subjects. Attendance at these lectures seems to have been unrestricted. There was standing room only in the large auditorium.

In the fall of 1841, shortly after Engels had begun his military service, Friedrich Joseph von Schelling, who the Prussian king had invited to the University, gave his inaugural lectures. The event was highly political. Schelling, with whose Romantic and mystical-religious ideas the king sympathized, had been given the Chair in Philosophy for the obvious purpose of counteracting the subversive rationalism of Hegel and his radical disciples. Engels, who attended the first lecture, describes the audience as including many University bigwigs and students, as well as people from all walks of life, nations, and religions. He may, for all we know, have sat next to Kierkegaard, who was among this audience. Engels himself went in his new uniform, and described himself in an article he published about the event in Gutzkow's *Young German Journal* as sitting next to grey-bearded staff officers with studied nonchalance.[48]

Not only did the young artillerist, only twenty years old, have the temerity to thus mix with his superiors, but he also had the gall to come out in public with criticisms of Schelling's lectures. The school dropout unhesitatingly took on the famous philosophy professor who was forty-five years older than he. He did so not only in the article just cited and in the satiric poem alluded to earlier, but also most astonishingly in a separate brochure that he published anonymously in the spring of 1842, in which he subjects Schelling's entire philosophy to criticism.

The brochure is a bold assertion of everything that seemed to him rational and progressive in Hegel's philosophy, a burning confession of faith in reason, progress, sensual pleasure, and the human species, and at the same time a denunciation of everything religious, mystical, and restrictive. It sums up the views of the young Engels, displaying all of the ideas that had germinated in him since he left school. It marks the culmination, but also the end, of the first major period in his intellectual development. Soon afterwards, he was to turn away from many of the ideas expressed in it with scorn. And yet this daring sally against the established philosopher provides an important key to the understanding of the mature Engels, for despite his repudiation of many of its ideas, the basic themes he struck in this brochure are the same that were to guide him through his entire life.

We find in this pamphlet his faith in the potential of the human race and the implicit assumption that we can all become like Renaissance men, like those "giants of intellect, passion and character, diversity and learning," men who are "everything but limited in the bourgeois sense," whom he described decades later with undiminished admiration.[49] We discover in it his conviction that the chief virtue of such men is self-consciousness. In the pamphlet against Schelling, Engels announced that a new world had come, a millennium in which everything rotten had been cast out, and the secret of salvation was self-consciousness. This secular Christianity had dethroned all gods. Anthropocentric in its conception of the Highest Being, it announced its alliance with the masses of the poor and the downtrodden. It was militant in spirit and military in its vocabulary, glorying in struggle for its own sake, counting both weapons and science in its arsenal, and ending in a call to action.

For all his life, Engels remained convinced that a scientific comprehension of the world would remain the most crucial weapon in the arsenal of the proletariat. In the pamphlet against Schelling, this comprehension of the world is stated in dialectical terms, and the point of departure is a theory of alienation and de-alienation. The world was alien to man, but it had become whole once again. Man had freed himself of his alienation from his own self. The split between the subject and the object within him had been healed. It may be that this impudent pamphlet states better than anything that has been written the spirit and beliefs of the Hegelian left.

The key to his criticism of Schelling, and the bridge to his new faith in the redemptive power of self-consciousness, was the need to reconcile the reasonable and the actual. "All philosophy so far," he wrote, "has posited itself the task of comprehending the world as rational, but of course, whatever is rational is also necessary, and whatever is necessary must be, or must become, actual. This is the bridge to the great practical results of contemporary philosophy." To this, he added Feuerbach's notion that man could become free only if he dethroned all gods and found the secret of all theology in anthropology. The tone of the pamphlet, particularly toward the end, suggests that from his reading of Hegel, and in response to Schelling's lectures, Engels had experienced an epiphany. Let us listen to its last pages:

"A new morning has broken, a morning has broken, a morning of the same significance for the history of the world as that morning when the bright, free, Hellenic consciousness broke forth from the semi-dark of the Orient... We have awakened from a long slumber. The nightmares lying heavily on our breasts have fled. We rub our eyes and look around us with astonishment. Everything has changed. The world that was so alien to us, Nature whose hidden forces frightened us like ghosts, how closely related to us they seem to us now, how much like home! The world that seemed a prison to us now shows itself in its true image as a magnificent royal palace where we go in and out, poor and rich, high and low alike. Nature opens herself up before us and calls to us. 'Don't flee from me. I am not evil, not fallen from the truth. Come and see. It is your innermost and your very own true being that gives fullness of life, and the beauty of youth to me also!'

"Heaven has descended to Earth, and its treasures lie strewn like stones by the wayside. Whoever desires them need only pick them up… The world has become whole once again, autonomous and free. It has blasted open the doors of its dark cloisters, thrown off its hair shirt of repentance, and chosen the free and pure ether for its dwelling. It need no longer justify itself to the unreason that could not comprehend it. Its justification consists in its magnificence and glory, its fullness, its power, and its life. How right that one was who dimly foresaw, eighteen hundred years ago, that the world, the cosmos, would one day replace him, and who therefore commanded his disciples to renounce the world.

"And the favorite child of Nature, the human being…has also overcome the separation from himself, the cleavage in his own heart. The bright day of self-consciousness has risen over him after an unthinkably long period of struggling and striving. Free and strong, confident in himself and proud as he stands…he has overcome himself and pressed the crown of freedom on his own brow. Everything has become open to his understanding, and nothing was strong enough to lock itself shut against him. Only now real life is opening for him. Where previously he strove groping in darkness, he now moves toward his goal with full and free will. Everything that seemed to lie outside of him, in foggy distance, he now finds in himself as his own flesh and blood… The jewel, the sacred, that he has found after such a long search was worth many a false trail.

"And this crown…this sacred thing is the self-consciousness of the human race. It is the new Grail around whose throne the people assemble with joyful shouting, and which makes all those who devote themselves to it into kings so that all glory and might, all government power, all the beauty and luxuriant wealth of this world lie at their feet and must sacrifice themselves for its glorification. That is our calling, that we become the temple servants of this grail, that for its sake we gird our loins with the sword and merrily risk our lives in the last holy war, which will be followed by the thousand-year reign of freedom. Such is the power of the idea that whoever has recognized it cannot cease to speak about its glory and broadcast its omnipotence, and when it so commands he will throw away everything else serenely and in good spirit and will sacrifice his body and his life, his possessions and his blood only to realize it, it alone…

"This faith in the omnipotence of the idea, in the victory of eternal truth, this firm confidence that it will nevermore vacillate or retreat, even if the whole world rebelled against it—that is the true religion of every genuine philosopher. That is the basis of the true positive philosophy, the philosophy of universal history. This philosophy is the highest revelation…in which every negation of criticism is positive. This urging and storming of nations and heroes, over which the idea hovers in eternal peace but finally descends into the midst of all activity and becomes its innermost, most vital, self-conscious soul—that is the source of all salvation and all redemption. That is the realm in which each of us will have to work and act… The idea, the self-consciousness of humanity, is that wondrous Phoenix that erects itself a pyre from the most precious things that exist in the world and emerges rejuvenated out of the flames that consume a bygone age.

"Let us therefore carry those things that are most precious and dear to us, everything that was holy and great before we became free, let us carry them to the pyre of this Phoenix. Let us not estimate any love, any gain, or any wealth too high not to sacrifice it joyfully for the sake of the idea. It will repay us all these things a thousand-fold! Let us fight and bleed, fearlessly look into the grim eye of the enemy, and hang on until the end. Do you see our banners waving on the mountaintops? Do you see our comrades' swords shining, their helmet plumes fluttering? They are coming. They are coming, streaming toward us from all the valleys, from all the hills, with singing and the sounding of horns. The day of the great decision is approaching, the day of the battle of the nations, and victory must be ours."[50]

CHAPTER 3

TOTALITARIANISM AND ANTI-COMMUNISM

As MUCH AS I enjoyed being at Harvard, teaching and doing research as well as administrative chores, my appointment there was not on a tenure track. In other words, I would sooner or later have to leave. I was therefore happy to be invited by the University of Washington to come for a year to substitute for one of their professors who would be on a year's leave of absence. Bill Ballis was going to spend that year in Munich with a research and propaganda institute he had helped set up some years earlier, with CIA financing.

I had met Ballis five or six years earlier. At that time I had felt some dissatisfaction with graduate studies and had inquired at the State Department whether they might have use for someone with my qualifications. I was invited to come to Washington for an interview with Dr. Ballis, who at that time was Chief of the Soviet Union branch of the Office of Research and Intelligence. We had a nice and lengthy chat, and then he told me that indeed he could use me, but that I might be well advised to get my Ph.D. degree first. That was good and friendly advice. He then suggested we pay a visit to his colleagues in the Central European Research and Intelligence office.

That is how I first met its chief, Herbert Marcuse, and his deputy, Otto Kirchheimer. In the 1960's and 1970's, Marcuse became the favorite guru of the New Left, the student counterculture. When I would tell my radical students how and where I had met their hero, they would be amazed and bewildered—even more so when I would add that Marcuse had transferred to the State Department from OSS, the precursor of the CIA.

To get to Seattle, we bought a Jeep station wagon and started on a long camping trip. Stefan was four years old. Vera was three. It would be the first of several trips from coast to coast that they were to take with us. The one I remember most vividly took place in the fall of 1955. I had just accepted a job in New York and had agreed to report for work on a certain day in early September. On the way, I hoped to attend the annual meeting of the American Political Science Association, which in that year was held in Boulder, Colorado. We had spent the summer on the Olympic peninsula, about 150 miles west of Seattle. Now, as we approached Seattle, Eva suggested we stop at her physician's office for a shot of penicillin, since she thought she was developing a throat infection. We did this, but by the time we were in Eastern Oregon, she had a fully developed strep throat. By the time we arrived in Boulder, Vera was sick also. I left them to sleep it off in our motel room, while I attended the Political Science convention, and then we moved on. We stopped in Bloomington, Indiana, where her Uncle Willi taught musicology, and by that time, Stefan was sick, too. After a night in Bloomington, I drove on, with three feverish patients in the car, and I did not stop until we arrived in Bridgeport, Connecticut. A terrible trip!

In Seattle, we rented a unit in a junior faculty housing project with barracks-like structures that had probably housed military personnel during the war. The project was a lively and very cooperative community of young professors from many fields. Our next-door neighbor was studying in the fisheries department. Across from us lived the biologist Ed Fischer, who recently won a Nobel Prize for his work on enzymes. Our best friends were in mathematics and physics, in English and sociology. Many of us belonged to a baby-sitting pool, which made going out for an evening easy, for there always was some colleague who was available to sit with the kids.

Seattle was beautiful. On clear days—and there *were* some occasionally—we had dramatic views of snow-capped craggy mountains from the city's many hills. The climate was mild, and the roses seemed to be in bloom for thirteen months a year. Lakes and an oceanfront surrounded the city and cut it into different areas. Fish, wild berries and wild mushrooms abounded for those who know where to look for them.

In no more than an hour's drive, we could reach the nearest pass in the Cascade Mountains, and skiing was possible the entire year.

On weekends, we would explore the beauties of this area. In order to spend the entire summer of 1954 there, I followed the suggestion of friends who had several times worked as fire lookouts in the wilderness of the Pacific Northwest. I applied to the U.S. Forest Service for a summer job and was hired as a fire lookout.

We spent that summer in a little ranger hut on the Northeast slope of Mount Hood. Before moving into the hut, I received a few days' training, and then, in early July, was sent up the mountain to begin my job. The road was still so muddy from spring thaw, however, and at about 4,000 feet elevation there still was so much snow, that our jeep did not make it all the way up. A few days later we succeeded.

During the summer, I issued camp fire permits, dug garbage pits, constructed an outhouse, patrolled lonely trails in the National Forest, and occasionally walked cross-country to chase suspicious smoke that had been spotted by the lookout above us. It was always a campfire, which some irresponsible campers had abandoned.

In the lake behind our ranger hut, Eva taught the kids how to swim. Across the lake, I gave occasional talks about forest fire prevention to the kids in a Campfire Girls camp. When I raised the flag in the morning and took it down at dusk, Stefan and Vera assisted me. Sometimes, deer would come to eat out of our hands. In a tree close by the hut, we saw a hummingbird nest, with tiny eggs in it that soon hatched tiny little birds. In my off-duty hours, by the light of a kerosene lamp, I re-wrote my doctoral dissertation so it could be published.

As a visiting professor of Political Science at the University of Washington, I taught various courses on Soviet politics and Marxist ideology. I had little interaction with my departmental colleagues. Most of them did not seem interesting or stimulating to me. In contrast, the scholars in the Center for Far Eastern and Russian studies were a group of very bright, learned, and cosmopolitan people, from whom one could learn a lot.

Some of them also were personally charming, and the social life of this group was lively, informal, and attractive. The parties in their homes were one of the pleasures of our stay at the University of Washington. Unfortunately, most of them were so bitterly anti-Communist that this sentiment tended to smother their general liberal tendencies. My aversion to anti-Communism prevented me from fitting in as much as I would have liked. That became apparent at the end of the year: The political science professor whom I was replacing was about to return, but a professor of Russian history was going to be away for a year. I applied for that temporary vacancy, but was turned down, since the historian preferred to hire one of his own graduate students. At the last minute, the graduate student decided not to take the offer, and, willy-nilly, they hired me. Yet one year later, the political science professor moved to another university, and again I applied for the vacant position. I was considered seriously for it, but, in the end, the answer was no. I was later told that the historian whom I had replaced vetoed my appointment for political reasons.

Anti-communism made many people behave strangely. While I was teaching at the University of Washington, the Physics Department hired Robert Oppenheimer to visit the campus for two weeks as distinguished visiting lecturer of some kind. Oppenheimer had been the scientific director of the United States program to develop the atom bomb. Since then, he had been denied security clearance because of his alleged involvement with people on the Left. Because of this, the President of the University vetoed the appointment. For weeks after that, he did not dare show his face in the faculty club, where he would have been booed.

I would have liked to stay in Seattle permanently. We liked the city and its spectacular environs. We had made friends with splendid people there. When my teaching duties at the University of Washington had come to an end in the spring of 1955, we spent the entire summer at a hot springs resort on the northern edge of the Olympic National Park, one of the most beautiful spots in the United States. Eva worked in the resort as a lifeguard and swimming instructor, a job for which she had prepared herself during the previous months through a water safety instructor course taught in the ice-cold waters of Lake Washington in

Seattle.

At the resort, our children roamed freely and found playmates among the children of some of the guests. I had taken plenty of reading along, mostly books about United States history and politics. A Park Ranger had his station near the resort, and once during that summer he and I took a three- or four- day hike to Bogachiel Peak on the northern slope of Mt. Olympus, trudging through lots of melting snow. Two mules carried our sleeping bags, cooking equipment and other gear, including the ranger's fishing rods, with which he caught plenty of trout for our suppers. Eva and I had time to explore other sections of Olympic National Park, including the fantastic northern rain forest on its western edge and a village of Native American salmon fishers, where we observed a large school of whales swimming by.

Among themselves, specialists in the study of the former USSR and its allies called themselves Sovietologists. This designation continued in use even after the Soviet Union ceased to exist. Sovietologist of the post-Soviet era became engaged in a somewhat abrasive post-mortem. Those who predicted that all communist systems would come to a bad end, and who now could say "We told you so," criticized those who made no such predictions for having failed to recognize the fundamental flaws, weaknesses, brittleness, and indeed evil of the Soviet system. Why, the critics often asked, did these people reject the image of the Soviet Union as a totalitarian system? Indeed, the debate among Sovietologists has for a long time been over the meaningfulness and adequacy of the totalitarian model.

Hitler and Mussolini first proudly used the term 'totalitarianism' to describe their governments, just as with equal pride they boasted that they were waging 'total' war. American scholarship after World War II adapted the term to distinguish communist and fascist regimes from democratic ones. One of the two courses I taught at Harvard in 1952 or 1953 was a survey of totalitarian ideologies and governments. I taught it together with Hans Rogger, then a graduate student, who became a highly respected specialist in Russian and German history.

In the 1950's, a number of attempts were made to define the term and thus establish a theoretical model of totalitarian systems. At the risk of oversimplification, let me summarize what most of these models looked like. Totalitarian systems were thought to be institutionalization of utopian ideologies—attempts to change the world on the basis of some mad image of the future, an image so unrealistic that desperate, cruel, inhuman efforts were required. These ideologies were qualitatively different from ideologies reigning in non-totalitarian countries. Brzezinski and Huntington, therefore, in a book comparing the Soviet Union to the United States, referred to the prevalent political ideas in America as a "belief system," not an ideology.

In order to change the world, the political system, and indeed human nature itself, totalitarian governments, according to the model, applied force and coercion in arbitrary fashion, in disregard of all laws and constitutions. They employed a political police and a wide network of informers and thus terrorized their populations. They punished people, not for having committed any crimes, but for having the potential to commit some crime in the future. Some scholars referred to this as prophylactic justice, and the uncommitted crimes punished most harshly as political ones as tantamount to heresy. More generally, in pursuit of all its aims, the totalitarian regime did not hesitate to impose the harshest possible conditions, including starvation rations and slave labor, on millions of its citizens.

From early on, advocates of the totalitarian model suggested that totalitarian regimes should be considered outlaw regimes, with which humane states could not deal, either in rational fashion or through normal diplomatic channels. In the 1930's, European conservatives had been criticized for 'appeasing' fascist and national-socialist regimes. Now those who advocated normal relations with the Soviet Union or China were told that would be a similar appeasement of a ruthless and cunning foe.

George Kennan, in his famous "Mr. X." article, argued that aggressiveness was built into the Soviet system, so that one could not negotiate with it, but could only contain it. Once it was contained within its present borders, it would collapse. Similarly, Nathan Leites, in a highly influential book, declared the collective personality of the Soviet communist leadership to be paranoid, and he suggested that one could not relate rationally with so deluded a group. One could deal with them only by force.

Those who elaborated the theory of totalitarianism argued that it was a novel phenomenon, which had originated only in modern times. They forgot or overlooked that the entire syndrome has occurred many times in past ages. The Holy Inquisition in Spain committed all the crimes attributable to communist and fascist regimes. The Hussite revolution, the Jesuit regime in Paraguay, the Anabaptist regime in Munster, the Puritan dictatorship in Massachusetts, the bloody rule of the Duke of Alba in the Netherlands controlled and abused their subjects with no less cruelty, murderous intent, thought control, and police surveillance than modern totalitarian systems. The Roman Empire under Constantine and many later emperors, as described by Gibbon, was a totalitarian system.

Moreover, the totalitarian model deliberately exempted the criminal regimes that the United States happened to support from inclusion in this model. The thieves and murderers whom we helped into power and kept in power for decades were given the label 'authoritarian' rather than 'totalitarian' by ideologists of the cold war—again in the attempt to make German National-Socialism and Soviet communism look uniquely heinous.

While the totalitarian model correctly characterized many features of Soviet politics, it failed to include many others and therefore was fundamentally flawed. The model paid little or no attention to continual debate and dissent within the top leadership of all communist parties, just as in the 1930's and 1940's it had been unaware of the deep cleavages within the Nazi leadership and of the remarkable disorder within Hitler's government. The model failed to take note of the many manifestations of silent resistance, deviation, disobedience, and citizens' initiative. It tended to deny the existence of any kind of social structure underneath the harsh dictatorship or the gradual formation of interest groups and pluralism.

After Stalin's death, the totalitarian model took no account of changes in ruling patterns that suggested the first beginnings of some sort of constitutionalism in the USSR. Harold Berman's observation that in some respects the Soviet Union was becoming a government according to law (he used the German term, *Rechtssicherheit*) made little impact. Few, if any, of the advocates of the totalitarian model were interested in the many benefits that Soviet rule had brought to the population. These included rapid upward social mobility for millions, free medical services (however inadequate), free education, social security, subsidized housing (however primitive), slowly rising living standards, and successes in war and in foreign policy of which the citizens could be proud.

The totalitarian model also tended to make numerous false assertions, positing a system that could not change, and in which the visible changes that did occur were a source of embarrassment. According to this model, the system would be able to accommodate the pressure for upward social mobility only by recurrent bloody purges. The bloody purges of political rivals were abolished under Khrushchev, however, and never reintroduced. The model attributed a compulsive aggressiveness to the Soviet Union, whereas in reality its leadership tended to conduct a defensive foreign policy, rather than an aggressive or expansionist one.

Perhaps the most serious error in the totalitarian model was its underlying theory of ideological determinism: the notion that all the actions of the Kremlin were dictated by plans for ultimate world domination formulated by Marx, Engels, and Lenin. The fact was that the Bolsheviks had come to power under the illusion that they were the cutting edge of an incipient world revolution that would bring communism to power throughout the civilized world. They quickly abandoned that illusion, however, and with it, the notion that in an isolated Soviet Russia the ideals vaguely formulated by Engels and Marx could be put into practice. Their aims became much more modest and, in a sense, realistic. The ideology of the revolution slowly but surely turned into a highly conservative doctrine that sought to justify the rule of the Party and the postponement of all utopian goals into the infinite future. From a revolutionary utopia, Soviet political doctrine turned into a conservative ideology. Instead of prescribing action to the Kremlin leadership, it served only to justify whatever they were doing. The advocates of the totalitarian model seemed unwilling to note this change and its implications for assessing the nature of the system.

In my own writings on the Soviet Union and other governments run by people who called themselves communists I stressed some of these points. I argued that these people had long ago abandoned any shred of a commitment to Marxism and Leninism in favor of unprincipled pragmatism; hence a study of their ideological pronouncements was no more than a study of public relations utterances. Instead of representing a conspiracy to achieve a world revolution, the Soviet Union was intensely preoccupied with its own problems: attaining economic growth, controlling a potentially unruly population, and securing the country from a world of hostile powers.

Nor could the sum-total of communist states be considered, as such, a conspiracy, because the antagonisms between these states and the cleavages within the ruling parties were too obvious. Instead of regarding the Kremlin rulers as a criminal gang of sadists or madmen, I made the outrageous assumption that they were human beings who, having risen to the top in a governmental apparatus coping with overwhelmingly difficult problems, wished to solve these problems to the best of their ability. Granting them this much, I was, of course, aware that political leaders everywhere are easily corrupted by the power that is given them and that, indeed, anyone who pursues high office anywhere is likely to harbor tendencies toward arrogance, paranoia, and cruelty.

In my writings I pointed out that there had been a succession of Soviet political systems, each devoting its energies to the solution of whatever problems seemed most urgent to the party leadership. In the first years of the revolution, the regime fought for sheer survival. In the next phase, it placed priority on the restoration of the economy and the healing of the wounds struck by the civil war. Both efforts were crowned with success: the regime survived, and then it managed to restore the economy more or less to its pre-war levels.

Each time, success also brought with it new problems, however, because nothing fails like success. Having won the civil war, the regime had alienated its population, and having restored the economy, it became aware that this was altogether insufficient as a basis from which to modernize Soviet Russia. This realization led to a fierce debate about policy alternatives within the communist party. The debate was also a struggle among different personalities over assuming leadership in the party. In the course of these discussions and personal conflicts, Joseph Stalin rose to power and then ruled the country for about twenty-five years.

That Stalin was a thug and a mass murderer, sneaky and vindictive beyond belief—a thoroughly despicable tyrant—there was no doubt. That political historians should equate him with Hitler, however, was much less clear. Hitler's aim really was to conquer the world, to enslave all non-Germans, and to exterminate like vermin all those whom he classified as sub-human: Jews and Gypsies, homosexuals, mental patients and people with genetic birth defects. These were the aims of a madman or a criminal.

Stalin's aims, compared to Hitler's, were much more 'rational'. He wanted to promote the modernization of the Soviet Union. He wished to mobilize his country for a heroic effort to overcome its economic, scientific, education, and cultural backwardness. Like millions of other Russians for the last several centuries, he felt this backwardness to threaten the very existence of the country. At the same time, he obviously was aware of the tremendous obstacles in the way of modernizing it. These included centuries of Czarist misgovernment, a wall of hostility from European powers and the United States, and a nation of peasants deeply committed to a way of life that left them unsuited for industrial work and urban living.

Stalinism was entrepreneurship on a giant scale, and Stalin himself could be compared to some of the legendary captains of industry of Western countries—Krupp or Carnegie, Rockefeller and Ford. All these men built huge industrial enterprises, with ruthlessness, determination, and cunning, and ran these mammoth organizations with an iron hand, unwilling to let go, until some of them became a menace to their own organization. The difference between the Soviet dictator and these many Stalins of Western industry was that they operated within the framework of countries that restricted at least some of their ruthlessness, whereas Stalin, having the entire vast country as his corporation, was subject to no such restraints. Moreover, the style of government under his leadership bore a strong resemblance to the tyranny practiced by Czarist regimes for about three hundred years, which made liberal-minded people in Europe and North America regard Russia as an evil empire long before the revolution of 1917.

In order to convert the USSR into a modern industrial country, Stalin and his lieutenants imposed strictest austerity on Soviet consumers. They reintroduced feudal bondage for the peasantry and virtually enslaved the working class. The performance goals they set for all their subjects were arbitrary and unrealistic, but failure to achieve them was treated as deliberate sabotage, a capital crime. I always described Stalinism as a 'crash program' of modernization: it was haphazardly conceived and implemented in chaotic fashion. Millions of lives were destroyed in the process, millions of people imprisoned, spied upon and terrorized. Stalin's method of modernizing the country was barbaric—which does not mean that it was necessarily self-defeating. Most countries that are considered modern and civilized have gone through barbaric periods. Still, for decades, a debate raged both in communist parties and among Western economists and historians whether, given Russian conditions and the difficulties caused by hostile Western countries, methods that were more benign might have been available to the Soviet leadership.

In 1960, I was invited by the Romanian government to participate in an academic celebration on the 100th anniversary of the University of Iasi. Romania at that time was virtually inaccessible to Americans, and some people in Washington, eager to see an American scholar visit the country, encouraged me to go and paid for my travel.

After the festivities in Iasi, our Romanian hosts took their foreign guests on a tour to some beautiful or interesting places, among them the spectacular Bicaz gorge and the deeply cleft valley of the Bistrica River, where a giant hydroelectric dam was being constructed. One of the foreign guests, the then Rector of the University of Vienna, knew a good deal about construction engineering. He explained to me that dams could be built in two ways. The sophisticated way was to gather all the necessary data to compute the precise curvature the dam should have so that it would withstand all the predictable water pressure, but with a minimum of construction material used. The crude method was to forget about complicated calculations and to just sink a massive, solid hunk of reinforced concrete into the valley. That was wasteful of material, but was quicker, simpler, and risk-free. The colleague from Vienna pointed out to me that the dam project we were being shown was being constructed in a crude and primitive fashion, probably by prison labor.

This could well be seen as a symbol of Stalinism: a crude, wasteful, primitive method of harnessing human energy and material resources for industrial growth. The method may also have been shortsighted. A crudely constructed hunk of concrete would withstand harsh conditions less well than a dam built by state-of-the-art methods. It would therefore degenerate more quickly. When a few years ago we passed through the locks of a power dam built across the Danube River in a joint Romanian-Yugoslav project, we saw many leaks in the concrete walls of the locks.

The fact was that Stalinism was both a spectacular success and a dismal failure. It succeeded in converting Soviet Russia into a major industrial and military power—a power that was able to defeat Hitler's armies, acquire a ring of dependent client states along its vulnerable Western borders, and, after the war, develop an impressive arsenal of modern weaponry. It did this, while also, very slowly, raising the general living standard of the population, providing rapid upward social mobility for millions of citizens and a wide array of social services for all.

Yet, ultimately, Stalinism failed, and the failure was built into the methods that allowed it to succeed. The crudeness of the crash program led to serious imbalance in the allocation, use, and production of resources. The arbitrariness of decision-making and the primitive enforcement methods seriously stifled initiative and inhibited innovation. At the same time, the habit of setting impossible performance targets promoted system-wide evasion of rules, cheating, hoarding, black-market practices, and other behavior that frustrated the planners and administrators. A swollen bureaucracy and police apparatus created inefficiencies of their own.

In retrospect, the Stalinist system was thus a success in building a vast industrial empire in a formerly backward, agrarian country. The method of creating that empire, however, while obviously effective in what initially it sought to accomplish, became an obstacle to further development, once the groundwork for industrialization had been laid. The talents and character traits useful for building an industrial empire were different from those needed to administer it, once it had been constructed. American industry offered many examples of great captains of industry who, once they had built their corporate enterprises with ruthlessness, cunning, and strict central control, were unable to loosen their reins and became a menace to their own corporations. Henry Ford was a good example of such a Stalinesque figure. The heirs of Stalin also were unable, unwilling, and insufficiently enlightened to relinquish party control over the economy and the society. Their control apparatus became top-heavy and ultimately collapsed.

Of course, the hostility of the Western world contributed to this. World War II had bled the Soviet Union dry, and, at the time of victory, the country was devastated and exhausted. The job of industrializing it had to be started all over again, and the former allies were not going to help. Lend-lease was stopped abruptly once the fighting ended, and Marshall Plan aid was offered in the hope that the Soviet Union would reject it. The task of reconstruction and further industrialization was severely handicapped by the arms race that Western hostility imposed on the Soviet Union. In the final analysis, the ring of American bases all around the USSR, the thousands of missiles, bombers, nuclear warheads, and ultimately Ronald Reagan's Hollywood 'Star Wars' fantasy, may have forced the Soviet Union to divert too many of its human and material resources into military preparedness and political vigilance. That broke the back of their economy.

In the 1960's, I wrote a book on the Soviet political system in which I elaborated on this image of the Stalinist project. I argued that we might understand the Soviet Union best if we regarded it as one giant nationwide corporate enterprise—a General Motors writ large. I compared the Soviet bureaucratic apparatus with overgrown bureaucracies in other countries, pointed at the slow emergence of interest groups and the embryonic development of constitutional processes, and suggested that the Communist Youth Organization had many things in common with Greek Letter fraternities and sororities in the United States. I believed that my overall image made a good deal of sense. But in the United States, hardly any attention was paid to the book (it received more careful attention among German specialists in Soviet studies). My deliberate effort to compare features of the Soviet system with analogous features in Western societies did not fit in the myths then prevalent in the West—the myths of anti-communism.

This book was written as an afterthought. For years I had taught courses on the subject, and then an opportunity came to write an entire book based on my lecture notes plus some supplementary reading in Soviet newspapers and journals. During a one-month trip to the Soviet Union in 1958, I had met a number of Soviet academicians. All of them naturally regarded themselves as 'Marxists.' They included a small number who were beginning to call themselves sociologists. That was a new discipline in the Soviet Union because the Party line considered sociology to be a false bourgeois ideology. When, in the early 1960's, an exchange program was instituted between the Soviet Academy of Sciences and the American Council of Learned Societies, I applied for inclusion in such an exchange. I suggested that I be allowed to spend a semester or two at the newly created Institute of Sociology in Moscow to learn what Soviet sociologists were doing. My application was successful. Both the American Council of Learned Societies and the Moscow institute of Sociology approved me for this exchange. I obtained a leave of absence from my university and, in the fall of 1963 spent some time in Europe visiting friends before picking up my Soviet visitor's visa. To my surprise, however, I was informed in the early fall of that year that my Soviet host institution had changed its mind about me, and I would not be allowed in. "Meyer," the President of the Soviet Academy of Sciences had written, "is not a scholar but only a professional anti-Communist."

In order to make use of my year of leave, I decided to study communist sociology in Poland, instead. A leading Party ideologist, Adam Schaff, offered to intercede on my behalf, but even he, though a member of the Party Central Committee, failed to get me admitted to Poland. With the greatest reluctance I returned home and read as much as I could to gather more material for my book on Soviet politics.

I also decided to do some exploring of Cuba, whose President had only recently declared himself a communist. Like all U.S. citizens who had a passport, I had a notice stamped in that document forbidding me to travel to Cuba. I therefore wrote to the State Department asking them to waive that restriction for me. The State Department did not answer my request, and then I asked the then Vice President Hubert H. Humphrey to intervene on my behalf. I had once testified on certain aspects of Soviet foreign policy before one of his Senate subcommittees. Humphrey intervened, and I received a very apologetic letter from the Passport Office lifting the travel restriction. Then the Cubans turned down my request for a tourist visa. Word must have got around among communist officials that I should not be welcomed. While American anti-Communists thought me too lenient in my judgment of socialist countries, officials in those countries considered me an enemy. I had offended the orthodoxies of both these ideologies.

I got it in the neck from both sides more than once. For instance, in 1970 I was invited to participate in an international conference that UNESCO had organized to commemorate Lenin's 100th birthday. The conference was to meet in the historic city hall in Tampere (Finland), where Lenin and Stalin had met for the first time. I gladly accepted the invitation and found that I was the only Westerner participating in it.

All the other participants were colleagues from the USSR and Eastern
Europe. They all presented papers with titles like "Lenin, the greatest
philosopher of all times," "Lenin, the greatest pedagogue of all times,"
"Lenin, the greatest historian of all times," and similar nonsense. After
a few days of this my patience snapped. I asked for the floor and gave a
reply in which I told the Comrades that Lenin had been a modest man
who hated saints and icons and stubbornly resisted attempts to make
him into a saint. If he were here today, I told my communist colleagues,
he would leave the room and slam the door as he had done in April
1920 when the members of the Party Central Committee organized a
surprise birthday party for him. I reminded my colleagues living behind
the Iron Curtain of the fury with which Lenin had reacted to this party,
and I told them that he was not at all a philosopher, historian or
pedagogue. He was a very skillful and successful political leader, nothing
else.

After I had delivered my reply, a number of younger colleagues from
the USSR and some East European countries thanked me for saying
what they wished they had had the courage to say. Other participants,
including the Editor of *Pravda*, no longer talked to me. A garbled
account of what I had said was reported in the Finnish press and made
its way into the pages of *Le Monde*. On the basis of this account the
editor of the CIA-financed cold-war journal *Encounter*, Leopold Labedz,
blasted me for attending a Lenin conference in the first place, and for
allegedly 'praising' Lenin as an astute political leader.

Ideologists typically see exactly what the high priests of their faith
tell them to see. If they are crusaders against some satanic force as
defined by the high priests, they will see Satan wherever they look. They
are subject to the not-so-well-known proverb, "Believing is seeing." In
my books dealing with Marx and Lenin, I never hesitated to criticize
some of the basic attitudes. I always tried to understand exactly what
they wanted to convey, however, to let them speak for themselves. I gave
them the benefit of doubt if their intent or meaning were not obvious.
That method of approaching them was not greatly appreciated by true
believers on both sides. These two books, one on Marx, the other on

Lenin, appeared in translations—the former in Spanish and Korean, the latter in French and Italian.

The Spanish and Korean translations of my book, *Marxism*, were commissioned by the U.S. Information Agency. Why, one might wonder. Undoubtedly because some cold warrior in this propaganda ministry, having read the book, decided that it was an anti-Marxist tract suitable to wean Latin American or Korean students away from their infatuation with Marxism. Why was the Korean translation unavailable in South Korean bookstores, however? Presumably, because the South Korean dictatorship so feared and loathed Marxism that it did not wish to even hear it mentioned in public, so that even a book presumably critical of it had to be suppressed. Why, too, was the Spanish translation of the same book offered for sale in *Fidelista* (left-wing) bookstores throughout Latin America in the early 1960s? Because Latin American rebels and revolutionaries, having read the book, believed it confirmed their own ideology. Which one was correct—the cold warriors in the USIA, the Korean censors, or the South American revolutionaries?

Anti-communism was a collective madness that gripped the United States, its political leaders, its media of mass communications, and its public, for many decades, with disastrous effects. Those who subscribed to the ideology of anti-communism accepted the totalitarian model dogmatically, often against all evidence, and denounced those who challenged it for being 'soft on communism' or 'soft on the Soviet Union.'

Anti-Communists took communist public relations seriously. I was told that John Foster Dulles kept two books on his night table—the Bible and Stalin's collected works. If that was true, it showed the extent to which this Secretary of State allowed himself to be taken in by Soviet propaganda, for everything Stalin wrote and had published was pure public relations without much relevance concerning actual policies he wished to pursue. Anti-Communists, in fact, were selective in what they did and what they did not believe of Soviet ideological statements. They accepted only the militant pronouncements and paid no attention to arguments that indicated willingness to compromise or to retreat from utopian goals. Nor did they take note of the recurrent conflicts within the Kremlin or between different communist parties and communist states.

When anti-Communists were confronted with evidence of such conflicts or of communist leaders' intentions to effect reforms rather than violent revolution, they dismissed them as sneaky efforts to deceive us. Anti-communism was a form of paranoia, which assumed that the enemy was everywhere and that he was implacable. Given such a preconceived notion, anything that communist leaders said confirmed their evil intentions: if they offered to negotiate, that was automatically assumed to be a trap and a confirmation of their hostility. If they made hostile statements, that, too, confirmed the anti-Communist's assumptions.

In 1960, Milton Rokeach published his study of dogmatism, *The Open and Closed Mind*. The book was based on psychological survey work that had been inspired by his dissatisfaction with another famous book, *The Authoritarian Personality*. In that work, the authors had developed a survey instrument to discover various attitudes and beliefs that constituted an authoritarian mindset. They had called this instrument the F scale. The 'F' stood for fascism.

Rokeach set out to develop some alternative survey methods that would reveal the authoritarian tendencies not only among people on the far Right, but also of people on the Far Left. His dogmatism scale sought to do that, and Rokeach decided to apply this instrument of measurement to an opinion survey of some communists; Professor Rokeach therefore composed a questionnaire that he could ask some communists to fill out for purposes of this survey.

Of course, in the late 1950's, when the hysteria of McCarthyism had just swept over the country, he could not find communists or people calling themselves communists in the United States. He did, however, find some in Great Britain. Imagine Professor Rokeach's surprise when he discovered that the British communists he surveyed scored lowest of all groups on some aspects of the dogmatism scale. For instance, more than any other group surveyed, they were ready to state that the USA and the USSR had things in common. They said that they would choose happiness over greatness, that they could tolerate disagreement with their views and dissent within their own ranks, and that one should not tolerate present injustices to achieve the future happiness of humanity.

These findings did not fit in with his preconceived image of all communists as inflexible, dogmatic, and full of anxiety. Had Rokeach been a dyed-in-the-wool anti-Communist, he might have explained this surprising finding by arguing that communists are so sneaky that they will lie even on psychological survey questionnaires. By dismissing their open-minded statements as unbelievable, he would thus have confirmed his own prejudices. He did not, however, use this kind of argument. Instead, he expressed his puzzlement and offered tentative explanations of these surprising findings. The notion that a communist might be genuinely open-minded was one that Rokeach was unwilling to accept, however.

Anti-Communists also demonstrated traits that Rokeach identified as symptoms of closed-minded dogmatism. They saw the entire world as divided into friends and enemies—those with us, and all the others against us. Into the camp of the enemy, they placed the Soviet Union and its client states in Eastern Europe, as well as China, North Korea, and North Vietnam, and all governments, leaders, and political movements that tried to remain uninvolved in the cold war. Neutralism was denounced as the cutting edge of communism. Movements of national liberation in former colonies and movements of reform in grossly repressive regimes—whether in Iraq or Iran, in Guatemala or the Dominican Republic—were all regarded as puppets of Moscow and as secretly led by the worldwide communist conspiracy.

Anti-Communists totally misread the anti-colonial trend that gripped the Third World after World War II and regarded all national liberation movements as communist conspiracies inspired and led by Moscow. Similarly, and against a great deal of evidence, communist parties everywhere were seen as acting in blind obedience to Soviet commands. The bitter conflicts among communist states were dismissed as attempts to throw sands into the eyes of gullible Americans.

Anti-communism was supported by chronic over-estimation of Soviet strength and Soviet capabilities. Some of these over-estimations, we know today, were deliberately and fraudulently concocted in order to persuade the Congress to appropriate more funds to close some alleged missile gap or bomber gap. More generally, the anti-Communist hysteria overlooked that the Soviet Union never was a real threat to the United States. It was too weak, far too preoccupied with its own economic and political problems, and much too conservative and isolationist to support foreign communist parties. As for the American Communist Party, a puny little sect far away from the political mainstream, it never presented any threat to the fabric of American politics, and to consider it dangerous was nothing short of paranoia.

Anti-communism in the 1950's was known as McCarthyism. This was the period in which the junior senator from Wisconsin accused Dwight D. Eisenhower, General George C. Marshall, Harry S. Truman, and many other prominent conservative leaders of being communists, and declared the New Deal and the twenty years of Democratic presidents as "twenty years of treason."

Joseph McCarthy was a thug—insecure, brash, and reckless—as well as a pathological liar. He seems to have been desperately trying to make up for a severely deprived background, and he made up for his own deficiencies by destroying others. He picked his targets at random and denounced them as communists or crypto-communists. He was helped in this by a group of shady characters—marginal people like the infamous Roy Cohn, and a number of former communists who had become paid informers. All that became clear with hindsight, but the relevant question was why the Congress, the President, the press, and the public fell for their paranoid ranting for five years.

McCarthyism, of course, was not entirely novel. There had been anti-Communist hysteria in the years immediately following the First World War. The vigilance against left-wing subversion was kept alive in various governmental and civic organizations, such as the Americanism Committee of the American Legion, and in the late 1930's, the House of Representatives set up the first House Committee on Un-American

Activities under Congressman Martin Dies. After the war, that Committee became a permanent institution, at least for a number of years. The Democrats—especially Truman and his Secretary of State, Byrnes—used the communist threat to sell the Marshall Plan and other elements of foreign policy, including the intervention in Korea, to the Congress.

The transformation of Eastern Europe into a group of communist states and the victory of the communist armies over those of the *Kuomintang* further encouraged anti-Communist sentiments. At the Yalta conference, Roosevelt and Churchill had agreed with Stalin to divide Europe into spheres of influence. By then, Soviet armies had overrun all or most of Eastern Europe. It would have taken another war to remove them. Besides, the Western generals told their leaders that we would need Soviet aid in defeating Japan. The atom bomb had not yet been tested.

American and British policies immediately after the defeat of Germany—the abrupt ending of Lend-Lease aid, Churchill's militant "Iron Curtain" speech, Truman's rude dressing-down of the Soviet foreign minister, Molotov, and many such incidents—were interpreted in Moscow as signs of deep hostility on the part of the West. In return, Soviet occupation forces in Eastern Europe rapidly converted the regimes in these country into governments dominated by communist parties and clearly dependent on the USSR. The iron curtain that Churchill had denounced was at least as much a product of Western policies as of Soviet design.

The American public, however, placed all the blame on the alleged communist master plan to conquer the world. Americans of Polish, Ukrainian, Czechoslovak, German, and other East-European origin were, naturally, very perturbed about developments in their former home countries and thus were receptive to explanations that blamed godless communism.

The transformation of Eastern Europe into communist dictatorships was followed by the victory of Mao's armies over the government of Chiang Kai-shek. For years, American diplomats and scholars had warned that the Nationalist government of China was corrupt and oppressive, and that millions of people in China were being alienated from it. They also pointed out that, during the war, Mao and his communist armies resisted the Japanese while the *Kuomintang* equivocated on this issue. The United States, such people suggested, would be well advised to dissociate itself from such a self-defeating clique, stop pouring resources into this 'rat hole,' and make friends with the revolutionary movement that was attracting overwhelming popular support. They correctly pointed out that the Soviet Union, led by its ruling party, was harshly critical of the movement led by Mao Tse-tung and gave it no support. The fact was that the USSR was the very last country to close its embassy in Chungking after the Nationalist armies had fled from the Chinese mainland.

The warnings uttered by the specialists remained unheeded. Mao's victory came as a shock to the American public, and a far-right interest group, the so-called China Lobby—one of the prime movers of the anti-Communist hysteria—laid the blame for our 'losing' China on those who had warned against this very eventuality. One of the results of the China Lobby's activity was a thorough purge of China specialists from the United States Foreign Service, a severe loss of many competent and thoroughly loyal servants. The China Lobby also served as one of the principal sources of financing, political support, and slanderous gossip for Senator McCarthy. John Birch, for whom a notorious far-right organization named itself, was an intelligence agent operating in communist territory in China.

In addition, the senator from Wisconsin tapped some populist rage and anti-intellectualism—sentiments that seemed to be recurrent elements of American democracy. More immediately, McCarthyism can be explained as the Republicans' revenge on the New Deal and on twenty years of Democratic rule in the White House. Their surprising electoral defeat in 1948 when Truman narrowly beat Thomas Dewey further embittered them and made them ready to go for the jugular.

McCarthy, under the cover of senatorial immunity, freely used slander, deliberate distortion of the record, illegal use of classified materials, and similar dirty means to get attention. After watching people like Senators Bridges, Hickenlooper, Wiley, and Henry Cabot Lodge resort to similar slimy tactics or at least abet them, I remained convinced that nothing was too dirty for those who wished to uphold the status quo or wreak political revenge.

Blame for McCarthyism should have been spread evenly, however. Perhaps more despicable than the opportunists on the far right were the spineless public figures considered to be liberals. People to the left of center in American politics played a pitiful role in the rise of anti-communism. They fell all over themselves to prove their loyalty and tried to outdo the McCarthys of the world in dissociating themselves from any socialists or communists, or from anyone who might be suspected to harbor left-wing sympathies.

Whether it was the American Civil Liberties Union or the labor movement, the Democratic Party or the American Veterans Committee, all of them quickly searched for people in their own ranks who might be vulnerable to McCarthyite attacks and threw them out of their organizations. American liberals, in short, joined the pack of red-hunters because of their cowardice. The anti-Communist hysteria had gripped them forcibly, inspired in part by a vast body of confessional literature written by former communists or sympathizers with communism. These now atoned for their political past by reminiscing about the misdeeds they had witnessed, or in which they had participated, and by denouncing the "God that had failed," the ideology that had misled them. Their turning away from supporting communism had been triggered by various key events, be it the Great Purge and the show trials of 1935-38, the signing of the Hitler-Stalin pact, or the behavior of the communist leadership during the Spanish civil war.

Parallel to this confessional literature, the 1950's saw a spate of influential books by political and religious conservatives—Clinton Rossitter, Waldemar Gurian, Erich Voegelin and others—who attacked the Enlightenment tradition with its materialism, rationalism, and humanism, in short, all the elements that constitute the democratic political culture.

Such denunciations of the Enlightenment tradition were echoed in the call issued by a number of former 'liberals' (David Bell, Raymond Aron, and others) for the end of ideology. This was a slogan that became quite popular among American intellectuals in the 1950's. It expressed the view that American politics since the Great Depression had been a success story: America under the New Deal had managed to create a decent and affluent democratic system that was functioning well. No longer did we need ideologies that depicted alternative futures or utopias. Indeed, utopian dreaming only would lead to totalitarian disasters. Having solved most of its social problems, America needed no ideology, but could or should go on making needed improvements through pragmatic tinkering.

Those who wrote in this vein often were intellectuals who had participated in Roosevelt's New Deal and were proud of what it had achieved. At the same time, they were eager to distance themselves from socialists, communists or Marxists whom many critics of Roosevelt rightly or wrongly associated with the New Deal. By calling for the end of ideology, the reform-minded New Dealers accepted the status quo and gave up their former critical stance. By the same token, they were implicitly joining religious and political conservatives who denounced intellectuals for tending to be excessively negative.

Anti-communism divided the world into two parties—the party of democracy and freedom, and that of a satanic conspiracy trying to destroy democracy and freedom: a set of people devoid of all human values, and a clear and present threat to everything decent. A society convinced that it faced so dire an enemy could resort to two measures to implement a final solution. One of them would be to expose the enemy and to ostracize it. The other would be to exterminate it. This was the response represented by the political witch-hunts of the forties and fifties staged by McCarthy, McCarran, as well as the House committees on un-American activities, the John Birch Society, and other guardians of Americanism. Their activity was designed to ostracize all alleged sympathizers with left-wing causes, to brand them publicly as subversives and to remove them from society by making it impossible for them to pursue their careers.

Meanwhile the United States helped promote the physical extermination of alleged socialists and communists by supporting and abetting death squad regimes in Central and South America, murderous dictators like Suharto in Indonesia, whose regime massacred hundreds of thousands of alleged communists, and similar practitioners of the final solution.

Those who criticized the anti-Communists, as I did, never claimed that Marxist-Leninist societies were virtuous or benign. What we did assert was that they had problems to solve and were trying to do so under great difficulties, and that in the name of anti-communism, our society, too, was abetting and supporting evil regimes, and losing our democratic soul. We pointed out that anti-communism was based on a ridiculously unfounded fear of the vulnerability and brittleness of the United States, which was a species of paranoia. In many cases, threatening talk, arms build-up, and foreign intervention by communist powers could easily be shown to have been a reaction to the threats, arms build-up, and interventions on the part of the United States.

The damage that anti-communism wrought was enormous. It seduced the United States and its allies into wasting hundreds of billions of our resources in a crazy and needless arms race. Had these resources been used for rational purposes, we would have been a richer and less troubled society. Much of the skewing of resources resulted from the wasteful and corrupt sweetheart arrangements between the Pentagon and American industry—the military-industrial complex against which Eisenhower warned us in his farewell address. Anti-communism also contributed to the ever-deeper penetration of police and intelligence agencies into the social fabric. It engendered witch-hunts that ruined the careers and lives of many decent people. Perhaps, most deplorably, anti-communism broke the spine of any meaningful opposition in American politics.

This readiness to measure political systems by two yardsticks, one for the left, another for the right, also greatly discredited the United States in many parts of the world. Moreover, in propping up those regimes that seemed to be of use to us in 'containing' communism, we have bet on many a wrong horse. We built up our chief competitors, supplying funds and weapons to many a regime that later used them against us. In the end, we helped bring about the collapse of the Soviet Union and its European client states, only to be confronted with a much more complex and dangerous world.

The ideologists of anti-communism, just like their counterparts in the communist world, developed a vocabulary of their own—a politically correct language that had to be used by anyone who wished to be taken seriously or wanted to be considered politically loyal and reliable. Together with certain words or concepts, some specific ideas also became politically taboo. Since the repression of concepts and ideas was an obnoxious totalitarian practice, I always rebelled against it, and since ideas that fell under this kind of tacit censorship often were the most interesting ones, I tended to subscribe to them.

One such idea was that of the mirror image of Soviet and American societies. Both societies subscribed to an official orthodoxy, according to which they understood each other as mortal enemies and menaces. Both armed themselves to the teeth to cope with this menace and accompanied that armament race with plenty of threatening words. The hawks on both sides thus provided arguments for the hawks on the other side in an attitude of mutually reinforcing paranoia.

Ideologists on both sides of the iron curtain denounced the idea of the mirror image because they were offended by the implicit notion that their country in any way resembled the evil empire confronting them. Similarly, cold war ideologists in the U.S. denounced those Sovietologists who, in their analysis of the USSR, applied terms or images usually used to describe Western societies. To interpret politics in the Communist Party as the manifestation of group interest or to argue that the rudiments of a constitutional order might be forming under Nikita Kruschchev did not fit in with the ideological notions about the inflexibility of Soviet totalitarianism. Moreover, my own habit of comparing the USSR with giant Western business corporations or the Communist youth organization with Greek-letter fraternities was an offense against prevailing orthodoxies.

Another offense of which I was guilty was my flirting with the so-called convergence theory. First suggested by Isaac Deutscher, convergence theory predicted that Stalinist systems would mellow and transform themselves into constitutional polities on the basis of a more democratic socialism. Meanwhile, it was foreseen that the West would also become more socialistic, so that both the U.S. and the USSR would one day become socialist democracies. Against such optimistic prospects that doubtless were based on wishful thinking, my own much bleaker expectations posited a different theory of convergence.

From observing the ruthless methods by which Stalinism sought to achieve nearly impossible aims and the top-heavy bureaucracy employed in this effort, I realized that the Party was not up to its task and that the USSR had become ungovernable. I foresaw that the resulting popular dissatisfaction would generate political unrest, and, in response to this, attempts to impose law and order from above. Similarly, I foresaw trends toward bureaucratization in corporate capitalism and political difficulties due to the growing ungovernable nature of the United States. My nightmarish version of convergence theory posited a tendency toward bureaucratic mismanagement and economic distress that would create political crisis and occasional interludes of fascism for both major powers. When, in February 1996, the right-wing Russian politician Zhirinovsky congratulated Pat Buchanan on his victory in the Republican presidential primaries, I thought that my gloomy predictions had not been so far off the mark.

In my own field of studies, the Cold War also imposed orthodoxy and thereby affected American political science deeply. The noble tradition in the study of politics and government had been that it should be critical. Politics being the continuation of warfare with other means (to misquote General Clausewitz), the political scientist studied the distribution, use, and abuse of power and then might come up with visions of an alternative future in which power could be distributed and used more acceptably. Under the pressure of the cold war, however, political science in the United States preferred to forego criticism of our own system in favor of celebrating it as the fulfillment of our democratic ideals. The prevalent paradigm for describing U.S. politics in the 50's and 60's was the pluralist theory worked out by David Truman and Robert Dahl. It saw the U.S. as democratic because competing groups in it contended with one another, each representing its own special interest. This open competition supposedly prevented domination by any single dominant group and thus insured democracy.

In the perennial conflict between interest groups, a group's resources, organization, and political skill determined the outcome, but only if these various sources of strength were evenly distributed. Neo-Marxists might identify the various elite groups that the pluralists talk about as the possessors of economic, political, intellectual capital, and then point out that underneath these competing elite groups there were the mass of working people without any property, who did not benefit from the conflicts within the elite. Pluralist theory seemed to acknowledge this, but in a half-hearted manner: Dahl and Truman made it clear that the underclass in the United States had none of the resources of the large interest groups. The unemployed had no money, no organization, no political party, and no political sophistication. They therefore could not make the system respond to their interests. They were excluded. Since democracy implies inclusion of all, to call the pluralist system as they described it democratic was dishonest.

Short of celebrating the American democracy in this fashion, many political scientists preferred to study trivia. At the University of Michigan, one of the topics studied most intensively was voting behavior and the psychic makeup of citizens casting their votes. These studies, based on survey research, doubtless were of interest to political campaign managers who marketed candidates. What studies of voting behavior usually failed to point out, however, was that the major parties offered little meaningful choice between alternatives.

In studying world politics, an analogous change in emphasis was the turn away from a preoccupation with morally inspired thinking about U.S. foreign policy to an attitude called "realism." From the time of Thomas Jefferson well into the 20th century Americans liked to believe that in interacting with the world at large the task of the United States was to spread the blessings of constitutional government and democracy to the entire globe. In the years of the cold war, political scientists and presidential advisers proposed to abandon such idealism and to opt, instead, for realism in the study and practice of international relations. Realism in this context stood for the Machiavellian belief that world politics had little to do with morality. Instead, it was concerned with power.

For the realist the world was a dangerous place. What mattered in this jungle was to pursue the national interest by keeping one's country strong and one's potential or real enemies weak. Squeamishness about the methods used to these ends was regarded as misplaced. After all, our enemies did not seem to be squeamish about their methods, either. The realists' approach to the study of world politics easily justified a general cynicism and seemed to make political scientists comfortable with the armaments race and the possibility of nuclear warfare. It enabled them to speculate about the 'rationality' of a first strike without noticing the insanity involved in this. The unthinkable had become thinkable. The morality rejected by the self-styled realists eventually returned through the back door as rhetoric to justify Machiavellian power politics. Whatever dirty tricks the CIA and other agencies of the U.S. government played, they were inevitably declared measures aimed at defending or restoring democracy.

Chapter 4

The Birth of Marxism

SO FAR WE have become acquainted with an exceedingly gifted, attractive young man who, because of an inner dynamic about which we can only guess, subjected the world of his parents and his peers to serious questions, again and again, and in that process defined his own role very differently from the wishes of his parents. He had sufficient emotional courage to repudiate both of them—the Philistine conformities of his father, and the submissive weakness of his mother—in order to serve humanity very much in a fashion of his own defining.

No human being, however, can ever be totally autonomous and self-defining, especially not an adolescent or a very young adult. Hence, having rejected his parents as role models, the young Engels had to search for substitute guides to thought and action. We have seen two such types of models—heroes of myth and fiction like Faust, Siegfried, and Don Quixote, and leading figures from history such as Jan Hus and Napoleon. In his attempt to shape his own self-consciousness, however, the young man, brash as he was, needed another sort of helper even more—he needed teachers. At least he seems to have felt a continual need for people who he could *consider* his teachers. He found these in contemporary or recent writers such as Goethe, Börne, Uhland, Heine, Freiligrath, Schleiermacher, Gutzkow, and Hegel. He also found them in his friends of the Doctors' Club, where he was by far the youngest member.

Engels adopted, however fleetingly, the method, views, and style of writing of whoever inspired him. Thus it might seem that he flitted in immature and fickle fashion from one to the other, in brief bouts of infatuation. One can also see this, however, as the method by which a young man with a gift for very quick apperception could learn, develop,

95

and indeed mature with astonishing rapidity. We might credit this talented young man with a rare gift for sensing, even on superficial acquaintance, the most salient points in a person's writings, but with unerring dialectical instinct also quickly perceiving its limitations. This, indeed, was the pattern of his intellectual development. Again and again, he was drawn to older men from whom he might learn, and whom in fact he was ready to serve, but each time he soon sharpened his own intellectual powers in debate with them, ending in rupture.

This pattern ended only after he had defined an ideology and a role for himself, and found an elder partner that satisfied him for the rest of his life. Even then, however, despite whatever self-assurance he seems to have felt, an occasional sense of insecurity became manifest. One can see it in his strange deference to Marx, but also once in a while in his relations with others. For instance, during his mid-twenties, Engels at times hesitated to assert himself within the circle of his fellow radicals. The reason he gave to Marx on one of these occasions was his self-consciousness in looking younger than his age.[51] We may possibly take this as the symptom of a general sense of immaturity that haunted him.

In his poem against Schelling, Engels had mentioned that ferocious black monster from Trier—Marx—whom so far he knew only by reputation. Despite many significant differences in their personalities, upbringing, and outlook, his and Marx's interests and general views at that time were remarkably similar, down to the very imagery of their early writings. In Marx's school graduation essay, at the age of seventeen, he had written:

"The chief guide that must determine our choice of a profession is the welfare of humankind, our own self-perfection. One should not assume that these two interests could fight each other as enemies, that the one must destroy the other. Instead, the nature of human beings is so constituted that they can reach their own perfection only when they work for the perfection and welfare of the world around them… History calls the greatest human beings those who ennobled themselves by working for the community. Experience praises these as the happiest who make the largest number of people happy…Once we have chosen the calling in which we can do the most for mankind, then burdens cannot bend us, because they are but sacrifices for all. Then we will not enjoy poor, narrow, selfish joy, but our happiness belongs to the millions, our deeds live on quietly but forever effective, and our ashes will be watered by the burning tears of noble people."[52]

We have only to compare this passage with Engels's 1842 pamphlet against Schelling, which struck such a note of high Romanticism, to note that, although Engels's vision may have been more exuberant, Marx was here expressing the same sentiments, in a similar spirit of Romantic idealism. The two writers—the peppery Jacobin and the black monster from Trier (Marx had strikingly dark features, black hair, black eyes, and a tan complexion; his nickname, *Mohr*, meant 'black man')—were soon to meet.

Having completed his military training, Bombardier Engels was transferred to the Reserve and could return home. There, his parents decided that he should now widen his horizon as a businessman and future senior partner of the family enterprise by going to Manchester and working in the recently founded cotton-spinning firm of Ermen & Engels. We must assume that his father consulted him prior to this decision, but we have no information about the motives that entered into it. His father may well have assumed that in Manchester his unruly offspring would be safely removed from corrupting intellectual and artistic influences and that in the cotton capital of the world he would willy-nilly turn to a life of solid respectability, especially if he were carefully supervised. Engels is not on record as having objected to the decision. He may have wished to comply with it, if only to continue receiving his parents' generous financial support. He may also have been aware, however, that Manchester, with its large concentration of proletarians, knowledge of whose miseries may have come to him by this time, was going to be the eye of the coming revolutionary whirlwind, and hence the proper place for a rebellious young bourgeois.

Since his return from Berlin, Engels had made an acquaintance that was to be of tremendous importance to his intellectual and political development. This was Moses Hess, whose book, *The European Triarchy,* he had read in Berlin. Hess in 1842 shared with Karl Marx the editorship of the left-of-center newspaper, *Rheinische Zeitung*, which he had helped create in the previous year. One of the first people in Germany who called themselves communists, Hess had shaped his views under the strong influence of Saint-Simon, from whom he had derived the central importance of the class struggle for understanding history and politics, the deleterious effects of private property, the determining influence of science and technology, and the notion that all history and social science so far had been written from the point of view of the idle and the privileged. The 'Marxian' slogan, "from each according to his abilities, to each according to his work," as well as the idea that only the productive should jointly manage the affairs of the community, had been advanced by Saint-Simon, and both Engels and Marx very likely heard about them first from Hess. In any event, their association with Hess doubtless helped them get acquainted with the writings of French socialists, and encouraged them to develop their interest in economic studies.

Engels visited Hess in Cologne in the editorial office of the *Rheinische Zeitung* some weeks before his departure for England. The two had a long and exciting conversation. Hess later claimed that in its course he converted Engels from a Jacobin to a communist by convincing him that Hegelian philosophy carried to its logical conclusion inevitably led to communism.[53] Engels called on Hess again on his way to Manchester, and at that time he also met Karl Marx, two and a half years his senior, who had only a few weeks before taken over the editorship of the paper. Marx, presumably because of ideas given to him by Hess, had only recently come to the conclusion that his own views were irreconcilable with those of the Left-Hegelians in Berlin and had made this clear to his former associates in no uncertain terms. Engels, however, still was in touch with the group and considered himself one of them. The two men thus had reasons to be suspicious of each other. The meeting was brief and frosty.[54]

If Engels's parents hoped that a stay of two years in Manchester would contribute to their son's training as a businessman and manufacturer, the young man himself obviously was firmly resolved to learn other things as well. In his discussions with his friends in Berlin and in his polemics against Schelling, he had cleared his mind in a certain fashion. Having embraced with boundless enthusiasm and panache the cause of human progress through revolutionary thought and action, he was aware that he was about to begin a totally new phase in his life. He had become a new person. In his pamphlet against Schelling, he had sworn fealty to the Holy Grail of revolutionary self-consciousness. He would now have to begin from the beginning all over again to work on himself, to train himself for his sacred mission. He was at once proud and diffident—diffident because of his interrupted education and the resultant feeling that he was inferior to some more learned people, proud because of what he had managed to make of himself.

When Arnold Ruge wrote to him still in Berlin, addressing him as Dr. Engels, he corrected him: "A doctor, by the way, I am not and will never be able to be. I am only a merchant and a Royal Prussian Artillerist, so please refrain from bestowing the title on me."[55] As to contributions for his paper, he added a few weeks later that instead of writing more articles, he was now resolved to do more studying. "I am young," he wrote, "and self-taught in philosophy. I have learned enough to have convictions and to voice them, but not enough to work for them effectively, and since I have not purchased my right to write philosophy with the union ticket of a doctorate, I must be better than most. Everything I have written so far has been a series of tests for me, indicating whether or not I was good enough to participate in the intellectual currents of the century. I believe I have passed these tests and now consider it my duty to study more."[56]

One marvels at the frankness with which this young man of twenty-one revealed himself in these letters, at the maturity with which he assessed his shortcomings and his accomplishments, at the daring with which he placed himself in the mainstream of coming intellectual and political developments, and at the modesty mixed in with this arrogance. One senses his regret at not having received academic training and the sense of inferiority he had when dealing with people who possessed doctor's degrees. Once again, however, this feeling of inadequacy may tell us something about the deeper self-image that he had—a sense, perhaps, of his own dilettantism, his inability or unwillingness to go into any matter in German-philosophic depth. Behind his confession we may also glimpse his awareness that in the past he had been intellectually dependent on others. Yet at the same time he was, here, expressing great pride in his own independence, his ability to come to terms with the world on his own, and his talent for dismissing models that he found unsatisfactory.

Engels lived in Manchester from December 1842 to August 1844, his stay interrupted only by two trips to London in the summer and fall of 1843. In later years, he was to describe this period as the most decisive years of his life, because during it he managed to define the world view that was to remain his forever.[57] What he had learned in Manchester, or as he put it, what he had run into with his nose, were three fundamental insights—the decisive importance of economic facts as an explanation of history (or at least modern history), the significance of economics as the basis of contemporary class conflicts, and the need to focus on class conflicts for an explanation of contemporary party politics, and hence of all political history.[58] This is much too modest an assessment of what Engels had learned, as we shall see presently.

Obviously, through his work in a manufacturing business dealing with customers and suppliers throughout the world, Engels learned much more than he already knew about the workings of the free-enterprise economy, and he learned it from within. He was no longer the apprentice he had been in Bremen. In Manchester, he apparently worked as a correspondent and accountant, and he may also have had occasion to watch proceedings at the Manchester cotton exchange. He found himself, moreover, in a highly political atmosphere different not only from his native Prussia but also from the exceedingly patriarchal Bremen. Here, everyone in the business world participated in public affairs. The press was free. Public issues were debated widely and freely. All his life, Engels remained impressed by these freedoms, even though his first published comments stressed their negative consequences.[59]

The participants in this political life were not only the representatives of the middle and upper classes. Soon Engels was to also meet men and women from the working class who were active in politics. During his visit to London in the fall of 1843, he met George Julian Harney, one of the leaders of the Chartist movement, and they became friends. Engels at once began writing for Harney's journal, *The Northern Star*, as well as for the Owenite paper, *The New Moral World*. He was tremendously impressed with the rapid political mobilization of the Irish proletariat in England's city slums. "England," he wrote, "shows that the lower the standing of a class in its society, the less 'educated' it is in the ordinary sense of the word, the closer it is to progress, and the more of a future it has. Altogether, this is the character of every revolutionary epoch, as has been shown particularly in the religious revolution that produced Christianity: 'Blessed are the poor,' 'The wisdom of this world has turned into folly,' etc.[60]

With his gift for rapid surveying and quick if superficial analysis of everything he saw around him, Engels was already sending articles on English politics and economics to radical papers on the Continent. In these articles, he was beginning to formulate principles that we would today associate with mature Marxism, such as the economic interpretation of history, the theory of ideology, which was derived from it, and the certainty of social revolution.[61] He read voraciously during his two years in England. The references he made in his publications indicate that he familiarized himself with the writings of the classical political economists, including Smith, Ricardo, Malthus, Say, and MacCulloch, and was critical of them at once. He also read the writings of the French and English socialists, such as Owen, St. Simon, Fourier, Cabet, and Babeuf, as well as Lorenz von Stein's treatise on them, *Der Socialismus und Communismus des heutigen Frankreichs*, which had been published in 1842. In addition, he read other radical writers, including Thomas Carlyle's *Past and Present*, and the muckraking novels of Eugene Sue.

From these books he derived a great deal of inspiration. He himself never forgot the intellectual debt he owed Ricardo. For Robert Owen he retained fondness and appreciation, and the writings of Fourier always, and to the end of his life, gave him great delight. One of the major inspirations he received from Fourier was the notion that labor is the specifically human activity, and that labor and pleasure are identical, but that in the present social order labor has been alienated.[62] By the fall of 1843, Engels had begun to call himself a communist.[63] As soon as he was acquainted with socialist doctrines, he began to formulate a theory concerning the relationship between French and English socialism, English industrial development, the French revolutionary tradition, German backwardness, and Hegelian philosophy, which has become the classical Marxist statement of the scenario leading from bourgeois society to the communist revolution:

"And so the three great civilized countries of Europe—England, France, and Germany—have all come to the conclusion that a thoroughgoing revolution of social relations on the basis of communal property has now become an urgent and inevitable necessity. This result is all the more impressive in that each of the three nations mentioned has come to it independently of the others. There is no stronger proof than this that communism is not merely the consequence of the particular situation in the English, or any other, nation, but that it is a necessary conclusion to be drawn from the premises given in the general conditions of modern civilization.

"It would therefore be desirable that the three nations come to understand each other, and that they come to know to what extent they do and do not agree with one another, for there must also be differences of opinion, since the doctrine of communism in each of the three countries has a different origin. The English have come to this result *practically*, through the rapid increase in the misery, the demoralization, and the pauperism in their country. The French have come to it *politically*, in that they began by demanding political liberty and equality and, when they found this insufficient, added to their political demands the demand for social liberty and equality. The Germans became communists *philosophically*, via conclusions from first principles."[64] On the basis of this notion, Engels then surveyed the history of socialism from the Corn Laws, Napoleon, and Hegel, to communism in its broad sweep. That historic sketch was to become part of the Communist Manifesto four years later.

In Manchester during these years, Engels also met his first love. Her name was Mary Burns, and all we know about her is that she was Irish and a woman of the working class—nothing else, not even her age. I have seen no pictures of her, neither photos nor sketches. Engels and his friends often exchanged photos, and it must be assumed that he kept some of Mary. Engels liked to sketch, and again it would be strange if she had not sat for him. We have no way of knowing whether Mary was literate or not, but if during their separation from 1844 to 1850 she ever wrote to him, Engels must have destroyed her letters after her death, together with every other evidence of her life. A fanciful account exists about their first meeting, but it is a totally fictitious prose poem supported by no evidence.[65]

There is a poem written by Friedrich's good friend Georg Weerth, which may have been inspired by her. Entitled "Mary," it describes a beautiful Irish girl working in a factory in England.[66] A poem is not a suitable source for a historian, however. Thus, in trying to write about Mary we gape into a black hole. This information vacuum attests to the urge Engels seems to have felt to keep his relations with this woman totally private. His bourgeois associates would have disapproved, his parents would have been horrified, and even his associates in the movement, beginning with Marx, thought his liaison with Mary was inappropriate for a variety of reasons. He himself may have sensed that it was an unequal relationship, that something about it was not quite proper, and that it should remain hidden.

What she contributed to Engels, besides her love, can only be surmised. She obviously introduced him to the life of the Manchester working class. Accompanied by her (and, perhaps, by her sister Lizzy, who very early became a partner in some fashion in their relationship), he wandered through the Irish slums of the city. How much real contact he had at that time with the wretches that inhabited these hellholes is not entirely clear. He may have gone through their dwellings more like a horrified voyeur. Engels later asserted that the first real proletarians he met were the German friends he made in London, in 1843, who had formed the League of the Just, but then it may also be that he did not consider the permanently unemployed residents of the Irish slums in Manchester to be 'real proletarians.' In addition to introducing him to the working class quarters of Manchester, Mary instilled in Engels a lasting love of Ireland and the Irish people, as well as in their history. In 1850, when he settled in England permanently, she became his steady companion, although they were never formally married.

In calling himself a communist, Engels was dissociating himself from the ideas of the older men who had been his drinking companions and teachers in Berlin. He was beginning to repudiate their emphasis on salvation through self-consciousness and their preoccupation with the criticism of religion. Not that he was less critical of religion than they, but he wanted to go further in his criticism. He was still enough of a Hegelian to assume that Hegel's philosophy could be overcome and transcended only by immanent criticism, in which the form would be shattered but the contents left preserved. Precisely in this he felt the Left-Hegelians were not sufficiently consistent.

The great inspiration for him at this time was Feuerbach. To be sure, not long after and for the remainder of his life, he would criticize Feuerbach for implying that a new ideology of love might help human beings to transcend their alienation. Indeed, he would later assert that this was a thoroughly anti-revolutionary ideology: "But Love—yes, Love is everywhere and always the magic-working god who in Feuerbach must help us out of all difficulties of practical life, and this in a society split into classes with diametrically opposite interests. With this, the last residue of revolutionary character has disappeared from his philosophy, and only the old refrain is left: 'Love ye each other, fall ye into each other's arms without regard to differences in sex and social status'—a general stupor from reconciliatory euphoria!"[67]

This reference to class division shows what Engels had learned from the French socialists—truly human sentiments like love cannot develop in a society rent by conflict, and if we make these sentiments into a religion, we cause them to atrophy within us even more.[68] If the socialists had given him an awareness of the class struggle, Feuerbach's method provided him with a key for the criticism of contemporary society from a broader point of view. That key revealed all existing institutions to be based on "hypocrisy (or, as we Germans call it, theology)."[69] Now Engels said this in reverse. Not only is hypocrisy religion, but also all religion is hypocrisy. The first word of religion is a lie. "Does not religion begin by showing us something human and asserting that it is something superhuman, something divine? Because we know, however, that all these lies and immorality is the result of religion, and that religious hypocrisy (theology) is the archetype of all other lies and hypocrisies, we are justified in extending the label 'theology' to the entire untruth and hypocrisy of the present, as this was first done by Feuerbach and B. Bauer."[70]

Religion is hypocrisy, he claimed, because it falsified human history into divine history and thus denied the validity of the real history of the human species. The communists, in turn, sought to reclaim the contents of history. They saw in it not the revelation of a god, but the revelation of humankind.[71] Real human history, he now asserted, was reducible to economic life. On the basis of his personal observations, together with a reading of the classics of political economy, Engels in Manchester wrote a lengthy essay on the economics of capitalism. Entitled "Outlines of a *Critique of Political Economy*," it was published together with his review of Carlyle's book. The "Outlines" are an important milestone not only in the intellectual development of Friedrich Engels, but also in the formation of Marx's own thoughts. Many years later, Marx called it a work of genius[72] and later yet argued that it had not lost its validity.[73] Even Engels, despite his customary modesty, admitted in his old age that he was proud of this article, though it was full of mistakes and out of date.[74]

In April of 1844, the young German playwright Friedrich Hebbel wrote to a friend that he had just read the first issue of a new journal, the *Deutsch-Französische Jahrbücher*. On the whole, its contents disappointed him. "Nonetheless," he wrote, "these Yearbooks contain two excellent contributions by a Prussian, Friedrich Engels, in Manchester—*The Condition of England* and *Critique of Political Economy*. Of these, it is particularly the latter that reveals the monstrous immorality on which all commerce in the world is based." What pleased Hebbel especially was that the article had confirmed some grotesque idea he had had for his latest drama. "My fantasy," he thus added, referring to Engels, "has been limping behind his understanding."[75]

The essay that both Marx and Hebbel liked so much contains, in sketchy form, a description of free-enterprise economics, a summary of the laws of capitalism later presented by Karl Marx in his large economic writings. Only one element is missing in the "Outlines" to make them a full statement of the Marxian theory of capitalism, and that missing element is the theory of surplus value. In his article, Engels singles out private property as the hidden blemish of the contemporary economic system and identifies the compulsive urge to accumulate as the prime mover of the system. Economics, he argues, should therefore be called *Bereicherungswissenschaft*—the study of accumulation or enrichment.

Accumulation in the contemporary economy, he stated, is a private urge and a private activity. There is no such thing as the wealth of nations. "The term 'national wealth,'" he wrote, "has arisen only as a result of the mania that liberal economists have for making generalizations. As long as private property exists, this expression is meaningless."[76] What is called political economy, he argued, should really be called *private* economy, "for its public relations exist only for the sake of private property."[77] By implication, Engels was asserting here that the ideal state of Hegel's theory did not exist and could not exist as long as there was private property. Two articles that Marx had contributed to the same journal issue that carried the "Outlines" argued that very same point, though in much more abstract philosophical fashion.

Property, Engels further argued, is a form of alienation, because it entails the sale of the self. Hence, the institution of property destroyed the human being as a member of a species, rendering him an isolated atom without species consciousness. The essay further anticipated Marx's refusal to recognize rent as reasonable: "To barter away the Earth itself, which is our One and All, the primary condition for our existence, was the last step toward the bartering away of ourselves. It was and is, to this day, an immorality exceeded only by the immorality of self-externalization."[78] That he meant this quite literally is made clear toward the end of the article, where he denounces the institution of private property for "having turned the human being into a commodity, the production and destruction of which depends only on the demand (that the market makes for it).[79]

Competition is described as a phenomenon as contradictory as private property, and as disastrous in its consequences.[80] Its contradictions, he asserts, bring about the anarchy of production that rules with the certainty of a natural law, and eventually yields the business cycle, which Engels describes as an ever-worsening spiral of recoveries and crises. He speaks of the minimum wage for workers as the natural price for labor as Ricardo had claimed, describes or predicts the concentration of capital in fewer and fewer hands, as well as the growth of the dispossessed proletarian masses and the consequent inevitability of the proletarian revolution. The final crisis is the *crise pléthorique*, the result of having accumulated more productive forces than the established system of social relations is able to utilize rationally.

"The struggle of capital against capital, labor against labor, soil against soil," he wrote, "urges production into a feverish heat in which it turns all natural and rational relations upside down. No capital can tolerate competition of the other unless it is brought to the highest level of activity. No piece of earth can be cultivated profitably if it does not raise its own productivity all the time. No worker can hold out against his competitors without devoting all his energies to his labor. In general, no one who enters the competitive struggle can sustain it without the highest possible exploitation of his own forces, without giving up the most truly human purposes. One consequence of the excessive tension on the one side is the inevitable atrophying of forces on the other. When the ups and downs of competition are negligible, when demand and supply, consumption and production nearly equal each other, then a period has to begin in the development of production in which there is so much excessive production force that the vast mass of the nation has nothing to sustain life, and the people starve because of all the abundance."[81]

Capital is alienation, Marx asserted later in all his work. It is the accumulated wealth that enslaves its own producers. The more workers produce, the more firmly do they forge their own chains and produce their own misery. This is the essential message of Marx's writings, and in the essay Engels wrote in 1844 the message is broadcast clearly. Engels ended his article with a sketchy vision of a more rationally organized collective economy organized according to principles suggested by both Fourier and Saint-Simon. "The productive force at the disposal of humankind is immeasurably great," he wrote. "The productivity of the soil can be increased to infinite proportions by the application of capital, labor, and science... If this immeasurably great productive potential were used consciously and in the interests of all, the labor to be done by human beings would soon be diminished to a minimum..."[82]

What Engels produced in this outline of the laws of capitalism is Marxist economic theory in a nutshell, less the theory of surplus value. If George Lukács later praised Marx for having "detected, both theoretically and historically, in the microcosm of the English factory system, in its social premises, its conditions and consequences, and in the historical trends that both lead to and in turn eventually threaten its development, precisely the macrocosm of capitalist development as a whole," he obviously did not know that Marx first read these ideas when Engels's article appeared.[83] Engels himself, we might add, often was careful to point out how much of these ideas he owed to Fourier, Ricardo, and others.[84]

In two articles written about the same time and published in a radical journal in Paris with which Marx also appears to have had connections, Engels added yet another important observation. In these articles he dealt with the rise of industrial towns and the development of a new class, the industrial proletariat. Three classes now constituted

English society—landlords, financiers, and workers—he wrote, applying ideas advanced by Ricardo and Malthus. The former two, he pointed out, constituted the classes of power, while the workers were both poor and powerless.[85]

Philosophically, Marxism can be defined as an inversion of Hegelianism, and Karl Marx did so define it. More generally, however, it can be defined as an inversion of liberalism, an inversion being that kind of intellectual operation that accepts all or some of the major assumptions and premises of an ideology, but changes their relationship or their function and sees the totality of these ideas in a decidedly different context, so that the ideology is revealed as untenable. Indeed, most of his life Marx sought not so much to invert the philosophy of Hegel, but the political economy of Smith, Ricardo, and Malthus. All his important later works are titled or subtitled "Critique of Political Economy." They all aim to show that a society of free producers, in increasing the general wealth, does not raise everyone's well being to a higher level as Adam Smith had claimed, but rather produces and reproduces human misery on a mass scale. The very rules of free enterprise, he sought to demonstrate, defeat the free enterprise system. These early articles by Engels first suggest how and why they do that.

At the very same time that Engels discovered the laws of capitalist development and the crucial position of the urban working class, another member of the Doctors' Club, Max Stirner, was working on his book, *Der Einzige und sein Eigentum*, in which he, too, discovered the poor. He, too, saw the poor living in a symbiotic relationship with the bourgeoisie, arguing that the bourgeoisie had a need for paupers in order to enhance its own worth. In short, he saw the need as purely psychological, and relationship was not in fact symbiosis, but rather parasitism. The pauper received nothing from it. We can recognize these notions as applications of Hegel's famous remarks about the master-slave relationship, but also of his assumption that property was required for being fully human.

The observation Engels made about the working class may ultimately have been suggested by the same Hegelian writings. We must note differences, however. First, although he does stress the exploitative side of the relationship between bourgeoisie and proletariat, he makes it more truly symbiotic because the workers are seen not merely as urban rabble, but as the real producers who are essential participants in the functioning of society. The bourgeoisie, in other words, does not need paupers for the purpose of flattering its status consciousness, but workers who provide for everyone's survival. The degree of abstractness with which Marx at that time was still writing about the proletariat suggests that he was still closer to Stirner, and that the contributions of Engels may have had a profound effect on him.

Engels's brief articles on the history of cities, city slums, and the working class, were pilot studies for the first major book of his own, for which he gathered material during his stay in England. This was *The Condition of the Working Class in England*, for which he made observations not only in Manchester but also in a fairly large sample of other industrial towns that he had occasion to visit in England. He did not finish the manuscript until after his return to Barmen, quite fittingly because he meant also to describe the condition of the workers in Germany, including his hometown.[86]

It is easy to discern behind this a repudiation of his own father's way of life and source of income, and hence as another milestone in his Oedipal rebellion and in the establishment of his own ego autonomy. He also intended the book to be a flaming accusation of the English bourgeoisie, however. "Before the entire world, I accuse the English bourgeoisie of murder, theft, and all other crimes on a mass scale," he wrote to Marx, and added that he would send the book to many public personalities in England. "Those chaps shall think of me," he added.[87] Engels here was voicing a sentiment shared by many leading avant-garde intellectuals of the time. Working-class slums in England and elsewhere had by that time become a public scandal, and middle-class consciousness was beginning to express its feelings of outrage, as is evident from the writings of such men as Carlyle, Dickens, and Ruskin, as well as the commissions formed to investigate the conditions of the poor—conditions whose reports would become such important material for the writings of Marx. Steven Marcus is quite correct in identifying

Engels as a radical spokesman for this middle-class consciousness.[88]

Written down in Barmen during the winter of 1844-5, the book reiterated the laws of capitalist development that Engels had sketched in his "Outlines for a Critique of Political Economy.[89] It further gave a history of the industrial working class, largely derived from Peter Gaskell's book, *The Manufacturing Population of England*, which had been published in 1833. In this context, Engels painted a rather idyllic picture, which in later years he acknowledged to have been overdrawn, of a pre-industrial working class living a rather cozy existence, in which work and leisure alternated with each other pleasantly, both being varied. Life for the English yeoman farmer, according to this sentimental picture, was simple and healthy, although it was also stupid and narrow, and in this sense not worthy of human beings. In almost the same words, Engels would no more than five or six years later sneer at the petty-bourgeois ideal.[90]

Having drawn an idyllic picture of labor in pre-capitalist periods, Engels then gave a chilling account of the alienation of labor since the industrial revolution. The pertinent passages make it clear that he assumed the basic dignity of labor, believing that human fulfillment could be attained only in productive work undertaken on one's own free will. He went on to argue, however, that in the modern factory all work was forced labor. He eloquently described the loss of self resulting from such alienated labor, the transformation of the individual worker into a commodity bought and sold on the market, the failure of modern factory work to engage the full faculties of the human being, and the resulting withering of most of these faculties—the dehumanization of the worker. These passages were not written down in their final form until 1845, but a comparison of Marx's "Economic-Philosophic Manuscripts" of 1844 with Engels's book indicates clearly that in drafting this fragment, Marx drew on the oral accounts that Engels had given him.

The main body of Engels's book was devoted to vivid descriptions of life in the working class slums of Manchester—the crowded, filthy dwellings totally without sanitary facilities, the inhuman conditions of work and their consequences in disease, maiming, infant mortality, and shortened life spans, the ruthless exploitation of women and children, and the total dissolution of family life. Dreary statistics culled from official reports and schematic drawings of dwelling units illustrated the devastating narrative, which included provocative theories of city planning and slum development under capitalism. Engels argued that one prime concern of the bourgeoisie was to conceal slums from public view, especially from the view of the businessmen riding to and from work every day. The development of slums in industrial cities was a theme to which he returned decades later in his articles on the Housing Question.[91]

In discussing the layout of Manchester, with its squalid quarters carefully hidden from the businessmen and their wives who might pass through them on their way to do their shopping, Engels pointed out that there was a belt of lower-middle-class districts separating the filthy inner city, with its destitution and despair, from the other ring of wealthy homes. It is remarkable that he did not develop the broader theoretical realization that one might have discerned behind this—that in the relationship between owners and workers, between the beneficiaries and the victims of capitalism, the mediation of interstitial classes and layers played a crucial role. Not to have seen or expressed this clearly is indeed one of the major weaknesses of Marxism as a political theory.

In concluding his account, Engels compared the condition of the workers to that of the medieval serfs in all essential respects, with the differences that serfdom under feudalism was open, while the slavery of the wage slave was dishonestly concealed from himself and from all others. However, he continued, part of this scheme of deception was the libertarian ideology of capitalism that promised freedom to all, and the exploited would see to it that this principle of freedom would be realized. Meanwhile, the various forms of criminality flourishing in the slums were the first, crudest, and least effective modes of the noble struggle waged by the workers against capitalist exploitation.[92] The book ended with expressions of confidence that the workers' alienation from their work and from their masters would surely develop their consciousness as a class, and that a bloody revolution would soon erupt that would right the wrongs. The revolution itself, he wrote, was a certainty, but its savagery and bloodiness would be inversely proportional to the development of the workers' consciousness, rationality, and capacity for self-abnegation.

Engels here, as later throughout his life, stressed the importance of self-consciousness as a precondition for assuring the rationality of historical process and outcomes. This should be noted, because later interpreters, overlooking his emphasis on self-consciousness, gave a narrow determinist interpretation to his writings. We should also note how clearly his views could already be distinguished from those of the Anarchists. Just as he did not share Stirner's glorification of the *Lumpenproletariat* as the salt of the earth, so he here repudiated Bakunin's belief in creative violence. Although at times both Marx and Engels reveled in the foretaste of power and revenge, as we will see in their more responsible statements they made it clear they wished to eliminate coercion and bloodshed from human intercourse and hoped for a revolution that would be as non-violent as possible.

In later years, Engels would concede that even the certainty of the coming of the revolution expressed in this book had been an illusion due, he argued, to his youthful ardor. The book nonetheless remained one of his favorite works. Marx, too, appreciated this ardor. Twenty years after the book appeared, he wrote to Engels: "Re-reading your work has made me aware, regretfully, of my senescence. How fresh, passionate, keenly anticipating, and free of learned and scientific scruples, is the way in which you attack the subject! And even the illusion that tomorrow, or the day after tomorrow, the result will come to light in history, too, gives the whole thing a degree of warmth and joyous humor against which the later 'gray-in-gray' makes a damned unpleasant contrast."[93]

Appearing no more than a year after the great Silesian weavers' riots, which had focused attention on the condition of the working cities in Germany, the book attracted a good deal of attention there. Its first edition was sold out in three years, and a second printing was published in 1848. Ironically, several conservative authors reviewed it quite favorably, finding it a convenient argument against the threat of liberalism. This would not be the last time that German conservatives thought they might have useful allies in those who spoke for the workers' movement.[94]

Contemporary opinion about the book ranges widely. Marcus hails it as a classic of Victorian radicalism and the best work Engels wrote, a stirring, pioneering book that pointed an accusing finger at conditions many others had noted, but none had pilloried so mercilessly. Henderson criticizes it as a tendentious piece of propaganda based on slipshod use of insufficient evidence, opinionated in its interpretations, unfair in its portrayal of the factory owners, and its major prediction based on wishful thinking. Both of them may be right. It was meant to be a conscience-raiser, hard-hitting, and charmingly direct—a polemical tract, not a scholarly treatise—and, at least for a short time, it made precisely the impact it had intended. Moreover, even Henderson concedes that it became a milestone in the development of Marxist thought. It is all the more curious that among contemporary Marxists, at least in the West, the book is not discussed very much.

All his life, Engels planned to do more than he had time or energy to accomplish. One of his unfinished (or even not started) projects in Manchester was a translation of Feuerbach's book, *The Essence of Christianity* into English.[95] Although there may have been other projects that were not carried out, one must agree with Engels that his two years in Manchester constituted a decisive period for him. Surveying what he had learned, I am tempted to argue that he had become a Marxist before Marx, that he had made the transition from the Hegelian Left, and its rather directionless radicalism so reminiscent of the American New Left in the 1960s, to a much more structured world view, which he himself later came to call materialist, and in making this transition he had at least in passing made most of the points that later made up the Marxist system of ideas, and which became milestones in Marx's own repudiation of the Hegelian Left.

Most of the important milestones of this transition mark Engels's

Manchester writings—the destruction of the human being as a 'species being' and the alienation of labor in a society based on private property as the end to the means of production, the contradiction between the abundant productive forces in capitalist society and its irrational and immoral production relations, the humanist inversion of both theology and the bourgeois state leading to the 'materialist' conviction that the real life of a society goes on in its productive activities, the recognition of the crucial role played by the industrial revolution in the development of modern England and the resolve to study all civilized societies in the light of the effects of this industrial revolution.

Other important aspects of his writing during this period include the attention given to the class struggle as the essence of politics and to the working class not only as the chief victim of capitalism but also as a liberator class, and of course the first outlines of a theory of capitalism, complete with the laws of accumulation and concentration, the anarchy of production, the increasing misery of the proletariat, the business cycle, final crisis, and revolutionary overthrow. Moreover, Engels called himself a communist before Marx did, and made important attempts at tracing the history of socialism from its utopian to its 'scientific' forms.

In later life, Engels would modestly and falsely attribute all these discoveries to Marx. True, in his *Geschichte des Bundes der Kommunisten*, he was bold enough to assert that in Manchester he himself discovered the determining forces of economics in modern history and the importance of class struggles as the substance of politics, but added that Marx was making the same discoveries at the same time, although he expressed them at first in much more abstract form.[96] Engels here was referring to two contributions Marx had published in the same journal, which featured his review of Carlyle and his "Outlines of a Critique of Political Economy." In one of these articles, Marx used a discussion of Jewish emancipation to offer a stinging criticism of the entire world of commerce. In the other, he applied the technique of immanent criticism through the inversion of subject and predicate that Feuerbach had used to dethrone all gods for the purpose of dethroning the state, especially that of Hegelian theory, and to proclaim civil society to be the secret of the state. Both articles were milestones in the intellectual development of Karl Marx, just as the "Outlines" were for Engels.

The two young men read each other's contributions and seem to have recognized at once that they were in complete agreement with each other on all essentials, and that by separate paths they had come to identical and novel views. Each obviously had a great deal to give the other. Marx had given up the editorship of the *Rheinische Zeitung* in the spring of 1843. During the subsequent summer, he had negotiated with his friend Arnold Ruge concerning the creation of a new radical journal, the *Deutsch-Französische Jahrbücher*, and in the fall had moved to Paris.

The first and only volume of the new journal, containing his and Engels's contributions, had appeared in February of 1844, and he must have read Engels's manuscripts before that time. They must have had a tremendously great influence on him, and may well have been the impetus he needed to begin the intensive study of classical political economists. In other words, Marx's attempt to write a critique of political economy might never have been made if he had not read Engels's manuscript. That the last section of these fragments, dealing with the alienation of labor, is obviously based on Engels's account of his impressions in Manchester deserves emphasis, although it is not clear when Engels had the chance to convey these impressions to Marx.

In the late summer of 1844, on his return to Barmen after his two years in Manchester, Engels stopped in Paris for a visit with Karl and Jenny Marx. He stayed for ten days, during which he not only sealed his friendship with his future partner, but also met some of the leading radicals then living there, including Michael Bakunin. It is likely that before his visit to Paris, Engels and Marx already corresponded with each other. Once they began conversing, they found themselves, according to Engels's later accounts, in total agreement on every essential point, and a relationship began between the two men that seems unique in Western intellectual history. For both of them, the meeting was the most decisive moment of their lives, and they seem to have been aware of that. "Dear Karl," Engels wrote shortly afterwards, "I have not felt so joyous and humane as I did during the ten days I spent with you."[97]

What was it that they gave to each other? What were the contributions by which they complemented each other's knowledge and understanding in so harmonious a fashion as to make them fast friends? We have seen Engels's contributions. He had introduced Marx to the proletariat as a concrete phenomenon. To be sure Marx had already begun to be interested in the poor and the exploited. Two years before his meeting with Engels, he had written brief articles about the plight of the peasants in the Eifel region, but even in his 1844 article on Hegel's philosophy of right, he had not mentioned the proletariat. It had required Engels, who had observed the condition of the working class in his native Barmen and in the slums of Manchester with a discerning eye, to place the working class centrally into the thinking of Marx.

Even then, the proletariat in Marx's writings at first remained an abstraction, the Hegelian opposite of wealth and property, and therefore its abolisher—a class that had no merit and gave no promise except as a destroyer, indeed a destroyer of its own self. For Engels, who had roamed through Manchester's Irish ghetto with his lover, the workers were more than an abstraction. They were the subject of sympathetic study, an object of compassion, and a class with which he identified. Ever since his first stay in Manchester, Engles spoke in his published utterances of workers as the only decent people in an otherwise evil world, and as the only people who always treated him decently. "No worker...has ever treated me as a foreigner," he wrote in his book.[98]

Engels had also introduced Marx to the study of economics, and had provided in his "Outlines" an important preliminary statement of their later views. Many years later, Engels summarized the most noteworthy theses of Marx's *Das Kapital*—that the concentration and accumulation of capital and the accompanying and commensurate process of accumulation of excess labor force make the social revolution both necessary and possible.[99] That, however, is no more than a summary of what Engels himself had asserted between 1842 and 1844. Furthermore, Engels contributed certain talents to the partnership—an orderly mind, a quick intelligence, a fabulous memory for detail, and a remarkably journalistic talent for writing clear, forthright, informative, and stimulating pieces on the shortest possible notice and, it must be added, with a minimum of factual knowledge.

These talents were aided by what came to be an encyclopedic though, again, often superficial knowledge of history, languages, geography, science, technology, and the wide and complicated world of commerce and industry. The last of these areas of competence made Engels very much a practical man of the world, who knew his way around wherever he went and who could give sound practical advice in many situations. Finally, he brought to the partnership his lifelong urge to attach himself to men older and more learned than he, together with the unshakeable conviction that in Karl Marx he had found the greatest man to whom anyone might be able to play second fiddle.[100]

What impressed Engels about his friend is not all that easy to formulate. Obviously, Marx impressed all those who met him as a man of immense learning in a wide variety of fields, ranging from the classics of antiquity to contemporary studies in politics, economics, and history. He had an extraordinarily quick and agile mind, a sardonic wit, and a magnificent gift for generating hypotheses on the bases of vast and complex information. The subtlety of his thinking, the power of his formulas, and the combination of simplicity with infinite complexity that runs through everything he wrote impressed all those who met him, at least as long as they shared his views. Moses Hess, after his first meeting with him in 1841, described him as the greatest if not the only real philosopher living then, a man who combined deep philosophic seriousness with cutting wit. "Imagine Rousseau, Voltaire, Holbach, Lessing, Heine, and Hegel *united* in one person—" he wrote, "I say *united*, not thrown together—and you have Dr. Marx."[101]

According to Engels, this remarkable mind worked best in situations of crisis, when vast amounts of disparate knowledge had to be integrated and transformed into tactical decisions, on the spot,[102] which means that Engels regarded Marx as the ideal revolutionary leader. He did not hesitate to claim that in less troubled times his own judgment was sometimes better than Marx's. Even in those calmer moments, however, if at times he did not agree with Marx's judgment, he never ceased being impressed by his theoretical talents. "Marx," he wrote toward the end of his life, "stood higher, saw further, surveyed more and more rapidly than all we others. Marx was a genius, and we others at most talented people.[103]

Engels also greatly admired his friend's cool detachment, his contempt, whether stoic or cynical, for all manifestations of emotion and sentiment, even in the face of his own and other people's misery. Marx had an inhuman talent for steeling himself against softness and for shutting out unpleasant realities with a bitter joke. We may well consider this one of his most serious human failings, and the symptom of deep neuroses. For Engels, however, this studied coldness was an indicator of Marx's intellectual superiority. This from a person like Engels, who as a boy gave his pocket money to the poor, and who as a young lover agonized over the misery of the Manchester proletariat! This from a kind, sunny, open man, who never lost his capacity for compassion and righteous indignation, and whose entire life effort was an attempt to make it possible for all people to be human toward each other!

If such a man could be deeply impressed, indeed awed, by Marx's icy reserve and cold-nosed cynicism, it shows to what extent he was trying to combat or curb his own human sentiments, or as he would have called it sneeringly, his sentimentality. The assumption suggests itself that in resisting all tendencies toward sentimentality, he was combating the 'weakness' he condemned in his mother and in bourgeois wives in general.

When these two young men met in Paris, they had read each other's articles and had concluded that they were in basic agreement. Engels reported that Marx meanwhile had worked out a set of terse, concise sentences representing the gist of what both of them later liked to call "our theory." He claimed that he recognized these formulations as superior to his own and as an exciting synthesis of his own empirical work with Marx's philosophic prolegomena. As he put it, when presenting a summary of their theory, Marx had "elaborated this idea into its final form and placed it in front of me in words almost as clear as the summary I have presented above."[104] Having steeped myself both in Marx's turgid prose and in the clear, concise language Engels could write, I wonder whether once again Engels was not too modest. One might argue that there was no clearer statement of their theory than Engels's own essay on political economy. What he undoubtedly meant was that Marx had the ability of stating the insights they shared in much more profound, suggestive, and provocative philosophic terms.

It is tempting to speculate on the balance of the contributions made by each of the two partners. While the quantity of ideas contributed by Engels was far greater at this stage than those supplied by Marx, the latter's searching mind appears to have provided the critical mass of theoretical integration. At the same time neither could have made his own contribution without the other, and by working together they produced a theory of far more profound impact than either would have been able to elaborate by himself.

During the ten days they spent together in the summer of 1844, Engels and Marx formulated their ideas in a way that excited them both. They had another epiphany—the vision of a revolutionary communist movement based on the scientific comprehension of empirical facts about economic life and the class struggle. No longer, wrote Engels years later, would they use their fantasy to think up the most perfect, ideal society. Instead, they now knew that the task was to develop a rational, scientific grasp of the nature, conditions, and resulting general goals of the struggle waged by the proletariat.[105]

That they, themselves, as the spokesmen of this revolutionary movement, would end on the scaffold before long they seem to have taken for granted, and the idea does not seem to have frightened them.[106] The immediate corollary of their conversion was that two new and vast tasks opened up for them. One was that of elaborating their views scientifically in all relevant areas of knowledge. The other was to win the German and European proletariat over to their ideas.[107] These two tasks meant nothing less that rewriting all history and social science, together with philosophy and other branches of learning, and helping to bring about the final social revolution.

The first joint project for them, however, was to clarify the differences that separated them from their former friends in the Hegelian Left. Left Hegelianism might be summarized as a series of attempts to use Hegelian concepts and assumptions in highly speculative fashion as a means to criticize reality, instead of justifying it, as Hegel tended to do in his mature period. Engels and Marx had been part of that group, but had grown beyond their ideas. The collaboration between them began as a manuscript of about thirty pages, drafted by Engels, tentatively entitled "*Kritik der kritischen Kritik*," a loose collection of short essays in which he bitingly sought to expose the high-sounding but empty phrases and the factual ignorance of several third-rate scribes who by this time had begun to take an interest in the poor and to call themselves socialists.

Before he could finish the manuscript, Engels left Paris to return once more to his hometown, leaving the unfinished work with Marx. He came back to Barmen a very different person from the one who had left for Manchester two years before, and the changes he had undergone were to re-induce conflicts and dilemmas he had faced more than once before. Once again, and with greater urgency, he would be compelled to make decisions about his career. In addition, the ideological commitment had had made by teaming up with Marx was to provoke a crisis—by no means the last one—in his relations with his parents. Further, his stay in Barmen appears to have been a major turning point in his relationship with women. Finally, he continued to develop his mind by an active program of reading and discussion.

One of the first books he read at this time was Max Stirner's recent manifesto of anarchist individualism, *Der Einzige und sein Eigentum*. This book was at that time the last word in the development of the Hegelian Left. Stirner's work was, to a large extent, a reply to Ludwig Feuerbach's work on Christianity. Feuerbach had argued that speculative philosophy would never solve human misery, because philosophy was itself a manifestation of alienation. Instead of solving problems in one's mind, one should instead liberate oneself from speculative philosophy and religion entirely. Feuerbach's answer to merely intellectual solutions was the advocacy of materialism and sensuality. In his reply, Stirner had argued that Feuerbach had failed in his effort because the concepts he used, and indeed his entire conception of the problem, were part of the very philosophy he was trying to criticize.

What Stirner advocated, therefore, was the repudiation of all ideals and ideologies as self-enslaving, alienating, and oppressive fetishes of the mind. He denounced not only Christianity and his modern, secularized variants including the entire Enlightenment tradition and the doctrine of universal love advanced by Feuerbach, but also the most recent socialist and communist doctrines. In their places, he proposed absolute individualism and egotism based on the repudiation of all authority other than the individual will, including the authority of any revolutionary creed or organization.

In short, Stirner advocated anarchism, and his book was written in anarchist style, that is, with seemingly deliberate disregard for structure and orderly presentation. Some of its ideas coincided with those Marx and Engels had just worked out. It denounced Feuerbach's solution as inadequate. It recognized the state as a manifestation of alienation analogous to religion, and it identified the poor and exploited as the rebellious force that would deliver mankind from religious and political oppression. The differences with Marx and Engels's ideas, however, were more important. Stirner's individualism was compatible with the notion of universal competition, as well as with the institution of property. In the opinion of Marx and Engels, it therefore amounted to a defense of bourgeois society. Further, his understanding of history as a succession of different modes of consciousness, different illusions dominating human minds that could be overcome as soon as mankind rid itself once and for all time of them, was totally opposed to the sociological understanding Engels and Marx had gained.

Engels read the book immediately upon its publication. He thought it to be the work of a madman, but so consistent in its madness that it would lend itself to a dialectical inversion, in Feuerbachian style. "We must not throw it aside," he wrote to Marx, "but exploit it precisely as the perfect expression of the existing madness, and by *inverting it,* build on it. This egotism is so exaggerated, so mad, and at the same time so self-conscious, that in its one-sidedness it cannot maintain itself for a moment, but must change at once into communism… We must make a cause into our own selfish cause before we can do anything for it… In this sense, it is for selfish reasons that we are communists, for selfish reasons that we want to be *human beings*, not mere individuals… Feuerbach's 'human being' is derived from God. He has come from God to 'man,' and hence 'man' is still crowned with the theological halo of abstraction.

"The true path of arriving at 'man' is the reverse. We must take the ego, the empirical sensual individual, as our point of departure, not in order to get stuck there, like Stirner, but, from there, to rise to the 'human being.' 'Man' is always a spectral apparition as long as he does not have his base in empirical human beings. In short, we must take empiricism and materialism as our points of departure… Altogether I am getting more and more annoyed with all this theoretical chatter, and every word I am using about 'man,' ever line I have to write or read against theology and abstraction, as well as against crass materialism, irks me. It is a completely different thing to deal with real living things, with historic developments and results instead of with all these figments of hot air… That is still the best thing, as long as we are forced to use nothing more than our writing pens and cannot yet realize our ideas immediately with our hand, or if necessary with our fists."[108]

Marx read the book shortly after, and at first thought that Engels had overestimated its importance. Apparently, however, he changed his mind. By far the largest portion of the major work they wrote jointly a year later, *The German Ideology*, is taken up by a critique of Stirner, in response to his challenge that communism, like Christianity, would lead to the destruction or enslavement of the individual. The letter from Engels must be considered one of the sources for the sketchy remarks Marx wrote down about fifteen months later, which are known as the *Theses on Feuerbach*, which in turn constituted one of the germs from which that important book sprouted.

From August 1844 to April 1845, Engels stayed at his parents' home. He worked on the notes he had collected in Manchester and finished the book based on them, his first major publication. In his letters to Marx, he sought to spur his friend on to finish his own project—Marx was to write a critique of political economy, presumably a book-length synthesis of Engels's earlier essay and Marx's philosophy of alienation. Engels also suggested other publication projects they might undertake to spread their views, including a series of translations from French socialist literature.

As soon as he had arrived in Barmen, he had watched for signs of social progress that would confirm the millennial optimism that gripped him, and he had seen what he wished to see—that the younger generation was training its parents to treat servants more decently, thus signifying the growth of radicalism and a social conscience among the bourgeoisie. He talked about the increase in political participation and other signs of progress—the growth of the town, the rapid development of industry. Entire forests had been cut down, he noted with satisfaction, unaware that he sounded like a modern strip-mine owner. Meanwhile, he noted with pleasure that the workers no longer were accepting their miserable condition passively. Instead, they were taking their revenge against the exploiters by increasing their criminality. "The streets of Barmen," he wrote, "are no longer safe at night."[109]

The same optimistic belief that the proletarian revolution was imminent led Engels to become active in and around his hometown trying to make contact with the working class, but even more to win adherents for his ideas among people of his own class. This propaganda work culminated in a series of lectures he and a few friends, including Moses Hess, gave before large gatherings of the Elberfeld bourgeoisie in February 1845. He summarized for his listeners—businessmen and professionals—the laws of development of capitalism and warned them about the coming revolution that, he predicted, would be bloodier and gorier than the terror of 1793. All this, he argued, could be predicted with scientific assurance. The only way in which the coming war of the poor against the rich might take milder forms would be through the rapid assimilation by the proletariat of communist doctrines. The higher the level of class consciousness, the less vengeful would be the revolution, and if the entire proletariat could be taught communist ideas before the final cataclysm, the entire revolution would take a peaceful course.

Engels was just then writing down these same ideas in his book on Manchester. To these warnings, he added some vision of a better society to come in which all that would have to be sacrificed would be the false needs created by capitalism—that false semblance of enjoyment created by evil conditions, which in fact went against both the reason and heart of the same people who now enjoyed false advantages. The new order would create the kind of environment for all people where each individual could freely develop his own human nature, live in truly human relations with his neighbor, and need not fear convulsive changes in his life situation. "The truly human life, with all its conditions and needs," he said, "is something we have no wish to destroy. On the contrary, we really want to make it possible."[110]

After a few of these meetings, the city authorities forbade further propaganda assemblies of this kind. Just at that time, the manuscript Engels had left for Marx in the fall appeared as a book under their joint names. To the thirty pages of Engels, Marx had added over two hundred more, and had published the book under the sacrilegious title, *The Holy Family*. Its principal idea was based to some extent on Engels's letter cited above. "The 'idea,'" Marx wrote, "has always made itself ridiculous to the extent that it was different from 'interest.' On the other hand, it is easy to understand that every mass interest that comes through in history, when it first enters the world stage goes far beyond its actual limits in the 'idea' or the 'imagination' and mistakes itself for the 'human' interest, pure and simple. This 'illusion' constitutes what Fourier calls the 'tone' of any one historic epoch."[111]

Clearly, Marx and Engels wanted to dissociate themselves from high-sounding phrases about general human values. A few years later, in another joint work, they rejected the term "humanism" as "that phrase with which German confusion artists from Heuchlin to Herder have tried to cloak their embarrassment."[112] They wished to identify themselves with what they called the 'movement,' and by this they meant the development of human activities and relationships, the changing framework of institutions, and changes in aims and interests. Their statement of this resolve took the form, in this book, of a huge diatribe against Bruno Bauer and his circle. For Engels, the book was a source of keen embarrassment that he remembered for a long time. Since he had contributed so little to it, he felt ashamed at being listed as the first author. He also thought that the work was an attempt to shoot at mice with a cannon. "The thing is too large," he wrote Marx. "The sovereign contempt with which the two of us come out against the *Literatur-Zeitung* is in glaring contrast with the 22 pages we devote to it." Moreover, he thought it so esoteric that the public would not be interested in it, and he knew that the blasphemous title would embarrass him vis-à-vis his family.[113]

Ah, yes, his family. It is not clear whether his parents had any inkling of what kind of person their first-born son had become since leaving school almost seven years before. Now, however, when they observed his inflammatory activities before their very noses and perhaps saw his copy of *The Holy Family*, it was clear to them that he had turned into a godless communist and had fallen into bad company, indeed. His parents reacted with shock, anger, and reproaches. They sought to persuade him to return to a respectable business life, and made offensive remarks about his new friends. They watched him, spied on him, tried to censor his mail, and interrogated him. He felt humiliated and tortured. "I cannot eat, drink, sleep, or let out a fart without that same damned face with its droopy piety being right in front of my nose," he wrote to Marx about his father. "I might go out or stay at home, be silent or speak, read or write, laugh or not laugh, I might do what I wish, and at once my 'old man' will put on this infamous grimace."[114]

Engels had no intention of giving up his new convictions. Indeed, his parents' anger and sorrow, their silent or spoken reproaches, their prayers in his presence, and their whispers behind his back made him stubborn and defiant. Yet, neither did he wish to break with them because of the love he felt for his mother, and also because he did not wish to cut himself off from the financial security his family represented.[115] Persuaded by the mediation of his brother-in-law, Emil

Blank, with whom he got along well, he even spent a few weeks in his father's business office, trying to like the work. "But," he wrote, "I was sick of it before I started the work. Huckstering is too abominable, Barmen is too abominable, the waste of time is too abominable, and most especially it is too abominable to remain not just a bourgeois but even a manufacturer, i.e. a bourgeois actively working against the proletariat…

"And it may well be possible," he added, "as a communist, to be outwardly a bourgeois and a huckstering animal as long as one *does not write*, but to do communist propaganda in grand style and at the same time practice huckstering and industry—that won't do." In addition, he thought himself much too exuberant and bohemian for the quiet, sedate, pious, and solidly German life of this business town.[116] What profound irony this letter represents. Not only was Engels proving at the very time he was writing it that one could quite successfully combine a business career with writing communist tracts, but for another twenty-five years he was going to do precisely what he said he could not do—be a bourgeois and a manufacturer *and* write communist propaganda in grand style!

If family ties and a feeling of financial dependence caused Engels to try working in his father's firm, another reason for this was that he was in love. Upon his return from Paris he had at once plunged into a hectic social life, including flirtations with a number of "lovely women." Now, one of these flirtations had turned into a serious emotional involvement. Nothing is known about the woman he wooed so ardently during the winter of 1844-5, except that the courtship ended in disaster. From the bitterness with which he subsequently would describe the bourgeois marriage market, it can be hypothesized that the woman he courted was from his own class, and that she turned him down for someone whom she or her parents considered a better match.

That was the last time Engels seriously contemplated a liaison with a bourgeois woman. Henceforth, he would scornfully refer to all upper- and middle-class women as whores, and for the rest of his life would have sexual relations only with women from the working class or the peasantry. In the light of his professed feminist views, this is noteworthy. His genuine belief in sexual equality expressed itself in a predilection for women who were strong—self-reliant women who could fight side by side with men as partners. Yet, all his life, he surrounded himself with women who, at least in education, were his inferiors, who could not share all his interests, and who therefore were condemned, at least partly to a servant role.

With this crisis in his love life resolved in so disappointing a manner, Engels and his parents resolved the crisis in their relationship, as well. Obviously, Engels wanted to leave. Likewise, his presence in Barmen had become so embarrassing to his parents that they must have been glad to see him go. What may be surprising, however, is that they agreed to pay him a fairly generous monthly allowance, seemingly with no strings attached. With perhaps one interruption shortly after he left, they seem to have paid him regularly for the next three years, and in other ways he maintained friendly relations with his family. In the summer of 1846, he spent a vacation with them at a Belgian beach resort. Engels thus was free to become a full-time professional revolutionary.

Departing from Barmen in April, he joined Marx in Brussels, where the two friends plunged into a hectic life of political organization and agitation, journalism, and more ambitious writing. They traveled much, alone as well as together, including a lengthy joint adventure in England. When in the early fall of 1845 the two friends returned to Brussels from this trip, Mary Burns accompanied them. In Brussels, she went with her lover everywhere, including to meetings with his radical friends. This apparently caused resentment. Mrs. Jenny Marx, the daughter of a nobleman, snubbed the proletarian lover of her husband's comrade, and would do so the rest of her life. Some of the workers and craftsmen in this circle of radicals also appear to have resented the spectacle of the young bourgeois showing off his pretty working-class mistress.

We have here another instance of the difficulty Engels often had, despite his claims to the contrary, in getting along with men of the working class. Certainly he was aware that they suspected him and Marx because of their higher education.[117] The contempt he often expressed for workers in his private correspondence may have been manifest to them, however, if only by his dignified bearing, his spirited and obviously learned style of conversation, and the elegant, solidly bourgeois fashion in which he dressed. Marx, too, in his speech, manner, and clothing, never made the slightest attempt to appear anything other than bourgeois.

Whatever the motives of the friends in Brussels, they treated Mary Burns with a degree of hostility that Engels never forgot nor forgave, and she returned to Manchester. Henceforth, he would keep her more or less concealed not only from his bourgeois acquaintances, but also from his radical associates, including the Marx family. Until her death, he mentioned her only once in all his voluminous correspondence with Marx, and in Marx's letters there is only one contemptuous reference to her.

In the summer of 1846, the two friends decided that Engels should go to Paris to establish contact with like-minded people there, and to counteract the influence of an ideological rival, Karl Grün. There, too, he had little influence on the workers he met. The cultural and intellectual gulf separating them from him was great, and if Engels thought his bohemian lifestyle would bridge the gulf, he was in error. Indeed, Engels in Paris was in his most bohemian phase. On his trip there, a pretty young woman, Sybille Peach, accompanied him. She was the common-law wife of Moses Hess, who married her some years later. Hess had asked Engels to help Sybille across the border into France. Soon, Engels was including gossip about her in his letters to Marx. He repeatedly wrote about the grand time he was having in Paris, where the working-class women were pretty, and of easy virtue, and were succumbing to his charm in large numbers.

During his days in Paris he tried to mend his political fences, while at night he flitted from one dance emporium and one woman to another with much pleasure. That sex was much on his mind at the time is shown also by the fact that in February 1847, he wrote a pornographic satire on the Lola Montez scandal, about which he gleefully reported to Marx. Lola Montez, a scheming woman with a shady past, had been the mistress of the King of Bavaria, who got rid of her after she became too involved in matters of high policy. Unhappily, Engels's naughty piece has been lost or is buried deeply in some archive.

"If I had an annual income of 5,000 francs," he wrote to Marx a few weeks afterwards, "I would do nothing but work and have fun with women until I was kaput. If French women did not exist, life would not be worth the trouble, but as long as there are *grisettes*, OK! (*Mais tant qu'il y a des grisettes, va!*)"[118] After his disappointment in love and his liberation from a business career, he apparently thought of combining his revolutionary journalism with a bohemian life, if only his monthly allowance from his father were sufficient.

Later that year, he and Sibylle Hess had an affair. While getting drunk with Stefan Born, one day, he had bragged about it, and Hess may have heard the news from Born. Whoever the gossip was, Hess found out, accused Engels of having raped his wife, and threatened to shoot him. "If that ass," Engels wrote, "should insist on his absurd lie about rape, then I am able to serve him some earlier, contemporary, and later details that will blow his mind. For instance, last July, this she-ass of Bileam, here in Paris, made me a declaration of her love in *optima forma*, with resignation mixed in, and entrusted me with the most intimate nocturnal secrets of her ménage. Her rage against me is nothing but scorned love.

"Besides," he continued, "in Valenciennes I thought of Moses only in the second instance. In the first instance, I wanted to revenge myself for all the meanness they showed to Mary… For the rest of it, he is free to take his revenge on all my present, past, and future mistresses, and for this purpose I recommend him[119] (1) the Flemish giantess residing in my former quarters, 87 Chausée d'Ixelles, on the first floor, whose name is Mademoiselle Josephine, and (2) a French mademoiselle Felicie, who will be arriving in Brussels on Sunday, the 23rd, with the first train from Cologne, on her way to Paris…"[120]

During this period, Engels not only took obvious delight in the company of working-class women, he also gallantly defended them against sexual exploitation by others, and this got him into trouble. The story is told that in January 1848, he had learned that a French count that had lived with a working-class woman had suddenly thrown her out without making a financial settlement with her. Engels confronted him and threatened to make the matter public if the nobleman did not make amends. The gentleman apparently had friends in high places, however, complained that he was being blackmailed, and Engels was deported as an undesirable alien.[121]

Let us now leave Engels's sex life and turn to the work he and Marx sought to accomplish in these first years of their collaboration. One of these tasks was literary, involving not only the production of major book-length statements, but also a great deal of political journalism. Wherever they were, they were forever eager to have journals at their disposal so that they could have their views published, better yet to get paid honoraria for their contributions, and best of all to control a journal of their own. Some of the landmarks of their lives involved new relationships with one journal or another.

The other activity in which they were engaged much of their time was organizational. They wished to mobilize the working class, convert them to their views, and lead or guide tem in the coming revolution. This sounds more grandiose than what in fact Marx and Engels managed to do in the first decades of their collaboration. The only following they could muster for many years consisted of small groups—a few dozen, rarely as many as a hundred—and the political reliability of these few followers or sympathizers was always doubtful. Few, if any, in the early decades, were proletarians. If Engels or Marx called them workers, it must be understood that they were tailors, weavers, shoemakers, carpenters, or practitioners of other crafts—in short, members of the petty bourgeoisie.

For influence over these few small groups of radicalized craftsmen, the various socialist and communist intellectuals fought with tenacity and incredible bitterness, and an inordinate portion of everyone's energies, including those of Engels and Marx, was spent throughout their entire lives on vicious squabbles fought with no holds barred over issues that, in retrospect often seem unworthy of so much venom. If they shot at mice with artillery, however, or if they went for the jugular with personal invective little short of slander or won a vote in some committee through connivance and trickery, it was because their antagonists' false theories and disastrous strategies had to be totally discredited. Indeed, their rivals had to be destroyed. These, after all, were not tame academic disputes. The fate of humanity was at stake.

Engels spent much of his time and energy on this fight against various rivals. He seems to have enjoyed these fights and gloated over every real or imagined victory, however shabby the means by which it was won. Within the community of radical exiles, some people considered him to be Marx's hatchet man, and hated him for it. Marx, however, showed many times that he had no need of anyone to do the dirty fighting for him. He himself was not only the undisputed master in invective and intrigue, but he was also far more implacable in pursuing antagonists, however puny, and far more ready to drop more important tasks for such vendettas. Perhaps Engels enjoyed these fights only when he was winning, or when he thought he was winning. In fact, more often than not, these polemics alienated many radicals from Marx and Engels, suggesting again that they were inept at converting people to their views, especially people from the working class.

Some years afterwards, at a time when he and Marx found themselves almost totally isolated from other radicals, Engels wrote about the style of these squabbles with detachment and insight. He did not lose his taste for them for long, however. Indeed, his whole biography could be written by focusing on them. I, for one, however, have found them so tedious that I am going to say no more about them than is necessary for an understanding of Engels's intellectual and political development.

Since it has become fashionable these days to claim that Engels and Marx did not agree on any fundamentals of philosophy, theory, or political strategy, it must be stressed that in these formative years of their collaboration, from 1845 to 1850, they wrote and acted totally in tandem, freely representing each other. We have no record of any substantial disagreement between them. This is demonstrated most clearly by the major work they began to write during their stay in England in the summer of 1845. One glance at some of the manuscript pages shows that it was a joint work in which the two partners freely corrected and amplified each other's statements, so that it is difficult to say precisely what was written by whom. This work is *The German Ideology*. Because of its impudence, subversive message, and excessive length, Marx and Engels did not succeed in getting it published. It did not help that the very people who had at first agreed to publish it were mercilessly attacked in the manuscript.

The German Ideology was a broadside fired against the Bauer brothers, Max Stirner, and other former friends of theirs in the Hegelian Left, as well as against ideological rivals that had made their appearances more recently. It was a detailed denunciation of all philosophic speculation and an assertion that it must be replaced by positive science. "Where speculation ends," they asserted, "with actual life, positive science—the depiction of the practical activity or process of development of human beings—begins. The phrases about consciousness cease, and actual knowledge must take their place.

"Independent philosophy loses its medium of existence once actuality is depicted. Its place can be taken at most by a summary of the most general results that can be abstracted from the contemplation of the historical development of human beings. By themselves, separated from actual history, these abstractions have absolutely no value. They can only serve to facilitate the ordering of the historical material and to suggest the sequence of its discrete layers. The do not, however, in any way, like philosophy, give a recipe or scheme by which the historical era can be trimmed into shape. On the contrary, the difficulty begins precisely at the moment when one endeavors to contemplate and order the material, be it that of an era gone by or of the present."[122]

In other words, just as science had to replace speculation, so revolutionary action had to replace mere verbal criticism.[123] As the title of the book indicates, it was directed against *ideologists*, that is, against idea-mongers, meaning at one and the same time people who believed that ideas made history and that a change in outlook would have historic consequences, and also people whose ideas were speculative and hence illusionary. Ideologists were described as members of those social strata that had the privilege of indulging in illusions—schoolmasters, students, and political conspirators.[124] They were also denounced as elitists. The holy aims of an ideology were always the aims of *someone* who was inspired—some savior or miracle worker.

All theories of salvation divided the human race into shepherds and sheep. For ideologists, every revolutionary movement existed only within the head of some chosen individual, and the history of the world depended on the accident of whether this individual would be able to pass on his revelation before some rock hit him in the head. "The idealistic Dalai Lamas," they wrote, "have in common with the real one that they like to tell themselves that the world which nourishes them cannot continue existing without their holy excrements. As soon as this idealist madness becomes *practical,* its malicious character becomes apparent: their priestly lust for power, their religious fanaticism, their charlatanism, their pietistic hypocrisy, and their pious fraud."[125]

Comparing ideologists to parasitic plants,[126] Marx and Engels described them as thriving particularly in backward and reactionary countries like Germany, and depicted their work itself as reactionary. "This demand to change our consciousness," they wrote, "is tantamount to demanding that we should interpret the existing state of affairs differently, i.e. to recognize it by means of a different interpretation. Despite their allegedly 'world-shaking' phrases, the Young Hegelian ideologues are the biggest conservatives."[127] In an unpublished essay about German socialism, which Engels wrote shortly after his work with Marx on this manuscript, he applied the same criticism to Goethe, a genius who reflected many sides of his contemporary world, sovereign and colossal as a poet, but politically impotent. "Even Goethe," he wrote, "proved unable to defeat the misery of Germany. On the contrary, it defeated him, and this victory of the misery over the greatest German is the best proof that merely 'from inside,' it cannot be transcended."[128]

Here, in this casual remark about Goethe, we have the intent of *The German Ideology* in a nutshell. In discussing Germany, intellectuals since the beginning of the nineteenth century were preoccupied with two hostile cultures that vied for the souls of all Germans—that of Prussia and that of Weimar. Prussian, in this view, symbolized authoritarianism, patriarchal conservatism, and reliance on military power. In addition, it stood for religious conformity and a narrow, pragmatic preoccupation with efficiency. Weimar, whose acknowledged high priest was Goethe, implied a spirit of free inquiry and free imagination, and non-conformity in manners, religion, and sexual relations. It stood for a Romantic humanitarianism interested not so much in practical results as in a feeling of oneness with the universe. Hegel's philosophy could be seen as an attempt to create a grand synthesis of the two cultures, and the Hegelian Left as a return to the humanitarian spirit of Weimar.

The point made by *The German Ideology* was to denounce this return as a retreat into impotence. The book denounced all forms of socialism and communism based on notions of Christian love, human brotherhood, universal ideals, sentiments, or morals. It renounced all doctrines of humanism in no uncertain terms, putting in their place the call to class warfare and the emphasis on class interest and class position. What concerned the authors of the book was indicated neatly by the fact that the League of the Just, once it came under their influence, changed its name to the League of Communists, and for its old slogan, "All Men are Brothers," it substituted "Workers of the World, Unite."

The bulk of the book was a bitter, sometimes vicious, often tedious lampooning of their rivals, some of the people of such puny intellectual stature that once again we sense that the two friends were firing cannonballs at mice. Strewn in with the critical dissection of minor works, however, were statements about their own premises and assumptions. The Hegelian language in which these statements were couched was deceptive. The language was used mockingly, for the book was in large measure a repudiation of the Hegelian heritage in favor of a more positivist stance, which in this book they called naturalism, but in later years both referred to as materialism.

The basic premise from which all inquiry must start, they asserted, was that human beings existed in a reciprocal relationship with Nature.

"As long as human beings exist," they said, "the history of Nature and the history of humankind will condition each other."[129] Human beings differed from animals in that they produced their means for survival, and this ability was a function of their physical development. Different modes of production determined differences in culture. "The manner in which people produce their means of existence..." they stated, "is a definite manner of manifesting their lives, a certain 'mode of life' of these people. As the individuals manifest their lives, so they are. Hence, what they are coincides with their production, both with *what* they produce and also *how* they produce."[130]

Specifically, the mode of production conditioned all human intercourse, both the relations between different nations and also the entire inner structure of these nations. The level of production was indicated by the refinement of the divisions of labor, the first major division of labor being the division between city and country.[131] (Forty years later, when the feminist movement had exerted some influence on him, Engels would assert that the first division of labor was that between women and men.) Finally, the division of labor was expressed in property differences. Private property was merely a different expression of the division of labor.[132] In briefly discussing property, Marx and Engels provided a history of its forms and of the different modes of production associated with them.[133]

If in the beginning of the book they outlined their basic assumptions, toward the end they sketched their vision of the future. Once the division of labor was abolished, alienation—the domination of human relations over human beings—would be abolished as well. The division of labor would be abolished because of the fantastic development of productive forces, for which the division of labor and private property had now become fetters. Private property could only be abolished, however, under the condition that all individuals developed their talents in all directions, for only such individuals would be able to appropriate the present productive forces and use them for the common good.

The individuals of the present society *had* to abolish private property because, under private property, the productive forces had turned into destructive forces, and because the class conflict had been exacerbated to the point of no return. And they would do so, so that private property and the division of labor would yield to a free association of individuals on the basis of the productive forces already existing.[134]

"The 'all-round' (*allseitige*) dependency," they wrote, "this naturally-grown form of 'world-historical' cooperation of individuals, will be transformed by this communist revolution into the control and conscious domination of those forces which, generated in the reciprocal action of human beings upon each other, has until now been imposed on them as a thoroughly alien force and has dominated them."[135] If until now, such a society had not yet been created, it was precisely because all previous steps toward freedom had been constrained by the limitations inherent in the insufficient development of productive forces.

Since there was no abundance, the liberation of some always had to be purchased by the enslavement of others, and this in turn always compelled even the beneficiaries of liberation to be limited, both in their freedom and in their humanity. As Marx and Engels pointed out, their conception of what was human and humane was conditioned by the state of the productive forces, just as their conception of what was inhuman was nothing else than an attempt to negate these existing conditions.[136] Similarly, they argued that their conception of true and false human needs changed from one historic period to another.[137]

Working on *The German Ideology* with Marx was a very happy period for Engels, and decades later, when he had occasion to visit the Chetham Library in Manchester, with its large alcove and the ancient oaken desk at which they had worked, he reminisced about their collaboration there.[138] Late in his life, he called it the most impudent work ever written in the German language, and wanted excerpts from it printed.[139] This very impudence, however, and its inflammatory message, together with its excessive length, had led to their failure to get it published at the time, much to their chagrin.[140] However, a twenty-five-page pamphlet they wrote a little more than a year later was printed quickly and became famous at once. This was the *Manifesto of the Communist Party*.

In 1843, during his first stay in London, Engels had met three German craftsmen who were members of a small communist sect, the League of the Just. They were Heinrich Bauer, a shoemaker from northern Bavaria, whom Engels later described as a little guy, lively, bright, and resolute; the watchmaker Joe Moll, from Cologne, whom he said was strong as an ox and the most intelligent of the three; and Karl Schapper, a forestry student from Hessen, who later worked in other professions, had participated in political conspiracies in Germany and Savoy since the early 1830s and was, according to Engels, the very model of a professional revolutionary.

Though Engels called them the first proletarians whom he met, they were not industrial workers at all, and their League was made up primarily of craftsmen and journeymen. Yet, Engels found them receptive to his ideas and, much later, expressed amazement that people such as these would already have the beginnings of proletarian class-consciousness, despite their residual craftsmen's prejudices.[141] The League discussed socialist ideas, initiated strikes, formed shop associations, and founded production cooperatives—activities that, in retrospect, Engels criticized as being too scattered. "It was forgotten," he wrote, "that the main purpose should have been to win political victories and thus to conquer the territory on which alone such things could have been carried out in the long run."[142]

What happened to Engels in his first meetings with French and Belgian workers happened in London, also. There was an initial mutual suspicion—on the workers' part because they distrusted the educated bourgeois, and on Engels's part because he felt a certain bourgeois arrogance toward them.[143] These suspicions, however, were apparently overcome. The visit Engels and Marx paid these men in 1845 appears to have been cordial and fruitful, and by 1847 the leaders of this London organization, now renamed the League of Communists, had become sufficiently impressed by the theoretical views of the two friends that they requested them to write a brochure outlining the views and aims of the League in a relatively popular form. The two men consented, and Engels began the work by writing a couple of first drafts.

These drafts took the form of a political catechism, in which Engels sought to explain the nature of capitalism and the class struggle between bourgeoisie and proletariat, sketched out the inevitability of a social revolution to abolish private property, and outlined the political program of the communists until the time of such a revolution. Finally, he spelled out the consequences of the abolition of private property, which included the disappearance of economic crises, the rapid development of industry so that everyone's material needs could be satisfied, the abolition of class differences and of the division of labor, the consequent development of a new kind of family in which the dependence of wives and children on the patriarch would disappear, and the emergence of a new type of human being, trained universally in all areas of endeavor, and capable of doing many kinds of work well.[144]

It is likely that in transmitting these drafts to Marx, Engels also included copies of other materials he had written—published articles about other schools of socialism, or unpublished drafts such as his piece on "The Status Quo in Germany."[145] Marx also had at his disposal a polemic against Karl Heinzen that Engels had published in their Brussels outlet in October 1847.[146] All these minor articles deserve to be mentioned because passages from them can be found in the *Manifesto*. In sending Marx his catechism-like Principles of Communism, Engels expressed dissatisfaction with the form he had chosen for the pamphlet and urged Marx to rewrite it in a more suitable fashion. Marx accomplished this task brilliantly, closely following the outline and the basic ideas Engels had given him, but amplifying them and presenting the whole in stirring language.

In describing the development of capitalism, Marx was particularly eloquent in paying tribute to the revolutionary tasks carried out by the bourgeoisie in mercilessly removing all obstacles to science, industry, and acquisitive instincts. As Engels had suggested in his draft, however, he then pointed out that these accomplishments of the bourgeoisie were the very things that now threatened bourgeois rule, because they had made it superfluous. Marx's language was also more dramatic than that of Engels's drafts in denouncing the miseries that private property in the means of production imposed on workers, although the *Manifesto*, being a brief summary, was much more abstract than Engels's book on the condition of the working class in England. In outlining the strategies of the communists, Marx also elaborated on what Engels had provided him, but did not say anything essentially different.

The *Manifesto* ends with a survey of other socialist ideologies and parties, all of it a summary of numerous short and long pieces the two men had written since their first important meeting three years before. Engels thus furnished the first statements of the general content of the pamphlet, suggested the general outline, and also suggested the title, probably after a piece written by Moses Hess a year or two earlier. Marx added the final form, the grand style, and some of the specific formulations. The genesis of the Communist Manifesto thus fits into the pattern I have sought to establish for the genesis of Marxist doctrine in general, a pattern according to which Engels provided the stimulus of furnishing ideas and materials, whereas Marx synthesized them into their brilliant final form. With the publication of the *Manifesto*, however, this pattern ended, partly because the basic views of the two friends had now been stated, and the task for them now was to elaborate rather than formulate. Meanwhile, thunderclouds were gathering on the political horizon. The revolution expected and hoped for by the two friends was about to break out.

CHAPTER 5

THE MOVE TO MICHIGAN

FOR THE NEXT two years, we lived in New York City. My in-laws lived within a couple of hours' drive in Connecticut. They were pleased to have our children once in a while, and, for an entire year, they took complete care of them while Eva pursued a graduate program in Physical Therapy. She had discovered her interest in that field during the summer of 1955, which we spent at a hot spring resort in the Olympic Mountains of Washington, and where she worked as a lifeguard and swimming instructor. For the next two years, she took all the science courses she had carefully avoided in college, such as physics, chemistry, and biology. She did well in these science courses and eventually was accepted as a student in the graduate program in Physical Therapy at New York University.

In New York, I directed a research program on the history of the Communist Party of the Soviet Union. This program had been set up at Columbia University by a committee of four senior professors—Phil Mosely and Gerold T. Robinson, of Columbia, Harold Fisher, of Stanford, and Merle Fainsod, of Harvard. My duties were to dole out grants to young scholars working on projects in this field and to solicit memoirs from surviving veterans of the Russian Marxist movement. I was also given instructions on how to deal with the complex financial bureaucracy of Columbia University. I enjoyed the opportunity to support young colleagues, and I found some of my encounters with remnants of the Russian, Caucasian, and Baltic revolutionary movements fascinating. I was not a good administrator, however. Indeed, after two years of running the program, my records were in a mess, although no money was missing or had been misspent; Phil

Mosely's trusted old secretary had to be called in to straighten things out.

My relations with the committee of senior scholars were further strained by my belief that the project had been poorly conceived, and suffered from misplaced priorities. The first task of the committee was to commission someone to write a comprehensive history of the Soviet Communist Party, and then, once that history was written, do more detailed research on discrete periods. I thought that the comprehensive history ought to be the capstone, not the foundation, of the entire project. One does not usually start with the conclusions until all the evidence is in. Doing it the other way around made me suspect ideological motives.

At the end of the second year, the project and I parted company. What funds were left were to be spent on a detailed study of a relatively short period in the history of the CPSU. Merle Fainsod proposed that I be the one asked to write that study, but because of the mess I had made of the financial records of the project, the other members of the board opposed me. Fainsod must have fought hard on my behalf, for when the meeting was over and I accompanied him to Grand Central Station, he cursed all the way, angry with me and even more with the two Columbia professors who had opposed him. Fainsod was not only a great scholar and teacher, but also sweet and soft-spoken, a gentle, even-tempered man who never raised his voice in anger. When I told other former students of his that I heard Merle Fainsod utter obscenities, they didn't believe me.

In 1957, the Political Science Department at Michigan State University hired me, and in the fall of that year, I moved to East Lansing. For the next year, I lived there by myself, while Eva was at New York University studying Physical Therapy and, in the following summer, served internship at a hospital in White Plains, New York. Once she received her certification as a physical therapist, she specialized in the treatment of brain-damaged children and infants, a fascinating field in which she later took specialized courses. During this twelve-month period, we left our children with Eva's parents in nearby

Bridgeport, Connecticut.

In East Lansing, I had been promised an apartment in a bachelor faculty housing project owned by the University, but when I arrived, no apartment was available. So, I unloaded my U-Haul trailer and stored my belongings in the basement of the Housing Office, and then lived for a few weeks in a flea-infested rented room a few blocks away from the campus, until at last they had an apartment for me.

The Political Science Department at MSU was large and run by a group of exceedingly enterprising young men. Their entrepreneurial spirit expressed itself not only in the large number of new faculty members they were hiring—I was one of fourteen new members that year—but also in the quality of the new members, all of them with degrees from prestige universities and with respectable publication records. The Department prided itself on being at the cutting edge of the profession, which meant that most of its members, though by no means all, were committed to the latest fads and methods in behavioral studies and quantitative research.

It was up-to-date also by being one of the first political science departments in the country to have a formal relationship with the Federal government to furnish a team of advisors to one of our client states. The client state was the Republic of Vietnam. Political Science professors from MSU were in Saigon, working as personal advisers to the dictator, Ngo Dinh Diem, and setting up a school for bureaucrats. Professors from the School of Agriculture were advising Diem on how to reform property relations and farming methods in the countryside, while professors from the Department of Police Administration set up his presidential security guard and the VBI, modeled after the FBI.

The twelve or fourteen newly hired members of the department—as well as some of their older colleagues—were academic entrepreneurs. Within a few years, most had moved on to other universities. The faculty turnover, at least while I was there, was rapid, which made it a very unstable department. The entire university, in fact, was a prime example of what academic entrepreneurship could achieve in the period after World War II. Its principal entrepreneur undoubtedly was its current

President, a man of formidable administrative and entrepreneurial talent named John Hannah. Founded as a land grant college under the Morrill Act in the 1850's, the university had once been called Michigan Agricultural College, and a smokestack with the initials 'MAC' still graced the campus. Sometime before the war, the college added some departments and was renamed Michigan State College. Finally, around 1950, it added a business school and some other units and became Michigan State University, one of the three autonomous universities of the state. The new university also acquired a powerful football team and a persuasive Athletic Director, Clarence "Biggie" Munn, and parlayed its way into the Big Ten athletic league. Thus being on the map, it could also hire a good faculty.

A few times during my nine years of teaching there, I got phone calls from the Athletic Director. "Hello, this is Biggie," he would say, introducing himself.

"What can I do for you, Professor Munn?" I would respond (one of his titles was Professor of Physical Education). He would then recommend that I give a lenient passing grade to whatever member of his football team was taking one of my courses. I never promised anything.

The growth of Michigan State University to national distinction had been rapid and uneven. The Political Science Department was known in the profession as an avant-garde department. History and Psychology, to mention just two other departments, had excellent people. Agricultural Economics probably was one of the two best departments in the country, and there may have been others, including an excellent art school. The university did not have an adequate library, however, and large concerts were performed in a huge Nissen hut originally built for agricultural exhibits, which our choral conductor called The Barn.

The school actively recruited National Merit Scholarship finalists from all over the country, and prided itself on being able to attract more of them than some Ivy League schools. Once these young geniuses had come, the university, in my opinion, did not do enough to make staying there attractive to them, and some of these high achievers rued the day they had succumbed to the lure of the scholarship money MSU had offered them.

For a while, I served as faculty adviser to a mock fraternity/sorority that a group of such Honors students had founded. It was called Ypsilon Alpha Alpha, which stood for Underachievers Anonymous. One of the members of YAA later published a novel with the title *No Transfer*, which was a bitter caricature of Michigan State University.

One of the complaints of these very bright students focused on the courses all first- and second-year students had to take in English, the social sciences, the humanities, and the natural sciences. These courses were taught in a special unit called the Basic College. They were taught to huge classes, sometimes with lectures transmitted over a TV screen. The faculty in the Basic College sensed that they were considered second-class faculty. The students felt they were being taught in assembly line fashion. To me, the Basic College seemed to be an institution unworthy of a good university.

These were the years in which universities still considered themselves obliged to function *in loco parentum* (as substitute parents and guardians), and they particularly sought to guard the students' virtue— their virginity and their sobriety. Girls' dormitories as well as sorority houses were run by housemothers, who made sure that all their residents signed out when they left and signed in when they returned, and made doubly sure that everyone was back before curfew, when the doors to the dorm would be locked. Housemothers also saw to it that their charges behaved properly in all other respects. One of my students was upbraided for reading subversive material when her housemother saw her carry a copy of Problems of Communism, a journal published by the U.S. Information Agency. I used to marvel at what I thought was the skewed hierarchy of offenses at MSU. Students could be expelled for being found with a beer can in their possession. For cheating in an exam, they could expect to get a failing grade in the course. For administering cruel treatment during hazing, however, fraternity members might only get a warning. Parental supervision was also exercised over the daily newspaper published by the students, and I know that the faculty adviser to the paper more than once prevented some item from being printed.

Sometime in the 1960's, a judge in Lansing informed me that the subversives unit of the State Police, the so-called Red Squad, had kept a file on me. In conformity with a recent court decision, I had a right to inspect my file. I went to the address that had been given me and was shown a very small quantity of documents, the contents of which was so trivial that I no longer remember what they were. One document, however, caught my attention, and to describe it, I have to tell a somewhat elaborate story.

In early September, on the first day of a new academic year, I picked up the "Welcome" issue of the *Michigan State News*. It was as thick as a Sunday *New York Times*. A section carried the day's news. Another section summarized what had happened during the summer. There was a section on sports, another on fraternities and sororities, yet another on fashions, and also one on movies and other entertainment. After reading the paper, I wrote a letter to the editor, congratulating him on the amount of diligent work that he and his colleagues had put in to bring out this welcome issue. But, I continued, why was there no section on the academic side of the university, on schools, departments, degree programs, faculty, and the like? Should this not also be contained in the first paper of the new academic year?

I received no answer to my letter, and it was not printed in any subsequent issues of the State News. So, one day, I phoned the editor and asked him why he had not printed it. He said he had discarded it because "it was not representative of campus opinion." I thanked him and then sat down to write an account of this episode, beginning with my letter to the editor and his reason for not printing it. I ended my account by asking my readers to tell me whether they agreed with the student's statement that my criticism was unrepresentative of campus opinion. I made a number of reproductions of the letter and sent it to various friends among the faculty and the student body. It was one of those reproductions, which the Red Squad had in its file. One of my colleagues or one of my students must have considered my criticism of the State News to be subversive.

I know that the university administration thought of me as a dangerous person. Early in my tenure at MSU, a group of undergraduate students had come to see me. They wanted to create a Socialist Club at the university, and needed a faculty adviser in order to be recognized as a legitimate student organization. They had approached a number of professors, but everyone had refused to be associated with such a group. I readily consented to serve as their faculty sponsor, since I believed that every political opinion had a right to be represented in an institution of higher learning. A few years later, when one of the members of the club ran for student President, the campus administration called a meeting of fraternity presidents and other 'big men' on campus to urge them to form a united front against this candidate. During that meeting, my name came up as sponsor of the club. I knew of at least one student of mine whom the campus police tried to recruit to spy on me.

Altogether, the university, when I was there, was run in highly authoritarian fashion. Deans talked to faculty members in a tone of voice that lacked any trace of collegiality. Administrators monitored faculty performance as if the place were a factory, and tried to keep statistics on the proportion of time they spent on teaching and counseling, as well as research, administration, and other duties. When I had to submit such reports, the total percentage of the time I spent on these activities always far exceeded 100, because, I argued, I worked more than full time.

Promotions and salary raises depended on the amount of scholarly work a faculty member had gotten published. Rumor had it that in making decisions concerning promotion and raises our Dean counted the pages published during the preceding years. That encouraged faculty members to inflate their accomplishment when writing their annual reports, listing reviews as articles, articles as monographs, and monographs as books. One of my colleagues even listed 'unpublished publications' in his annual report. I assume that rubric included manuscripts submitted but not accepted, papers read at conferences, or perhaps even lectures given to Rotary Clubs.

Administrators also meddled in the professors' private lives in a manner that would not have been tolerated in old, established colleges or universities. I remember a very jolly party in the basement of our little house. A jazz combo provided dance music. Our guests included colleagues, neighbors, students, and friends. The trumpeter in the jazz band was a janitor. A day or two after the party, the Dean of the Business school, to which our department then belonged, called in my department chairman. "Were you at Al Meyer's party the other night?" he asked him. When my chairman said that, indeed, he was, the Dean asked: "Were any undergraduates at the party?" My chairman denied it.

All these shortcomings notwithstanding, I was happy at Michigan State University. I taught my courses and did my research. I felt that my colleagues as well as my students appreciated and respected me. The salary increases given me attested to this judgment.

Eva, who joined me in the fall of 1958, found work as a physical therapist, first in a local hospital, and then in a special education school for physically handicapped children, specialized work that she enjoyed a great deal. We bought a comfortable house on the banks of the Red Cedar River and enjoyed a reasonably active social life with a large group of friends. Every summer, we would escape the oppressive mid-western heat by moving to our vacation home in Maine.

In the summer of 1958, however, Eva was still busy doing her Physical internship in White Plains. During this time, I followed up an invitation from the Free University of Berlin to teach a seminar and a lecture course during their summer semester. For the month following this guest professorship in Berlin, I had obtained a grant for a trip through the Soviet Union. Until 1957 the USSR had been inaccessible to American scholars, and now Khrushchev had given permission for them to enter the country as tourists.

Travel grants such as the one I had obtained were given to many of my colleagues so that they might get some actual glimpse into the country they had been studying from long distance for years. My trip had an inauspicious beginning: I had bought an air ticket from Berlin to Warsaw and, in the beginning of August took a taxi to the East Berlin airport, only to learn that my flight had been canceled for some reason. Luckily, an East German airline employee went out of her way to help me obtain a railroad ticket, visas, and other necessities. I took off by train in an elegant sleeping car, where I shared a roomette with a young, intelligent and talkative official of the Polish Ministry of Foreign Trade, who discussed with me the problems faced by the Polish economy from a rather stiff communist point of view, yet frankly and without trying to conceal various difficulties. He was a member of the communist managerial elite, conscious of his intelligence and his responsibilities—the Polish analog of a Harvard Business School graduate.

In Warsaw, where we arrived the next morning, I saw the ruins created in August 1944, when the Germans destroyed the city in retaliation for the uprising. Strolling around town on subsequent days I saw that the Poles had carefully and lovingly restored some of the older quarters to look exactly as they had in the 18th century. Whether this slavery to old tradition was what the people either needed or wanted was a matter of controversy in Warsaw. I stayed at the Grand Hotel, still in the process of being built. Its decor, personnel, and its guests were a strange mixture of shabbiness and flashy elegance. Very different was the Warsaw journalists club, where I dined the next evening at the invitation of one of its members. The quiet pre-war elegance of this villa with a lovely terrace and carefully kept gardens served as a refuge for intellectuals and a hide-out for privileged characters, which is indeed what journalists were in Poland.

I needed more than two hours, the next day, to buy a railroad ticket to Leningrad. The ticket office was staffed with an insufficient number of personnel, a long line of people waited for their turn, tickets were still written by hand, and the price was calculated in cumbersome fashion. In the middle of the morning, the clerk at the window simply left for a while, presumably to get a cup of coffee. He came back munching a sandwich. I decided that Polish officials had a rather lackadaisical attitude toward time, an attitude that I would have associated with the Orient.

The summer of 1958 was an interesting time to be in Poland. Two years before, reform-minded intellectuals in the ruling party had rebelled against some of the harsh policies and the doctrinal rigidity of the regime. An unorthodox journal, *Po Prostu*, put out by rebellious students, had given voice to such 'revisionist' ideas. In 1958, the Party had closed it down, but the rebellious spirit was still alive, and young Party members still engaged in frank discussion of the need for reform. I met quite a few people who seemed eager to discuss these matters with me. On the bookshelf of a young journalist whom I visited in his home, I was surprised to see Koestler's *Darkness At Noon* and other anti-communist literature. I was equally astonished by his suggestion that I send him my book on Lenin so that he might review it for *Przeglad Kulturalny*, a journal formerly published under the auspices of the Ministry of Culture, but now, he said, independent.

I spent one evening in a tavern on the beautifully restored Old Market in free discussion with a large group of reform-minded young communists, all of whom expressed their commitment to liberty and democracy. As if to underscore the favorable impression these people made on me, two young Party bureaucrats from East Germany, spending their furlough in Warsaw, joined us. They were depressed because of the open antagonism that they, as Germans, had encountered in Poland, and as true-believing Marxists-Leninists of the Walter Ulbricht school, who could talk only slogans and litanies, they were appalled by the heresies that were uttered by their Polish comrades.

When they heard me speak German their eyes lit up and they joined me, obviously thinking I was a comrade from the German Democratic Republic. I was sorry I had to disappoint them. Once I steered our conversation toward the topic of Marxist-Leninist ideology, however, they discovered to their horror that I knew Lenin's writings much better than they did, and was able to ask them challenging questions. This shook them up so badly that they promptly drank themselves into a stupor and had to be carried out of the tavern. For fanatics of any religion, including Marxism-Leninism, the proverb applied: "Beware of the Devil quoting Scripture." I still managed to have a stimulating conversation with a senior historian and a group of communist youth leaders, with whom I discussed the many causes of the poverty still prevalent in Poland.

A nasty hangover the next day admonished me to be more careful when mixing vodka with wine. That morning, I boarded a train for Leningrad. All the compartments were occupied, and even the corridors were full of people, but about an hour before we reached the Soviet border the car got emptier. At last, I was alone in my compartment with a couple of Belorussian farmwomen who were returning from a visit to their relatives in Poland. They were laden with bundles containing clothing and food. When the Soviet customs inspector came in to hand them customs declaration forms, the women were too scared or too illiterate to fill them out; and so I did it for them. We arrived in Brest, on the Soviet side of the border, with some delay, and I found out that the connecting train that was to take me to Leningrad had left already. This gave me time to stroll around town a bit, treat myself to dinner at the station restaurant, observe an orthodox service of great splendor in a nearby church, and watch the life in the streets.

On my arrival in Brest I had expected to be received by representatives of *Inturist*, the agency that served foreign visitors to the USSR. Since they did not show up, I sought them out, and they were surprised and appalled to see me: despite my repeated reminders, the man in Warsaw who had sold me the ticket had not notified *Inturist* of my coming. Now my connection to Leningrad had left. With profuse apologies, *Inturist* told me they would put me into another train that would arrive in Leningrad no earlier than 7 o'clock. Fine with me.

The train turned out to be a slow local train, my car an ordinary dormitory car with wooden shelves on which to sleep, double-decker style. Every passenger was given a thin mattress, a pillow, and bed linen. The motherly matron in charge of the car sold hot tea and cold soda pop. The passengers, who had changed into pajamas or dressing gowns, brought out their food baskets and supped on rye bread, hard-boiled eggs and raw cucumbers. The public was decidedly lower class, the atmosphere quiet and restrained. Brueghel would have been able to transform the scene into a marvelous picture.

The *Inturist* people in Brest had told me, somewhat apologetically, that my train would arrive in Leningrad at seven o'clock. I thought they meant seven o'clock the next morning. At that time, however, the train stopped in Orsha, a small town in Western Belorussia. I asked how long we would stay at the station, and was told about ten hours. A train coming from Kiev would pick us up in the late afternoon. In order to use all this time fruitfully, I decided to go into town, even though it was raining cats and dogs.

A bus took me to town. With my camera hanging from my neck, I strolled around its wide muddy streets, looked at the wooden dwellings with their flower and vegetable gardens, visited the *kolkhoz* market, where vegetables, eggs, mushrooms, fruit, and live poultry were being sold. I bought a pound of delicious egg tomatoes—my first breakfast in the Soviet Union. Little wagons filled with hay stood around. Low, ramshackle wooden buildings surrounded the market. The entire scene, with the thick crowd of people, made me imagine the Klondike during the gold rush. Cobblers sat in the open mending shoes while-U-wait. It was, in short, a big once-a week carnival.

On the top of a high hill the scars of war could be seen—old trenches and blown-up bunkers. In town, some buildings were still in ruins. The Germans left not a single stone building standing, but much had been rebuilt since then, some apartment houses, administrative buildings, schools, and a theater. I was about to take some pictures when an eager-beaver 'activist' came up to me and demanded that I give him my film: taking pictures is forbidden here, he said. When I asked him who might give me permission to do so, he directed me to the local police. I went there, saw the chief, explained why I was in town, and got his permission to photograph 'cultural institutions', whatever that may have meant.

I resumed my strolling about town and along the pretty banks of the Dnepr River. Clad in American clothing, with an expensive camera on my chest, I felt or saw myself observed, sometimes covertly from behind windows. As I stepped from the riverbank onto the street, a man in a business suit with a briefcase in his hand eyed me intently until I was out of sight. Ten minutes later, a truck carrying a lieutenant and eight men stopped beside me. I was told to come along and was taken to the police station, where one of the cops explained that someone had reported that a suspicious-looking foreigner with a camera was walking around town. I explained to the officer that I had already seen the police chief and was released, with apologies. The entire incident seemed a real lark, and an auspicious beginning of my tour through the Soviet Union. After leaving the police station, I treated myself to a good dinner at a local restaurant and then returned to my train. Late that night, I arrived in Leningrad.

The next day I took a leisurely stroll through this beautiful city that combined the grandeur of Paris with the charm of Amsterdam. On *Nevsky Prospekt*, the main avenue, I ran into a friend from the Harvard Russian Research Center. Together, we visited an Economics professor at the university for an animated three-hour conversation. I also browsed in a couple of bookstores. I had discovered that the USSR was a nation of readers. One could observe them reading or studying in parks, streetcars, subways, and trains, and eagerly searching through card files in the bookstores. I very much wanted to see those parts of the city where working-class people lived, but *Inturist* did not wish to accommodate me. I therefore told another *Inturist* agent that I had written a book about Lenin and wished to visit all the places in the proletarian parts of town in which he had hidden from the Czarist police. That kind of pilgrimage to holy places suited them fine, but I am not sure whether it gave me a realistic image of how Soviet workers lived.

I also was eager to attend some sessions of a court of law and asked the *Inturist* people to tell me where I might find a courthouse. I was told that they did not know, but would inquire. I was being given the royal run-around, and decided that the *Inturist* bureaucrats would never tell me how to find a courthouse. Eventually, I stepped in front of the hotel and asked the nearest cop to show me the way to the courthouse, which he did. The cases I heard were mostly divorce cases.

Later that night, my friend and I took in a vaudeville show in a nearby park. I was interested in the kinds of jokes told by one of the performers, and in the general behavior of the people in the audience. I found it exciting to be among these people and to notice many little details about them, some of which were surprising. The beauty of the city and its historic significance complicated the task of gathering impressions. Every building breathed history. Some famous person lived here, some czar was assassinated there, and in that building, *Pravda* was printed secretly. Leningraders were proud of their city, and even of fictional events associated with it. Two people pointed out to me the little canal in which Liza—the fictional heroine of Pushkin's "The Queen of Spades"—had drowned herself.

I did some conventional sightseeing—for instance, a boat tour to Peterhof, the luxurious palace that Peter the Great had built for himself. The construction must have cost the Russian people dearly, and the splendor of this residence fit ill with Peter's famous personal modesty and frugality. The Germans totally destroyed this palace, and the Stalin regime restored it. In my letters home, I compared this splendor with the shabbiness of my hotel and the lackadaisical service there. The next day, I visited the Winter Palace and the Hermitage—an art historian's paradise, but a tourist's nightmare. I also visited a fine exhibit of German graphic art, then a soccer game in the huge Kirov stadium—Zenith Leningrad vs. Dynamo Moscow.

Afterwards, I had a lively conversation over a few glasses of beer with some soccer fans. I was amazed by the freedom with which they discussed problems of Soviet life, and expressed their curiosity concerning life in the United States. I had the same experience in subsequent days when I visited Moscow. I also encountered a few people who wanted to buy dollars or some of my clothing from me, as well as some who complained about American tourists trying to sell or buy things in the black market.

In the Museum of the Revolution, I noted how much of the history of the Party was being falsified, how many formerly prominent leaders of the revolution had become non-persons or, if they show up on old photographs, were simply not identified. A few days later, I sat at lunch with a very bright university student who had taken her compulsory course on the history of the Party. I examined her on that topic, and on the life of Lenin, and found out that she knew absolutely nothing, just some empty phrases.

Walking in Moscow, I noted many details—the rush of traffic and the thick crowds of people, long lines in front of stores, restaurants so overcrowded that service was painfully slow. I observed the large number of TV antennas over the roofs of the houses, the prevalent hobbies: fishing, hunting, and stamp collecting. I was surprised to see that Soviet citizens could freely buy hunting rifles. I was impressed by the cleanliness of the streets, by the recklessness of the motorists who honked and gave gas as soon as the traffic light turned green, paying no attention to the masses of pedestrians trying to cross. I saw lots of drunken people staggering along the streets.

I was strolling along Gorki Street, with my trench coat slung over my shoulder, when a drunken man stopped me to ask why I was walking around like that. My answer, that it was warm enough to go without my coat on, did not satisfy him. To end the stupid conversation I put it on. He then looked at the coat and asked what the shoulder straps were for. Was I an officer? I told him I had been one during the war, but the shoulder straps were meaningless decoration like his lapels or the buttons on his sleeve. He asked me what medals I had earned and what I had done for humanity to deserve such a fancy coat. I told him I had done nothing special but lived in a country where lots of people dressed like that. He grew more and more bitter about the difference in clothing. His tirade could have come straight from some Hearst paper, with the names of Russia and America reversed. "You goddamned foreigner," he said. "You come here to snoop around and take pictures and subvert us. But we have got the goods on you. We know who you are and what you are doing. We don't like you Negro-baiters and capitalists, and when you come to attack us we are going to lick you." Strangely enough, we parted with a handshake.

Visits to the Kremlin and the Tretiakov art gallery rounded out my visit to Moscow. Later that week I made a pilgrimage to Iasnaia Poliana, Lev Tolstoy's noble and beautiful estate not too far from Tula. The estate was very pretty, and to look at Tolstoy's library and living quarters was of some interest. I did not care for pilgrimages, however, and did not visit the mausoleum where Lenin and Stalin were displayed. In the company of R.H.S, Crossman, MP, and John Scott, of TIME magazine, I traveled to Zagorsk to visit the holiest monastery of the Russian church and attend a solemn service celebrated by the Patriarch. With a young priest, I discussed the training of new priests in which he was engaged. Later that week, I spent a day at the Lenin Library, which in size and function was the Soviet analog to our Library of Congress. They received me courteously, asked me whether I was the Meyer who had written a book on Lenin, and gave me access to the facilities reserved for professors and members of the Academy of Sciences. They let me read most of what I requested for my research on the war scare of 1926/27, including articles by Party leaders who were later purged. The next day, I visited the Institute of History of the Academy of Sciences, and was received cordially. They suggested that I should spend a year with them to study Soviet history. I told them I would have to discuss that with my wife.

Wherever I went in the Soviet Union, officials tried to segregate me from Soviet citizens. At Vnukovo airport, waiting for my plane to Stalingrad, I wanted to sit at a table already occupied by a few people having a meal, when the headwaiter told me, "Don't sit there. There are nothing but workers there." I replied that I thought the USSR was a worker's state.

The ride from Moscow to Stalingrad was bumpy. After my arrival, an *Inturist* guide gave me a walk through this ruined city, where the decisive battle of World War II was fought that broke the spine of the German war machine. The place reminded me of Kansas City, the Volga being for Russia what the Mississippi is for the United States. It was a big industrial and agricultural center, lay in the middle of a fertile prairie—here called steppe—had the same continental climate, and was swept by harsh winds.

Founded in the 16th century as an outpost against the Tartars, it was totally destroyed during the war, its industries razed to the ground. Every existing building was constructed after 1945. High up on one of the new buildings, a big sign exhorted citizens to carry out the resolutions of the XXI. Party Congress. I asked my *Inturist* guide, a recent graduate from an interpreter school, what these resolutions had been. Her vague answer indicated that she did not know. I then I asked, "If you don't know, who does?"

"Everybody knows," she replied.

We made our way to the boat dock on the shore of the river, where I was surrounded by a number of Gypsy women. One wanted to read my palm. Another offered to make me rich quickly with a magic formula if I gave her some dollars. I was amazed to see such people still existing here. On the way to the riverboat, a derelict-looking young man followed me, and I let him catch up. He told me he had done time in a camp for theft, was unemployed now, and living more or less as a vagrant. Given the variety of people that talked to me, I wondered how typical any of them had been.

My guide took me across the Volga, where the biggest water power station in the world was being constructed. These and other river projects were matters of great pride to the Soviet Union. Nobody there pointed out to me the enormous numbers of prisoners who were forced to slave on them. During our boat trip down the river, through the Volga-Don Canal and across the huge flooded valley known as the Tsimliansk Sea, I saw many of these monuments to Stalinism. On a number of construction sites I saw that soldiers were doing the labor. I was now on the large side-wheeler "Aleksei Tolstoy," going from Stalingrad to Rostov-on-Don.

Traveling first class, I had a roomy cabin above water level with a large window and access to the deck. The weather was balmy. Passengers and some of the ship's officers promenaded on the deck in their pajamas. Occasionally, the ship would stop at a village to take on or unload some passengers. I saw touching farewell scenes as local families bade good-by to young lads departing for the army. The journey reminded me very much of Mark Twain's *Life on the Mississippi*. After all, the Volga served the same function as a major communications channel, and the Russian civil war was as fierce along the Volga as the American civil war had been along the Mississippi. I had an interesting conversation with a veteran of that Russian civil war. He had joined the Red Army in 1918 and fought for two years. He told me he was sick and tired of politics and was satisfied now to live on his pension. He talked freely of old commandeers who had been purged, some of them unjustly, he said.

In Tsimliansk, lots of people got on board, among them several Gypsy families whom the ship's crew treated very rudely. Once we were on the Don, an officer invited me to come to the bridge so that I could take photos of the countryside—Cossack territory. The officers were very hospitable, the atmosphere relaxed. We had a friendly political discussion and drank vodka together.

On arrival in Rostov, my *Inturist* guide took me to my hotel and warned me not to take pictures of the modest wooden dwellings along the street. She also introduced me to the headwaiter to make sure that he would give me segregated seating, away from Soviet citizens. Obviously, *Inturist* had orders to discourage fraternization between them and American tourists. They also seemed eager to keep foreign tourists under strict supervision. After a good night's sleep in the hotel, I got up very early and took a leisurely walk through Rostov, noting various interesting forms of architecture. When I returned after two or three hours, my guide was waiting for me in the lobby and immediately scolded me for going off independently. At dinnertime, the headwaiter led me to a separate table set for four people, and featuring an American flag. "Here you will be among your own people," he said. I replied that I had come to the USSR to meet Soviet people, not Americans.

As I said this, I spotted a table with an empty chair, went to it, and asked the two men sitting there whether I might join them. They invited me to do so, and so I had company: two young engineers working for the Rostov fishing fleet. They seemed thrilled to be with a visitor from the States, and we had a long and friendly conversation over dinner—a real party. Late that evening one of the young men looked at his watch and said, "My wife will be furious with me for coming home so late. I must go now." I suggested we all go to his home, bring a bottle of Champagne along, and continue the party with his wife. He agreed and called a cab. I bought a bottle of Champagne. Soon we were at his modest home. "Honey, I brought a visitor along," he called to his wife. They served me delicious smoked fish caught in the Tsimliansk Sea. We emptied the bottle and continued partying until the wee hours of the morning. Given the reluctance of Soviet citizens to have anything to do with foreigners, I felt triumphant.

The next day I traveled to Kiev by train and again had lively conversations with people sharing my compartment—a Soviet Lieutenant Colonel, a few Polish and East German tourists. My *Inturist* guide here was an intelligent and friendly young woman, who, however, seemed determined not to let me walk around alone or even see much of the city. When she found out that one of my hobbies was mushrooming, she took me on a mushroom walk through the woods. She also was eager to show me the insides of a cathedral built in the 19th century. When we entered, a service was going on, and the choir sang beautiful Russian church music, which seemed to make my guide feel uncomfortable. She wanted to show me the murals inside, however. I did not like them. They reminded me of the late-Romantic reactionary paintings of Ivanov, I told her. She was flabbergasted. "He is the one who did these murals," she replied. After that, I had her respect. We talked for a long time about art and politics and my negative views about Stalinist art. The next day I met with a few historians at the Academy of Sciences. After that, I took off by train for Prague, the first lap of my return to the United States.

I would have loved to prolong my stay in the Soviet Union, or to repeat such a trip. Five years later, the Academy of Sciences canceled an earlier invitation I had received to be an exchange scholar. The reason they gave was: "Meyer is not a scholar but a professional anti-Communist." I wondered whether my behavior during the trip in 1958 had anything to do with that judgment.

Eva and the children joined me in Michigan in the fall of 1958. The next summer, in 1959, we spent our first vacation as a family in Maine. The family connection to Maine had begun with Eva's uncle, Willi Apel, who lived near Boston, where he taught musicology, first at Harvard and later at one of the conservatories in or near the city. Back in 1937, he and his wife wanted to spend a vacation in a quiet, unspoiled rustic setting. They asked some friends to recommend a place and were told that

Mount Desert Island off the coast of Maine would be ideal.

Mount Desert Island was indeed a rare jewel. Surrounded by Frenchman's Bay and Blue Hill Bay, its hundred square miles lay within a few hundred feet off the shore, twenty miles south of Ellsworth. Steep mountains that rose directly from the rocky shore dotted its southern half. A genuine fjord cut through the mountains and divided the island into two halves. Several lakes provided fresh water and lovely views. Thick forests came all the way down to the shore. There was a sand beach for those who wanted to brave the icy surf. The island was a haven for forest animals and birds. It combined in one small spot all the features of beauty that northern New England had to offer.

In the middle of the 19th century, wealthy people from Boston, New York and Philadelphia discovered the island and began to spend their summers there. They bought choice properties. They built themselves fancy villas with fabulous views of the ocean, lakes, and mountains, moored their yachts in sheltered spots off Bar Harbor or Northeast Harbor, and enjoyed a social life in their exclusive clubs.

In time, the island became famous for its beauty, and more wealthy people began to move in, buy property, and build vacation homes. Even some not-so-wealthy people did the same thing. In 1888, Friedrich Engels was going to take a trip to the United States. He wrote to his old friend and fellow revolutionary, Friedrich August Sorge, then living in Brooklyn, that he was coming and wished to visit him. Sorge wrote back, saying, "If you are going to visit me, then why not come to my summer place on Mount Desert Island, where it is very beautiful?" To which Engels replied, in effect: "I have seen lots of islands in my life, and I will visit you in Brooklyn."

To the original elite crowd that had begun to 'rusticate' on the island, the influx of people of newer wealth was unwelcome, especially if these newly wealthy people had Italian, Irish, Jewish, or Slavic names. They wished to preserve their paradise unspoiled, and they found an ingenious solution to their problem. They bought as much land on the island as they could, especially looking for the more beautiful areas, and presented it to the federal government. All that land, and many additional lots, ultimately became Acadia National Park.

The fancy social life on the island took place around its two most important ports, Bar Harbor and Northeast Harbor. Uncle Willi and his wife Ursula found some bed-and-breakfast place on the Western half— or quiet side—of the island, and shortly before leaving again, they discovered a little hut for sale. Tucked away in a cove on Long Pond, accessible only by a swampy trail or by boat, it was the site of an old saw mill.

Willi's mother-in-law, who was with them at the time, was horrified by this primitive abode. "Children," she cried, "you cannot buy this. It is nothing but a goat stable!" They bought it anyway, along with several hundred feet of shorefront, and it was nicknamed the *Ziegenstall* (goat stable). It was an idyllic place, still without electricity or telephone. Water had to be pumped from a well, and the only source of energy for the stove and the refrigerator was bottled gas. Until about 1950, blocks of ice, which one purchased at an icehouse, provided refrigeration. Many of Willi Apel's books on musicology were written in the hut by the light of Coleman lamps in this abode.

I visited the *Ziegenstall* for the first time in 1947, shortly before Eva and I set off on our trip to Stanford. In 1950 or 1951 we visited again, and we learned that a developer had bought an entire undeveloped peninsula on the lake, divided it into lots, cut an access road, and wanted to sell these lots.

"Let's buy one," Eva said to me.

"Let's not," I replied.

All her relatives agreed with me. "This is not the time for you young people, just starting out, to invest in real estate," they said, "and, anyway, you don't know where you will be ten years from now. Suppose you are in Texas or California, what will you do with a piece of land in Maine? And can you really afford to pay for this lot?" In the end, Eva insisted, and we shelled out the $450 that the developer asked for the lot we had chosen, a pie-shaped bit of forest in a sheltered cove, with a lovely view of the Western Mountains, and virtually nothing but national park land on the opposite shore.

In 1959, therefore, we bought a wooden house trailer in a little town near Lansing, Michigan, loaded our children and five cats into it, and lugged it to our lot in Maine. A driveway had meanwhile been cut out of the forest, and, with an architect friend, we discussed plans to build a summer camp, as seasonal residences in the area were called. Construction of the house was started in the fall and completed the following summer. It became a second home for us from that time on, so much so that during my academic vacations, I did far less traveling abroad than most of my other colleagues.

In this second home, we lived our lives according to a markedly different rhythm from that of the rest of the year. One of the first things I did upon arrival there was to get rid of my watch. I didn't wish to be chained to time during my summer vacations. I also got rid of my shoes—sandals or sneakers were more comfortable. The only things to do of a regular nature were household chores, picking up the mail at the village post office two or three miles from our home, and a daily walk through the woods with our dog.

The national park, which covered about a third of the island, had many trails one could explore. One could take an easy, half-hour walk, or a more strenuous hike that required an entire morning or afternoon. In July and August, there are blueberries, huckleberries, raspberries, blackberries and cranberries to be picked, as well as many species of edible wild mushrooms. If you knew what you were picking, and refrained from picking what you didn't know, it was a safe hobby, and we practiced it for many decades.

The beauty of the island was famous. Part of the secret of this beauty was the great variety of views. Every house one visited has its own scenery, some of it lovely and gentle, some dramatic and exciting, and the pleasure of discovering ever-new sights never ceased. We had an active social life there with good friends. Various music groups provided as many chamber concerts as anyone would want to attend. We were on the board of directors of one of these festivals, and provided housing for some of its musicians. I sang with the Mount Desert Island Summer Chorale, a good group consisting of summer people as well as 'natives.'

I also sang with a group in nearby Surry, which performed entire operas. Occasionally, I also did some research work or some writing.

Long Pond was a deep lake. At its southern end, it filled a V-shaped valley between two steep mountains, and went down to a depth of about 120 feet. At that end, one could fish for land-locked salmon. Less ambitious people could catch small-mouth bass. Loons inhabited the shore of the lake during the summer, and we also saw many other kinds of birds—from hummingbirds to great blue herons and bald eagles. The wildlife we could observe included muskrats and beavers, deer, fox, raccoon, red squirrels and chipmunks. Eva once saw a moose swimming across the lake. I also ought to mention the swarms of mosquitoes that abounded in the early part of the summer. One got used to them.

Sometime in the fall of 1965, I received a phone call from Sam Eldersveld, then chairman of the Political Science Department at the University of Michigan. Would I like to join their department, he asked. The question was a bit unusual because it was politically risky for one major State University to raid another major university in the same state for personnel. The possibility of moving to the University of Michigan sounded attractive, however. I therefore told Sam to make me an offer, and I would respond to it.

The University of Michigan was an institution of higher learning with an international reputation for excellence. Scholars from all over the world flocked to its Institute for Social Research. Several of my colleagues at Michigan State University had found the rich holdings of the University of Michigan libraries an indispensable resource. The governing style of the University of Michigan was much more liberal than that of MSU, both with regard to the relations between the faculty and the administration, and to those between the university and the students. Ann Arbor hummed with a cultural life that made East Lansing seem culturally arid and provincial by comparison.

For some months after this phone conversation, I did not hear from the University of Michigan. I was unaware that the proposal to hire me was hotly debated among the senior members of the department, and that the man who had been chairman for two decades and run the department with an iron hand had stubbornly opposed my appointment. He did not know me, but I later learned that he did not care to hire Jews. Ultimately, he was outvoted, and the department decided, obviously with a go-ahead sign from the Dean, to offer me the job. Again, I received a phone call from Sam Eldersveld, who invited me to join his department. The salary he offered was less than what I was receiving at Michigan State University. I considered that an insult. On the phone, I gave a non-committal reply; but as soon as he had hung up, I wrote a letter, saying, in effect: The terms on which you propose to hire me indicate to me that you do not mean this offer seriously. I therefore reject it.

That letter prompted Eldersveld to phone me again. "We do mean it seriously, he said." He suggested I come to Ann Arbor, sixty miles from East Lansing, to discuss the matter. In his office, he explained that the University of Michigan had to be careful in raiding the MSU faculty and that the low salary they were offering me reflected that caution. He then took me to meet the Dean, Bill Haber, a labor economist who himself had previously taught at Michigan State and knew the place well. Haber chatted with me for an hour or two, presumably to assess my character and my priorities. In the end, he must have figured me out pretty well, because he said, "Meyer, you have got to make up your mind. Do you want star money from John Hannah or do you want to teach at a good university?" He must have guessed that my academic snobbism was stronger than my greed. I opted for teaching at a good university, even when Michigan State University then offered me a huge salary raise if I stayed. I never regretted my decision.

When I announced my resolve to leave MSU, the Provost (or Vice President for Academic Affairs) called me to his office and asked, "Al, what can we do to keep you here?"

"If you get rid of the Basic College, I will stay," I replied.

The Provost smiled sadly and said, "We'll be able to do that only after President Hannah retires."

The one condition I made before accepting the job at the University of Michigan was that Eva had to find employment suitable to her in or near Ann Arbor. That problem was solved quickly and easily. She was hired as a staff therapist at a school for physically impaired children run by the Department of Special Education at Eastern Michigan University, in nearby Ypsilanti. In later years, she also became an Assistant Professor in that department, teaching courses to better prepare students of Special Education to deal with physically handicapped and developmentally challenged children.

Thus, we moved to Ann Arbor. We bought an elegant home in a new neighborhood on the outskirts of town. Its living room was large enough to hold a grand piano that Eva's parents had brought over from Germany thirty years earlier. We had bookshelves in three or four rooms, which must have held up to three thousand volumes. Some interesting pieces of modern art that my father-in-law had collected in his younger days, together with some paintings and drawings we ourselves had picked up here and there, graced our walls, and a few oriental rugs covered the floor. The house stood on a large lot, the front of which was wooded. A carpet of trillium bloomed there in the spring, and during the summer the edge of the woods was lined with phlox.

Ann Arbor lay in the hills of the Huron River valley, forty or fifty miles west of Detroit, on one of the roads from Detroit to Chicago. The town offered a rich cultural life. With its millions of volumes, the University library system was an invaluable treasure. Among the faculty, there were people of erudition, wit, and sociability, with whom it was a pleasure to be associated, and we met equally interesting people who had no connection with the university. The students, who came from all over the world, were recruited from applicants that had distinguished themselves by high academic achievement. They were an intelligent and cosmopolitan group and I learned a lot from them. There was no day during the academic year on which the university calendar did not offer a wide choice of lectures, discussions, or seminars that one could attend free of charge. Every sort of political sect and religious denomination had its own organization among the students. Theater and dance performances competed with cinema societies that showed classical, foreign, or contemporary experimental movies. Some of the buildings belonging to the university were architectural jewels—the Clements Library, the Gerald Ford Library, Hill Auditorium, the Rackham Building, and the Law Library Annex.

Finally, and, for me, most importantly, there was a wealth of music, some of it performed by world-renowned artists in magnificent auditoriums. The university's School of Music invited all citizens to attend degree recitals, free of charge. The University Music Society had a rich program of concert offerings culminating in the annual May Festival, when some famous orchestra was invited to give three or four concerts on successive days. The Festival Chorus of the University Music Society also presented several performances of Handel's Messiah every December. I was a member of the Festival Chorus for ten to fifteen years, sang *The Messiah* every one of those years, and participated in many a May Festival, singing under the baton of Eugene Ormandy, Robert Shaw, Edo de Waart, Sergiu Comisiona, and other famous conductors. Later I joined an independent music ensemble, the Ann Arbor Cantata Singers, with which I sang for many years.

CHAPTER 6

THE REVOLUTION OF 1848-9

THE YEARS 1848-9 were a period of exciting activity for Engels. In retrospect, however, they appear strangely uninteresting and anticlimactic. Much was done, at times at great risk, but nothing happened. A revolution that he and Marx had hailed in advance had finally broken out, but it was not the proletarian revolution they had expected. Sporadic participation by workers or their spokesmen— especially during the Paris uprising of June 1848—bloodily suppressed, only served to frighten the middle-class liberals and petty-bourgeois democrats into a more compromising or timid stand vis-à-vis the conservative establishment. A few symbols of the old order were removed as a result of the revolution, among them King Louis-Philippe and Prince Metternich, but on the whole the causes of political liberalism, social reform, or national unification were not advanced appreciably.

When the revolutionary cycle began in Paris in February of 1848, Engels and Marx were in Brussels, relatively isolated from the community of radical émigrés there. Indeed, Engels had reported to Marx in September of 1847 that all their former associates were aligned against them. Engels and Marx had gained the reputation of being people who used their friends, treated them with contempt, and neglected them within their organizations. Engels himself admitted that they had treated some of them rudely, as they would do so often in the future. Now, their former friends were seeking revenge.[147] Engels was even involved in some physical fights with them.[148] The fact is that the two friends had become quite intolerant of all views conflicting with their own, and were making no bones about it. In a letter to Marx, Engels observed that people around him attributed differences he had with others to personal motives even when he insisted that they were based on disagreements in principle—a strange accusation from a man who in his polemics with former associates would so often use the very same *ad hominem* argument.[149]

The only persons who acknowledged Engels and Marx as ideological leaders or spokesmen were the members of the tiny League of Communists. Its central office was in Paris, though Marx, its organizer, was still in Brussels. In March, Engels, too, was elected to the League's central board. At the first news that a revolution had broken out in France, that the king had been deposed and a republic proclaimed, Engels reacted with boundless confidence. In an article published in the *Deutsche Brusseler Zeitung*, he declared himself surprised by this "brilliant success" and then predicted even more astounding achievements. "Our time is coming," he wrote. "The flames of the Tuilieries and the Palais Royal are the dawn of the proletariat. Everywhere, the rule of the bourgeoisie will now collapse from within or will be smashed from outside.[150]

A few days after this comment was published, the arrest of Marx and his subsequent expulsion to France hastened Engels's departure from Brussels as well. While the revolution was spreading to Germany with the March uprising in Berlin, he joined Marx in Paris only to leave for Germany the next month. A friend had suggested that they run for election to the new Prussian Diet, but instead they decided to go to Cologne with the aim of putting out a newspaper of their own. Engels first went to his hometown to organize support for the movement there, and to sell shares in their journalistic enterprise, if not to his parents, then to other local bourgeois. He found the Barmen bourgeoisie in a state of panic and highly suspicious of his political motives, some of them expecting him to proclaim the republic at once. Carefully concealing his true views, he spoke to them in tones of moderation and did manage to sell a few shares.[151]

By the beginning of May, he had rejoined Marx in Cologne, where they founded their newspaper, the *Neue Rheinische Zeitung*, a daily paper designed to appeal to radical democratic rather than socialist opinion, according to the belief that socialism could not be placed on the agenda before the completion of the democratic revolution. One year earlier, Engels had made this strategy clear in an article published in Harney's Chartist journal, *The Northern Star*. For the time being, he wrote in this article, the revolution that was about to begin would be of direct interest only to the bourgeoisie, but it was nevertheless a matter of concern for the proletariat. For as soon as the power of the bourgeoisie had constituted itself as a new government, a separate movement, which Engels still called democratic, would begin.

In the fight against autocracy and aristocracy, the broad masses of the people could play only a secondary role. The star role would still be that of the bourgeoisie. A bourgeois government, however, would be a new despotism, and then the democratic movement would enter the stage. The struggle would be simplified and reduced to two parties—the bourgeoisie versus the people.[152] Since Prussia was still a conservative and autocratic regime, in which the landed aristocracy remained the politically dominant class, demands that Engels associated with the bourgeois revolution would still have to be met.

Cologne was picked as the home of the new daily paper because the Rhineland provinces, being governed by the Napoleonic Code and having the institution of the jury trial, offered greater freedom for the editors of a radical journal. On the editorial staff, Engels tells us, Marx was the undisputed dictator, and Marx often had his hands full with the management of the paper, including its shaky finances, its legal fights against the Prussian authorities, and the easily ruffled political sensibilities of its bourgeois shareholders. There were periods, therefore, during which the major share of political reportage and editorial writing was borne by Engels. He wrote profusely about all the major political developments—the course of the revolutions in Paris, Vienna, and Prague, the war in Schleswig-Holstein, the debates in the Prussian Diet and in the all-German parliament in Frankfurt, as well as Prussian treatment of its Polish minorities in Poznan province, political justice in Antwerp, and conditions in England.

The chief concern of the paper was to secure the gains of the revolution. According to an assessment Engels wrote in June of 1848, some democratic freedoms had been won in Prussia, but power had fallen into the hands of the grand bourgeoisie, the most conservative section of the class. Hence, the revolution was not complete. Indeed, it was about to be betrayed, for the basically anti-revolutionary bourgeoisie feared the people so much that it had concluded an alliance with the reactionaries.[153] Henceforth, the paper's principal aim seemed to be to unmask this betrayal and to berate the timidity of all those liberals and democrats whose interests were being sold out. In writing about liberals and parties further to the right, the paper quite deliberately adopted an arrogant, insolent, contemptuous, and defiant tone. All his life, Engels continued to be proud of this and argued that the guts to speak of the establishment in such a tone was a precondition for self-liberation.

"That's the right way," he wrote to Bernstein in 1883, when a socialist Reichstag deputy had sharply satirized the German Minister of the Interior in a speech. "Not to twist and grovel under the beatings of the enemy, to cry and sob and stammer excuses—'We didn't really mean it'—as so many still do. To kick back—that's what one has to do—two or three blows for every one from the enemy. That has always been our tactic, and so far I think we have got the better of just about every antagonist."[154] In the same vein he wrote, very much like Frantz Fanon later, that only revolutionary violence could purge a people of its habitual submissiveness to authority. "The submissive subject," he said, "can be doffed only in the course of a bloody struggle for liberation.[155]

Such calls for violence were often made in a frank spirit of vengeance, stimulated again and again in him by the fury of conservative or counterrevolutionary repression. In 1848, Engels reported such bloody repression measures with a mixture of indignation and astonishment, as if he could not quite understand the rage with which General Cavaignac had wrought his vengeance on the Paris workers in June. Then, and on many subsequent occasions, he would call attention to the double standard according to which every misdeed against an establishment person was denounced while the misdeeds against many times more workers were left unreported and unlamented.[156]

It may well be that Engels had caught his spirit of vindictiveness from his old associate, Moses Hess, whose thoughts on this matter were summarized in a letter to a friend in which he wrote, "Nothing is right in the world until all money aristocrats have been hanged. There would be but few who would be executed innocent..."[157] To be sure, Engels was theoretically against vengeance for the sake of vengeance. Even the bourgeois, he had written not long before, acts as he does only because his position within the system compels him to do so.[158] His Christian spirit of vindictiveness often got the better of him, however. Marx frequently expressed similar ideas.[159]

The tone of defiance adopted by the paper corresponded to its policy line. The task for the movement on the left, Engels explained later, had been to be as radical as possible, to make the intermediate results of the revolution as clear could be, to dispel all illusions about its results, and to push for the realization of all rights so far attained only on paper. The *Neue Rheinische Zeitung* thus developed the principle of revolution-in-permanence,[160] in the name of which it would give enthusiastic support to all proletarian uprisings, wherever they might occur, and to every revolutionary nation and every war of liberation.[161] The editors wished to dissociate their movement from all other movements, their class from all other classes. If the democrats denounced the workers' uprising in Paris, the paper encouraged it. If the petty-bourgeoisie timidly wished for (at most) a federal German republic, the paper demanded a unified republic.

The notion that historical stages cannot be skipped, which later came to be associated with the Marxist theory of development, did not enter into the editors' heads much during the years of the 1848-9 revolution. Instead, although Marx and Engels were telling themselves in 1848 that this was yet another bourgeois revolution and therefore sought to apply the lessons of all previous bourgeois revolutions as they understood them, they were confident that the proletariat would join in so as to make this the first revolution led by a majority of the people. Shortly before his death, Engels conceded that neither economic conditions nor the consciousness of the proletariat had ripened sufficiently to warrant the success of a truly democratic revolution, much less a proletarian revolution that would abolish capitalism, not to mention the equally underdeveloped class consciousness of the bourgeoisie itself, about which Engels was to write at length in the 1850s.[162]

In European politics, the paper supported the unification of Italy, the restoration of Poland, and revolutionary war against the staunchest bastion of reaction—tsarist Russia. In fact, it could easily be argued that the *Neue Rheinische Zeitung* was the most nationalistic paper in Germany during the revolution of 1848-9. Intemperate sallies against non-German nationalities, especially those in the Austrian Empire, abounded in Engels's articles. His opinion about these nationalities was that they were the sorry residues of nations that once may have had their own independent existence, but now were hindrances to progress, or else that they were tribes whom history had passed by entirely—a notion derived from Hegel's theories about a-historic nations. Ignorant about the social conflicts in Eastern Europe and the position of various peasant nations vis-à-vis the aristocracies of dominant alien nations, he regarded these nationalities as the natural allies of tsarism and of the aristocracy, attributed to them a variety of historical misdeeds for which in fact their rulers should have been blamed, and advocated their absorption into more viable nations—Bohemia into German Austria, the Southern Slavs into Hungary and Turkey, and the Ukranians into a newly-created Poland.

Mixed in with his Hegelian assumptions and his sheer ignorance about Eastern Europe were current German prejudices against various non-German nationalities, against peasants in general, a belief in centralization that regarded all national interests primarily as disturbances, and the curious assumptions that there were revolutionary and counter-revolutionary nations. Thus, in the interest of the revolution, Engels called for a war of annihilation against Czechs and Croats. The next revolution, he gloated, would destroy some of these nations totally. "And that, too," he wrote, "is progress." The paper was openly anti-Semitic, regarding the Jews in general as enemies of the revolution and as archetypal exploiters, an opinion shared by many socialists and workers then and later. For Marx, Engels, and many of their followers, Judaism was identical with capitalism.[163]

Engels's treatment of these problems, both during and after the revolution of 1848, shows that the issues of nationalism and national dependence, oppression, and liberation, were much too complicated to be treated realistically by the grand simplifications of their theory. To treat such explosive issues as these as if they were a residue of past problems and would disappear with capitalism was politically naïve. Moreover, to the extent that political reality forced them to take sides, they had to do so on the basis of purely pragmatic considerations. Behind the pragmatism, many students of Marxism have argued, one could discern a more fundamental attitude—internationalism. That, by now, has been revealed as deceptive.

Marx and Engels were internationalists only in the sense that they believed the conflicts between European (or civilized) nations to be holdovers from the past. Viewed on a global scale, however, they were Europeans. For them, the history of the human race was one of social, economic, and political progress. Its meaning was the growth of civilization, or modernity, and the cradle of this civilization was Europe. This left out most of Africa and Asia. On the rare occasions when they thought of Africa, they saw only savage, uncivilized tribes. When they looked at Asia, they saw large nations without history, outside the mainstream of progress. In various parts of Europe, they discerned the sorry ruins of what had once been proud nations, which had lost their capacity for self-government.

A few years after the revolution of 1848-9, Engels summarized his views about these nations as follows: "Thus, the attempt of the Slavs in Germany to regain their national independence has ended for now and with all probability forever. Splintered remnants of numerous nations whose nationhood and political vitality have been extinguished long ago have therefore seen themselves obliged for almost a millennium to tread in the path of a stronger nation that has defeated them—such as the Welsh in England, the Basques in Spain, the Lower Bretons in France, and in more recent times the Spanish and French Creoles in those parts of North America recently occupied by the Anglo-Americans. These dying national tribes—Bohemians, Carinthians, Dalmatians, etc., have attempted to utilize the general chaos of 1848 for the purpose of restoring the political status quo of the year 800 A.D. The history of a whole millennium ought to have shown them that such retrogression is impossible.

"Even if the entire area east of the Elbe and the Saale rivers was once settled by Slavic peoples related to each other, this fact demonstrates only the historic trends and the physical and intellectual ability of the German nation to subject, absorb, and assimilate its old eastern neighbors. This absorption drive of the Germans has always been and still is one of the mightiest means of spreading Western European civilization in Eastern Europe. This trend can stop only when the Germanizing process comes to the frontier of a strong, solid, unbroken nation capable of leading an autonomous national life, like the Hungarians and to some extent the Poles. The natural and inescapable destiny of these dying nations, therefore, is to let this process of dissolution and absorption by their stronger neighbors complete itself."[164]

Work on the paper must have been a giddy activity that left no time for the fun and frivolity Engels liked so much. When he was not busy reading the newest dispatches from various parts of the world or writing articles, he plunged into other tasks. A large public assembly held in Cologne in September 1848 elected him to membership in a revolutionary Committee of Public Safety, and in a mass rally held in a nearby village on the banks of the Rhine, he functioned as Secretary. Soon afterwards, the public prosecutor began proceedings against him and others for conspiracy to overthrow the existing order. When arrest seemed imminent in late September, Engles fled first to Barmen and then to what seemed to him a safer haven, Brussels. There, however, he was promptly arrested and deported to France.

When he arrived in Paris in early October, he came to a gloomy city. The June uprising of the workers had been suppressed with extreme harshness. The Paris he had known, he wrote, had become a corpse. The city and its mood were so depressed that he decided to leave. Being healthy and vigorous, a few weeks short of his 28th birthday, he left on foot, carrying little money and no identification papers with him. He headed south, toward Orleans and the valley of the Loire, and then hiked through Burgundy to Geneva. He must have been a brisk walker, for he completed his trek in less than three weeks. His travel journal, left incomplete and not published during his lifetime, contains graceful landscape descriptions and deft sketches of the comparatively primitive but reasonably self-sufficient economy of the French countryside, where wine was cheap, bread tasty, and the standard of life was superior to that of Germany.

On his trip, he met workers employed in a public works project. Over a drink in a village tavern, one of the foremen offered him a job. If he had had identification papers, Engels might have been tempted to stay for a while. At the same time, however, the lack of interest these workers showed in politics depressed him. He thought that the short time they had spent away from the city had already demoralized them. Yet he found the workers sophisticated compared to the peasants, whom he called barbarians living amid civilization.

"The peasant's isolation," he wrote, "in villages off the beaten track with a small population that changes only with the generations, the hard, monotonous work that ties him to the soil more firmly than any serfdom, and which always remains the same from father to son, the stability and uniformity of all living conditions, the narrow limits within which the family becomes for him the most important, most decisive societal relationship—all these things reduce the peasant's horizon down to the narrowest limits possible in modern society. The grand movements of history pass him by. From time to time, they forcibly carry him along, but even then he has no idea about the nature of the moving force, the genesis, of its aim."[165]

For some decades, Engels clung to the opinion that peasants were ignorant, blind, erratic, stubborn, and limited. His favorite adjective for them was "*borniert,*" a term of contempt signifying just such qualities.[166] His observations of the peasants' stupidity led to sad reflections about their role in the recent revolution and its tragic outcome. His rage against them was even greater because he had foreseen a grand peasant revolution engulfing all of Eastern Europe, from the Baltic to the Black Sea.[167]

Once he was in Burgundy, the friendly landscape and the congeniality of its peasants cheered him. He listened with interest to the Burgundian dialect, but was even more interested in the grape harvest, which he witnessed at its orgiastic peak in the market city of Auxerre. Later, he came through a region where the grape harvest was still going on. "On the other side of Saint-Bris," he wrote, "there was a long climb to be made, but on this hill I climbed with very special pleasure. Everything here was still busy with the grape harvest, and a grape harvest in Burgundy is jolly in a very different way than even one in the Rhineland.

"At every step," he added, "I encountered the merriest company, the sweetest grapes, and the prettiest girls, for here, where there is a little town every two or three hours, and where the inhabitants because of their wine trade are engaged in a good deal of commerce with the rest of the world, a certain degree of civilization prevails, and nobody adopts this civilization more quickly than womenfolk, for they enjoy the most direct and most obvious advantages of it."[168] The travel journal breaks off abruptly after he has launched into a connoisseur's comparison between the peasant women of Burgundy and those of Germany and the Paris region. He preferred the Burgundians.

What a strange interlude! A professional revolutionary, at the first threat of arrest, runs away in panic and then, as if he had no responsibilities toward his cause or his comrades, takes a two- or three-month vacation from the revolution. He apparently felt that he needed it. He greatly enjoyed his hike to Geneva and his subsequent carousing with other exiles that he met there. Forty years later, he was still reminiscing about the jolly time he had in Geneva.[169] Toward the end of the year, he wrote to Marx that several weeks of sinful life had caused him to recover from hardships and adventures. His bohemian side had reasserted itself.

After leaving Paris, he had been out of contact with Marx for some weeks. Money that, for once, he had requested from his friend had not reached him. Meanwhile, his family made attempts not only to lure him back to a respectable business life, but also to sow seeds of discord between him and Marx. In a letter on October 25, 1848, his mother asserted that she had reliable information that Marx was no longer willing to take him back on the editorial staff of the *Neue Rheinische Zeitung*. Did Marx consider him a deserter? Engels was worried enough to ask Marx whether he could still count on him to be his friend, and was promptly reassured. "You will always remain my *intimus*," wrote Marx, "just as I hope to remain yours," and in a postscript he added, "Your Old Man is a son-of-a-bitch, to whom we will write an extremely rude letter."[170]

Having recovered his sense of purpose, Engels reported to Marx that he was ready to do some work again. He was eager to return to Cologne, but only if the criminal proceedings against him were dropped. He rejected the idea of going back only to be thrown in jail pending an investigation. In jail, he said, smoking was forbidden.[171] Ten days later, however, he said that he was so tired of sitting around in exile that he was willing to risk even going to jail in Cologne.[172] He was, as often, exaggerating his own laziness. In fact, shortly after arriving in Switzerland, he had returned to journalistic activities and sent articles to the *Neue Rheinische Zeitung*. Most of them dealt with Swiss politics. Soon after his arrival in Geneva, he had continued his trek in several stages to Bern, where he attended a congress of workers' associations and democratic clubs as the delegate of the Lausanne Workers' Association, and also listened to debates of the Swiss Federal Council.

He had already made clear what he thought of Swiss politics in an article published in November 1847. As a radical democrat, he sought to dissociate himself from the democracy of what he considered backward peasant countries, such as Switzerland and Norway. Democracy in civilized countries, he had written, aimed toward the rule of the proletariat. Democracy in Switzerland was the rebellion of stubborn hillbillies against the pressure of historic and progressive trends, of

barbarism against civilization. The Swiss peasants had exchanged the
feudal yoke of the Hapsburgs for the yoke of the Babbitts of Zurich,
Lucerne, Bern, and Basel.

Engels denounced the federalist principles of Swiss democracy and
came out strongly in favor of centralization. He poured scorn on the
pristine virtues of those backwoods people, and argued that these virtues
were in the process of being corroded by capitalism, French ideas, and
English tourists.[173] Much earlier, in remarks about Andreas Hofer, a
martyr of the wars of liberation against Napoleon, he had made clear his
contempt for backwoods peasants in mountain countries.[174] The articles
he wrote about Switzerland in early 1849 were variations on these same
themes.

By the middle of January 1849, Engels was back in Cologne and
working for the paper, having been reassured by the authorities that no
case was pending against him at that time. In articles dealing with the
war between Austria and Piedmont, and with the course of the
Hungarian revolution, he expressed his first interest in the military side
of revolutions, and for the rest of his life he remembered the Hungarian
developments because they had awakened this interest in him. In late
April and early May, Marx was away on a four-week trip, trying to
collect money to keep the newspaper in operation, and Engels was left
in charge. This was a politically dangerous period. The counter-
revolution had begun to rally and seemed prepared to strike back at the
forces of the Left. Engels believed that the Prussians were about to place
Cologne and other nearby cities in a state of siege, which would have
suspended civil laws. In the paper, he warned the workers to remain
calm in the face of provocation, and not to be lured into premature
revolutionary action under unfavorable conditions.

Meanwhile, new revolutionary disturbances broke out in various
parts of Germany. The Frankfurt Parliament had drafted an all-German
constitution providing for an Emperor as the head of state. A delegation
had gone to the King of Prussia to offer him the Emperor's crown, and
had been contemptuously dismissed. In the King's opinion, crowns were
conferred by the Lord above, and not by the rabble below. Most of the

larger German states had followed the Prussian example in refusing to ratify the new constitution, and the Parliament had no power to enforce it. Rebellions broke out, first in Dresden, then in the Palatinate and Baden. The Grand Duke of Baden fled, and his army declared itself in favor of the Reich Constitution. The Prussian Army then moved to quell the insurrections, and when it began to mobilize the older reserves there were refusals in scattered locations in Westphalia and the Rhineland.

At the very time Marx returned from his fundraising trip, the revolt had spread to Elberfeld, where the rebellious workers erected barricades and formed a revolutionary Committee of Public Safety. Engels at once left Cologne and, accompanied by a group of workers from neighboring Solingen, appeared in the town where he had attended school and placed himself at the disposal of the revolutionary committee. As an artillery sergeant in the reserve, he was made inspector of the barricades and the rebels' artillery, and he must have felt very much in his element. There is a story, plausible but unconfirmed, that adorned with a red sash he was standing on a barricade on Sunday morning when his father came by on his way to or from church. If that encounter indeed took place, it must have been a source of keen embarrassment for both, and a cause of deep sadness for his father. If it did not, then the elder Engels must have heard that his revolutionary son was in town and what role he was playing, and both parents must have suffered from the knowledge that everyone else in town had heard the same disgraceful news.[175]

Indeed, all of Engels's activities during the revolutionary years of 1848-9 brought his relations with his parents as near to the breaking point as they ever were, although even now the ties were not totally severed. While the precise point at which his father stopped paying him his monthly allowance is not known, this support certainly was not continued after his revolutionary adventure in Elberfeld. Financially, Engels was now without any outside support.

Four days after his arrival in town, the revolutionary committee asked him to leave again. Perhaps the bourgeois establishment had intervened with them. Maybe they, themselves, deeply distrusted his more radical views. In any event, the committee felt, or pretended to feel, that his presence among them was a source of political embarrassment or misunderstanding. Reluctantly, he returned to Cologne. There he learned that because of his activities in Elberfeld a warrant for his arrest had been published, and he fled again. (The warrant described him as five feet, six inches tall, with blond hair, blue eyes, a reddish beard, oval face, healthy color, and slim stature. A rapid manner of speaking and nearsightedness were listed as special features. An earlier arrest warrant had described him as being two inches taller, with dark blond hair and grey eyes.)

Two days later, on May 19, 1849, the *Neue Rheinische Zeitung* came out with its last number printed all in red. It contained, among other things, another admonition to the workers of Cologne to remain cool in the face of overwhelming enemy power, a summary of the revolution in Hungary written by Engels, a poem by Freiligrath, and a defiant editorial by Marx, in which he predicted the rapid revival of revolutionary energy.

Engels and Marx, having fled Cologne, believed that it might indeed be possible to revive the flagging energies of the revolution. They traveled to Frankfurt, trying to mobilize the more radical deputies of the all-German parliament to take charge of the insurrection in southwest Germany. Unsuccessful at this, they proceeded to this region to contact the leaders of the rebellion and persuade them to march on to Frankfurt in order to spread the movement. The two friends had no illusions about the relatively narrow aims of the rebellion. They thought of its leaders as petty bourgeois and of its program as illusory. In their eyes, the defense of a paper constitution was not a cause worth fighting for in its own right. They also believed, however, that it was a necessary or convenient way station on the road to the spread and radicalization of the movement.

Just as Engels had shelved his 'red' views when he placed himself at the disposal of a 'black-red-gold' (the all-German national colors) movement in Elberfeld, so now in dealing with the leaders of the rebellious troops in Baden and the Palatinate, Marx and Engels shelved their socialist views in cautious and limited support of a much less radical movement because they believed that this would intensify the revolution as a whole. In first commenting on the events in these two states, Engels had interpreted them as harbingers of the kind of revolution he himself wished to see. He perceived an all-European revolutionary war around the corner. "Another few weeks," he wrote, "a few days perhaps, and the armed masses of the republican West and the enslaved East will roll toward each other in order to wage the great fight on German soil, a fight in which the one and only question will be, 'Do you wish to be free, or do you wish to be Russian?'"[176]

The cautious reaction of the leaders of what Engels later called "this so-called revolution," discouraged him and Marx. The second article he wrote about these events was too radical for these leaders, and remained unpublished. Marx, by this time, had gone on to Paris, while Engels remained living what he later called the life of Riley (*Schlaraffenleben*)[177] in Kaiserslautern, the provisional capital of the rebel forces, observing the political developments and trying to stay in touch with Marx. He was offered several positions in the rebel government, but refused them.[178]

When Prussian troops marched into the Palatinate and he found his communications with Paris cut off, however, he could not resist the temptation of joining a battalion of revolutionary volunteers. He decided that August Willich, a former Prussian lieutenant who had joined the League of Communists, was a good officer, and he signed up as Willich's adjutant, participated in four engagements of the comic-opera war that ensued, and found to his satisfaction that bravery in the face of bullets whistling by one's head was a very ordinary quality.[179] He also thought it politically important that someone from the *Neue Rheinische Zeitung* participate in the fighting, a sentiment shared by Marx.[180]

Poorly armed, poorly led and organized, and with poorly defined aims, the troops fighting for the Reich Constitution were thoroughly beaten in less than a month, and either simply dissolved or crossed over into Switzerland. Engels made it to the safety of Swiss soil on July 12, almost exactly four weeks after signing up as an officer with Willich.

There, he began writing an account of the campaign and its inefficient conduct, dismissing it as a typically petty-bourgeois venture. He explained this by the backwardness of Baden and the Palatinate, where the class conflict that he thought had fully developed in Elberfeld had not yet begun seriously. Hence, the campaign never took a socialist direction.[181]

·In Switzerland this time, he met two people who became his lifelong friends—Wilhelm Liebknecht, who soon afterwards joined the League of Communists and was to remain an ever-faithful representative of their views within the German workers' movement, and Wilhelm ("Lupus") Wolff, a veteran of the struggle against Prussian autocracy, who later emigrated to England, settled in Manchester, and was for many years Engels's best friend there.

His Swiss exile did not daunt Engels. He was confident that the revolution was by no means over. On the contrary, it would soon pick up speed and develop into the proletarian revolution that was now destined to come. Marx, in France, shared his optimism.[182] This mood of confidence persisted in the friends for another year, despite the vicissitudes they meanwhile suffered in their personal lives. These included chronic financial worries, troubled relations with their families, intense and bitter conflicts with other exiles, continued police surveillance, and the problem of how to stay out of jail.

For the moment, in the summer of 1849, the more immediate question was where they should go. In late August, Marx reported that the French authorities had ordered him to leave Paris and had assigned him a swampy area in Brittany as residence. Unwilling to settle in such a notoriously unhealthy region, Marx had decided to go to London and was now imploring Engels to join him there. In London, he argued, the two could do business together, and if he did not wish to go for Marx's sake he should do so for his own. He could not go back to Prussia, where he would be shot at once, and Switzerland was no country in which to spend a lot of time.[183] Engels agreed, and on October 6, 1849, he sailed from Genoa, London-bound, on board the English schooner "Cornish Diamond," Captain Stevens in command. The passage, meals included, cost him 150 francs (about $28).[184] After a five-week journey, he landed in London.

For Engels and Marx, the beginning of their exile in England was not, at first, the end of the revolution. On the contrary, for another ten months or so after leaving the Continent, they were convinced that the more radical phase of the revolution was yet to come, and that soon they would be back in Germany, this time not to promote the democratic revolution that would usher in a bourgeois regime, but to organize the proletarian revolution. In other words, in the summer of 1849 they had moved even further to the left. In making this shift, they were extremely confident that they had their fingers on the pulse of history. "The difference between the present revolution and all previous ones," Engels wrote in their new journal in the spring of 1850, "consists precisely in the fact that we have at last discovered the secret of this historical process of revolution."[185]

This move to the left was indicated by their belief that the revolutionary situation had become simplified since the collapse of the hopes for a unified, democratic German republic. The choice, wrote Engels in the same issue of the new journal, was no longer one between various factions of the ruling classes, between Prussian authoritarianism and bourgeois democracy. The choice now was between the rule of the revolutionary proletariat and the Prussian ruling class. Nothing in-between was possible any longer, because the bourgeoisie as well as the petty-bourgeoisie had demonstrated their unfitness to rule.[186] In a circular to the League of Communists printed in March 1850, Engels and Marx declared that a new revolution was near. The task was to fan the flame and keep it alive, and in this task the chief enemy was yesterday's ally, the petty-bourgeoisie.

For several years, the two friends would now concentrate their attention on this villain, to whom so far they had paid little attention. To Engels, who saw himself in the forefront of modern development, this class of small, independent producers and traders was representative of an age long passed. Hence, its ideology was outdated as well. It looked backward, rather than forward. It was fundamentally conservative, even though in times of stress it could rise in revolt. Even then, however, its aims were basically reactionary. "The highest ideal of the petty-bourgeois and peasant of Baden," Engels wrote, "has always remained the small burgher-and-peasant republic such as it has existed in Switzerland since 1830. A diminutive area of activity for small, modest people, the state as a somewhat enlarged community, a 'canton,' a little, stable industry based on manual labor that forms the base of equally stable and sleepy social conditions—not much wealth, not much poverty, nothing but middle class and mediocrity.

"No prince, no bureaucracy, no standing army, almost no taxes—no active participation in history, no foreign policy, nothing but domestic petty local gossip and small squabbles *en famille*. No big industry, no railroads, no world trade, no social collisions between millionaires and proletarians—instead, a quiet, comfortable life of pious beatitude and honest decency amid the small, ahistorical modesty of satisfied souls. That is the gentle Arcadia that exists in most parts of Switzerland, the introduction of which the Badensian petty bourgeois and peasant have been dreaming about for years. If Germany could ever transform herself into such an Arcadia, it would then have descended into a stage of humiliation of which up to now she has had no inkling even in her most shameful periods."[187]

Engels here made no bones about his total commitment to the machine age and all its consequences, and about his contempt for people who would warn against the despoiling of nature, man's subjection to the machine, the curses of large size and scale, and other consequences of science and technology. Whenever modernization engulfed a formerly sleepy area of the world, Engels rejoiced. "It is desirable that the lazy peasant economy of Bavaria, the soil on which the parsons and the Daumers grow, be turned over at last by modern agriculture and modern machines," he wrote in a review of G. F. Daumers' book on contemporary religions, and on the same page made fun of the author's naïve wonder about the intricacies and beauties of nature, which Engels called childish. "Through science," he wrote, "we will revolutionize production as well as Nature, and through science we will make an end of this childish attitude of sovereign man toward Nature."[188]

This opinion remained with him to the end of his life. Two years before his death, he wrote to a friend who had given up his business work and moved to the Isle of Man to work as a surveyor that, for a short time, he might enjoy that kind of life, too. In the long run, however, he could not live without the excitement of the big city, where he had spent most of his life. Nature was beautiful, and for relaxation from contemporary history, one returned to it with pleasure. History, however, was grander than Nature. Nature had taken millions of years to produce conscious creatures, and now these conscious creatures had taken but thousands of years to learn to cooperate consciously, not only as individuals but also through collective action, pursuing common goals. "We have almost reached this stage now," wrote Engels, and to observe this process, this development of something unprecedented, seemed to him to be a spectacle worth watching. For his entire life, he had not been able to take his eyes off of it. Only once in a while, the active participant in this process got tired, and then the study of Nature was great relief and good medicine.[189]

Because of its commitment to a dead past, the petty bourgeoisie was politically untrustworthy. In his history of the campaign in which he had just participated, Engels wrote that the members of this class were big in their words, extremist in their ideology as long as there was no danger, but hesitant, cowardly, and vacillating as soon as anyone began to take them seriously. The petty bourgeoisie, he asserted, would betray all its allies for the sake of minor gains as soon as revolutionary action really started, and of course the reactionaries would always cheat them out of the fruits of their action.[190] The half-hearted revolutionary efforts of this class were useful only in that their abortive attempts tended to simplify the situation by making further mediation efforts impossible. The cowardice of the petty bourgeoisie ended up by sharpening the class conflict because it showed the masses that half-hearted revolutions were useless.[191] This judgment of the petty-bourgeoisie Engels never renounced.

Another villain that appeared in his writing for the first time in the summer of 1849 was the *Lumpenproletariat*. The word had a double meaning. *Lump*, in German, meant scoundrel, while *Lumpen* meant rags or tatters. Hence, *Lumpenproletariat* was both the scoundrel proletariat and the proletariat clad in rags. Engels later explained that this was the scum of degenerate subjects from all classes that established itself in the big cities.[192] In 1850, he pointed out that such people existed in all societies as vagabonds, hoboes, beggars, and day laborers, but that in bourgeois society they were more rotten than in previous societies, where it had still retained part of its healthy peasant nature.[193]

In England, he added, it was mostly of Irish origin and therefore constituted, among other things, one of the mainstays of the Catholic Church,[194] which Engels despised more than all other Christian denominations. Totally demoralized and totally purchasable, as Engels pointed out repeatedly,[195] the members of the *Lumpenproletariat* was readily at the disposal of the bourgeoisie as their butchers, hangmen, and cannon fodder, but in any event as the executioners of the real proletariat.[196] In Elberfeld, he related, as soon as members of the *Lumpenproletariat* got hold of the arms originally appropriated by him, they sold them to the bourgeoisie.[197]

Marx shortly afterwards cautioned that class labels used in their political writings did not necessarily refer to the actual interests of every single spokesman. Not every radical democrat was really a petty-bourgeois shopkeeper. "What makes them into representatives of the petty-bourgeoisie," he wrote, "is that in their heads they do not go beyond the limits which the latter cannot surmount in real life, that in theory they are driven to the same problems and solutions to which the latter in practice are driven by their material interests and the social condition. This, in general, is the relationship of the 'political' and 'actual' members of a class to the class they represent."[198]

Both Marx and Engels often asserted, however, that there were direct links between political attitudes and occupational or life experiences. Engels applied this particularly to the proletariat, differentiating between them according to the way in which their work shaped their mentality. For instance, dyers, he wrote, were robust, well paid, and crude. In their work, they relied on bodily strength rather than on skill. Such workers, he argued, tended to be reactionary. Other factors that he said had to be taken into consideration included the influence of alcohol and religion, the workers' concentration or dispersion, the amount of coercion and terror to which they were subjected, the lies spread about by the establishment (peasants, he asserted, were more prone to believe bourgeois lies than workers), or even their feelings of rage. An instinctive hatred of the bourgeoisie could blind the workers' political acumen. Another well-known fact, he thought, was that one could not make a revolution with workers during times of full employment.[199]

In contrast to the petty-bourgeoisie, which wanted no more than a few changes in the system that would accommodate their modest interests, Engels and Marx argued in their circular to the League of Communists that the proletariat must now promote revolution in permanence until all classes were abolished and the state as well as the major forces of production were in the workers' hands throughout the entire civilized world. From now on, they urged, the proletariat should no longer be considered an auxiliary force of a putatively revolutionary bourgeoisie. In their leftward turn, the two friends now argued in favor of proletarian hegemony in the bourgeois revolution.

Indeed, this circular was the most Bolshevik document they ever issued. In it, they exhorted the workers to compel the democrats to carry out the programs to which, according to their ideology, they were committed. They urged them to punish the old exploiters, warning them not to prevent any so-called excesses against persons or hated symbols of the old authorities. By making the most radical demands, they would be able to compromise with the half-hearted. They admonished them to maintain their own political organizations and armed forces not only during the revolution but also after a new democratic government had been created.[200]

The circular contained a political program to be adopted by the workers' movement, including the statement that after the breakup of the large landed estates the land should not be distributed to individual peasants, but should be nationalized. The distribution of land to freeholders, they explained a few weeks later, might look like a revolutionary measure, but it always led to the concentration of land in fewer hands, and the nationalization of all land was a more revolutionary program.[201] In this matter, too, their program of 1850 was much like that of the Bolsheviks before 1917.

Later in his life, Engels wrote that this move to the left was based on an illusion, which in turn rested on a false analogy with the French revolutions of 1789 and 1839. For him and Marx, the main lesson of their study of the French revolutions was that the radicals had to press for revolution in permanence in order to secure the more moderate gains, and hence that the communist movement had to secure the rule of the proletariat. Here was the proletariat, Engels wrote, powerful but unsure of itself; and here was the movement—thinking it knew exactly where history was going. For the first time, there was thus a small minority really speaking for the vast majority. Forty-five years later, however, Engels admitted that this had been an illusion, because the preconditions for doing away with capitalism had not yet ripened on the Continent. Without using the word, Engels acknowledged that in 1850, his and Marx's ideas had been ideology rather than science.[202]

Once Engels arrived in London he plunged into feverish activity, inspired by his vision of the new revolution soon to come. He joined the central committee of the League of Communists and the German Educational Association for Workers. Together with Marx, he attempted to found a new journal, and by early 1850 they had done so. The periodical, which they nostalgically called *Neue Rheinische Zeitung-Politisch—Ökonomische Revue*, was published in Hamburg, and several issues of it came out in 1850. It contained a series of articles by Marx about the course of the revolution in France, which Engels much later published as a book (*The Class Struggles in France*), as well as Engels's account of the four-week campaign in Baden and the Palatinate, with which in the fall of 1849 he had vainly hoped to make a good deal of money. In addition, it featured book reviews, an article by Engels on English politics, and chronicles of recent events written jointly by him and Marx.

Finally, the journal included two lengthy articles, later republished as a book, on the German Peasant War of 1525. Basing his account on the factual material presented in Wilhelm Zimmerman's *Allgemeine Geschichte des grossen Bauernkrieges*, which had been published in the early 1840s, Engels here developed a theme he had struck in some of his earliest articles on Switzerland.[203] This was his interpretation of the Protestant Reformation as a dress rehearsal for the bourgeois revolutions of subsequent centuries, with Luther playing the role of the vacillating and treacherous spokesman for the bourgeoisie, and the revolutionary peasants as premature radicals led by brave but misguided ideologists. Now, after the setbacks of 1848 and 1849, the story of the peasant war was also told to show that the cowardice shown by Luther and the ideological confusion manifested by Thomas Münzer were identical with, or similar to, the attitudes and beliefs that had played such disastrous roles in the most recent events.

In everything they did and wrote Engels, Marx, and their friends in the League of Communists sought to dissociate themselves from those radical émigrés whom they considered petty bourgeois and to discount them as both ignorant and cowardly. By the summer of 1850, however, the two men realized that the revolution was over for the time being. It dawned on them that the immediate cause of the revolution had been the economic crisis of 1847. They were dismayed by the speed with which the economy of Europe had recovered in 1849 and 1850, and saw the new boom as the immediate cause of the defeat of the revolution. From this they concluded that a new revolutionary upswing could come only in the wake of a new economic crisis, and that would entail a wait of seven to ten years, although then it would be a certainty.[204] Gradually, their confidence gave way to a mood of gloom. By February of 1851, Engels wrote to Marx that the present time was a period of growing reaction, and a few months later he confessed that the enemies of the revolution had won a crushing victory.[205]

In September 1851, they were ready to draw the political conclusions from this assessment. Instead of advocating revolution in permanence, they now adopted a wait-and-see attitude, and indeed a lingering reluctance to be involved soon in another revolution. As Engels wrote in the same letter to Marx, the revolution was a maelstrom that sucked in everyone with a blind elemental force, and the best thing one could do was to say out as long as possible, maintain one's independence, and be 'in substance' more revolutionary than everyone else.

Being 'in substance' more revolutionary than everyone else meant, in practice, lying low and being inactive for the present time. This was something that some of their recent associates, including Engels's old commander, Willich, were unable to understand. Now it was their turn to denounce Engels and Marx as cowards, and in September of 1850, Engels and Marx broke with the radicals in the League of Communists.[206] Engels later described Willich as a good soldier who was a communist out of sentiment, and therefore instinctively and secretly against their own critical brand of communism. Willich later immigrated to America and, like so many former friends of Engels, ended up as an officer in the Union Army during the Civil War. (Marx's own brother-in-law, to Marx's dismay, fought for the Confederacy).

Engels and Marx were now totally isolated. Toward the end of the year, the last issue of their new journal came out. During the following summer, they made feeble plans to start a publishing house of their own.[207] They were aware that no one else in Germany would have published anything they wrote under their own names.[208] At the same time the last issue appeared, Engels moved to Manchester to begin work in the cotton-spinning firm of Ermen & Engels. Only now, his exile was really beginning in all its bitterness.

CHAPTER 7

HIGHER EDUCATION AND THE STUDENT
COUNTERCULTURE OF THE SIXTIES

IN THE FALL of 1947, the Dean of the Graduate School of Arts at Harvard University asked graduate students who had been enrolled during the previous spring term to fill in a lengthy questionnaire. The form inquired into their background, their interests, and their opinion about the education that they were receiving. It also asked them where they thought they might be, and what they might be doing, fifteen or twenty years later.

Some weeks after that, the Dean called the graduate students together to discuss with them the results of the survey. The only thing I remember about this meeting is Dean Wilde's almost angry criticism of what he considered the students' unrealistic expectations. "Most of you," he said, "seem to be under the illusion that fifteen years from now you will have professorial rank at some distinguished university. But in the academic world one does not rise so fast, because there is not that much room at the top." The Dean advised us to be much more modest and much more realistic in our expectations.

Fifteen years later, most of those graduate students who had entered academic careers, were full professors at respectable universities or colleges. Some were, or had been, department chairs, deans or even college presidents. The ambitious expectations we had expressed in the questionnaire had, if anything, been too modest. The Dean was the one who had been out of touch with reality.

This turn of events was a reflection of the spectacular expansion of higher education in the United States, an expansion that might be compared to the analogous growth of the military establishment. Prior to

World War II, the military forces of the United States, consisting of the Army and the Navy, were relatively small and in many respects marginal to American society. Socially ingrown and often isolated from civilian society, this was a stern, authoritarian culture of service, where pay was low and promotion to higher rank came very slowly. Appropriations for the military were a tiny portion of the government's budget. This military establishment was appropriate for a country that considered itself far removed from the quarrels among the European powers. It was small and self-contained. If it had expensive military hardware, that might be found primarily in the Navy's battleships and in the large-caliber guns of the coast artillery. It was not a military establishment ready for major land warfare.

For instance, on December 16, 1941, a Japanese submarine shelled an oil derrick near Santa Barbara. After that incident, the military command quite reasonably considered it possible that the Japanese might launch a sneak attack on the United States mainland. They assumed that Christmas Eve or New Year's Eve might well be the dates the Japanese would pick for such an attack. Consequently, on those two nights, the soldiers stationed at the Presidio of Monterey guarded not only their post, but also were ordered to guard the town of Monterey. Both nights, I was on guard duty, as were most of my buddies. The place I had to guard was a railroad storage building. I was issued no weapon. There were not enough rifles or pistols stored at the post to equip every soldier doing guard duty. That's how marginal the pre-war military establishment was to the United States in terms of preparedness as well as budget.

Similarly, the pre-war colleges and universities were a relatively minor adjunct to American society, also rather remote from the mainstream and from Main Street; and, as regards their contribution to science and learning, American universities, by and large, were no match for the great academic institutions of Europe.

The explosive growth and flourishing of higher education in the United States was not only analogous to the growth of our military establishment. It was also, to some extent, a consequence of the militarization of American society. The first impetus for rapid growth came with the G. I. Bill, a generous law that guaranteed a certain amount of college or graduate education to any veteran of the war, depending on the length of time he or she had served. Augmented later by Pell grants, Fulbright fellowships, and other federal money, it enabled millions of high school graduates, who would previously not have dreamed of entering college, to continue learning and obtain degrees. The G. I. Bill initiated a process of democratization in American higher education that was expanded later through affirmative action programs. It thoroughly changed American higher education from elite institutions to those that served the masses.

While this was an indirect consequence of a war fought and won by a citizen army, other changes resulted much more from the nation's subsequent preoccupation with preparing for future wars. A large proportion of scientific research and teaching done at universities after World War II was defense-oriented and was sponsored and financed by the Federal government. This was true not only of research and instruction programs in the natural sciences, but also of the social sciences and the humanities. The numerous centers for Chinese, Russian, Latin American, African, and similar 'area' studies could not have existed without generous government financing. The same was true for many of the so-called think tanks and for some scholarly journals. Not only defense-related work received outside money, however. A vast amount of scientific work and training was sponsored and funded by business corporations of all kinds and by the great foundations—Rockefeller, Guggenheim, Ford, Carnegie, and the like.

This unprecedented influx of funding caused American universities to flourish, making them into the world's leading academic institutions. This funding provided rapid promotion, great prestige, and considerable affluence to the top ranks of the academic profession, but also led to a certain degeneration of the university as an institution by giving the 'production' of Ph.D.s and the pursuit of scientific research far greater priority than the education to be provided in the four years of college. This deflected universities from their obligation to teach undergraduate students.

Whenever anyone complained about that, university administrators and research scholars replied that research and teaching supported each other, and that professors enriched their classroom presentations by continually exploring the frontiers of knowledge and that undergraduate students could profit from participating in ongoing research projects. On rare occasions, indeed, research and teaching mesh in this fashion, and both scholars and students profited from this. The mutual support and enrichment of the two activities, however, was more often than not a myth. The fact was that most scholars engaged in research considered teaching a waste of their time. In the sharply competitive world of academia, what counted was the volume of published research a person had managed to produce. It was that volume, and its 'quality,' as determined by peer judgment, which determined tenure, promotion, salary, and those valuable offers from other institutions that could be used to extract even faster promotion, higher salaries, and—equally sought after—release from teaching duties.

Sometime around 1970, the University of Michigan installed Robben W. Fleming as its new President. He had made a name for himself, as Chancellor of the University of Wisconsin, by his shrewd and wise handling of rebellious students. He was ever ready to negotiate with them and to avoid confrontational tactics. He had learned this wisdom by having served on many occasions as a labor arbitrator. Some time after his inauguration as our president he invited all faculty members to an informal meeting so that we might get acquainted with him. At that meeting, someone asked Fleming how undergraduate education fitted in with his over-all plans for the University of Michigan. He replied that we could not afford to neglect undergraduate education, because, after all, that was an important part of our mission as defined by the citizens of the state. Moreover, the tuition paid by undergraduate students was an essential part of the university's budget. Undergraduates, he said in effect, are our bread and butter.

To me, this sounded meretricious. I interpreted it as a statement to the effect that we had to continue teaching undergraduate courses, even though it interfered with our more important missions of producing Ph.D.s and research. It sounded to me like an impatient dismissal of the undergraduate curriculum.

Not only had the relative importance of this curriculum changed; the content of undergraduate instruction had changed as well. Decades ago, for instance, the study of government and politics focused on political theory. This was essentially citizenship training. It was supposed to encourage reflection on the many ways in which communities could govern themselves, on the advantages and disadvantages of different institutional and constitutional arrangements, and on the moral choices determining one's preference for one or the other such arrangement. This kind of approach to the study of government and politics, past and present, was supposed to be part of the liberal education a college graduate was expected to possess.

I remember the commencement ceremonies at Harvard in June 1947. George C. Marshall gave his famous speech that day, introducing the Marshall Plan. When President Conant conferred Bachelor degrees, he said to the graduating seniors, "I welcome you to the ranks of educated men." When he conferred Master's degrees, he welcomed their recipients "to the ranks of professional people," and when he conferred doctoral degrees, his words were, "I welcome you to the ranks of scholars." Educated people were, by definition, not, or not yet, professionals. They were supposed to have shopped around in the supermarket of knowledge and acquired enough of a sampling to go on to many kinds of professional training.

On the scholarly level, however, the study of politics shifted from a concern with a broad education for citizenship to an emphasis on methodological rigor or scholarly professionalism. A scholar oriented on professionalism would be likely to stress his or her major interest also when teaching undergraduates. The courses taught by these scholars would then be technical. They would be pre-professional introductions to professional scholarship rather than conventional contributions to a liberal arts education. Techniques and methods, however, were of interest and use primarily to the student who wished to become a professional political scientist. The many students taking courses on politics as part of their general education were likely to consider the courses introducing them to professional methods boring and useless.

Conversely, those professors who could make their material—be it physics, literature, or sociology—come to life for a wide range of undergraduates, and who therefore were recognized as the great teachers, were the least likely to obtain tenure, promotion, or star salaries. Their popularity with undergraduate students might arouse envy among their colleagues or the suspicion that they catered to their students, and the style, contents, and range of their course offerings might suggest to their colleagues a lack of professionalism. Many fine teachers, in fact, left their departments under the impression that effective teaching of undergraduate courses was unprofessional behavior. So much for the myth that teaching and research supported each other!

These star entrepreneurs did not wish to waste their time teaching, or teaching well. Good teaching consumed time because it meant preparing courses, lectures, and reading lists, grading exams and papers, and perhaps conferences with individual students. The most fervent wish of many professors was to be relieved of teaching duties, especially for undergraduate courses. Because of this, graduate students taught a vast proportion of these courses. These teaching assistants were overworked and underpaid, and that is why almost every year classes at the University of Michigan were disrupted by a strike by teaching assistants.

Robben Fleming's remark suggested that our universities depended on the undergraduate students' tuition money for their continued existence. That was not entirely correct, however. True, they needed to teach college courses to justify their existence. The bulk of the money used by our universities did not come from tuition, however. In public institutions such as state colleges and universities, it came from government appropriations, as well as contributions to their school's endowment from wealthy and faithful alumni and alumnae. In addition, ever since the end of World War II, an increasing portion of the universities' budgets came from grants given for special purposes by agencies of the Federal government, by foundations, and by business corporations. In contrast to the regular government appropriations and steady income from endowments, these grants were known as 'soft' money, for which the university, and indeed every individual scholar or team of scholars, had to compete. Universities had become entirely dependent on the continued influx of soft money. The emphasis on graduate research and Ph.D. production over undergraduate education was one of the results of this dependence.

Another result was the rise to prominence of the academic promoter, or entrepreneur. The real stars in academia were those who brought in the research contracts, generated projects, formulated research strategies, got funded, supervised a team of assistants who do the work of collecting data, and then published the findings. They were also the ones who were most likely to get job offers from other institutions, which significantly raised their market value.

The academic profession had become very nomadic. At the bottom, the best teachers were on the move because they had difficulty getting tenure. At the top, the star entrepreneurs moved because they were self-promoters with little or no sense of loyalty to the university, or to the students who may have chosen that school specifically in order to study with them.

Some years ago, one of my colleagues in the Department suggested that it was time for him to be promoted to full professorial rank. A committee of two or three senior professors was asked, as was customary, to review his work, and I served on that committee. In my report to the assembly of full professors, I wrote that the man's teaching record was undistinguished, that his services to the department and the university had been valueless, and that his scholarly output was small in volume and poor in quality. I added that he was a successful self-promoter who managed, somehow, to obtain funding for various research projects and concluded by suggesting that our department needed yet another self-promoter "like we needed a hole in the head." The other colleague or colleagues who had similarly reviewed the man's work expressed general agreement with my judgment, but said they would not express it in such harsh terms. The senior professors then voted, 12 for, two against, to promote the man.

One other factor that contributed to the transformation of universities into corporate enterprises that marketed their research was the immense increase in the cost of doing research. The extraordinary expenses involved in sub-nuclear physics or astronomy could be met only by billion-dollar figures that the Congress had to appropriate. Many other fields, including some in the social sciences and the humanities, required expensive equipment, and all scholars needed money to travel to conferences and conventions—to spend time in 'the field,' whatever that might be in their case. Our best university libraries were in dire straits financially because of the proliferation of books and journals and their skyrocketing cost. Research had become terribly expensive, and access to research possibilities therefore became exceedingly competitive.

In addition, the ascendancy of academic entrepreneurship, the proliferation of sponsored research, and the growing dependence of the university on soft money, caused the rapid bureaucratization of the university. The age-old tradition, according to which university faculties were autonomous, self-governing communities of scholars and teachers, rotating in assuming the burdens of a dean or a department chair, had given way to the tendency to see huge increases in the administrative apparatus of the university. In the university budget, the undergraduate teaching program, primarily, bore the cost of this bureaucratization. From an institution of teaching and learning, American universities had turned more and more into corporate bureaucracies that marketed research. The obscenely high salaries paid to these governing bureaucrats by American universities became notorious. I was aware that similar trends toward the rise to dominant status of administrators and professional fundraisers had occurred in other cultural institutions— museums, orchestras, public libraries, theaters, and the like. Their operations, too, became ever more costly, and for their survival they became dependent on professional art and music managers.

Every once in a while, these overpaid bureaucrats realized that undergraduate teaching at their institutions was done poorly and routinely. Then they mobilized themselves into doing something it. The

President of the University of Michigan, for instance, once set aside a million dollars to solicit innovative proposals for the improvement of undergraduate teaching. A faculty meeting to discuss this venture was called, and the few professors who troubled to attend noted with concern that the one million dollars was to be taken from the departmental budgets—funds that were used primarily to pay for faculty salaries. That would have been like robbing from Peter to pay Paul and could hardly be considered a meaningful approach to the improvement of undergraduate education. Some faculty members then suggested to the President that the only honest solution would be to hire more teaching faculty, graduate assistants, and counselors. Any other use of the money was likely to turn into mere gimmickry and, instead of improving undergraduate instruction, would merely enrich those who were well trained in writing clever grant applications. The President did not accept these suggestions.

At the University of Michigan, I could divide the faculty roughly into two categories: the teaching faculty and the research faculty. The teaching faculty consisted of those who did research and a good deal of teaching and counseling, and the research faculty consisted of those who did research, a minimal amount of teaching, and often no counseling at all. In the social sciences and humanities, the research faculty did not produce much more research than the teaching faculty. Nor was the quality of their scholarship significantly higher. The people in the research faculty, by and large, were paid the star salaries, however. I noted, in fact, that the total time that faculty members spent with undergraduate students was roughly inversely proportional to their annual salary. Research faculty members also enjoyed ample support services, such as plenty of secretarial help, computer time, and graduate assistants, while teaching faculty often did their own typing and preliminary library searching. The entire system was rigged to cheat undergraduate students.

Our undergraduate students were bright, ambitious, and eager to do well academically. The GPA (grade point average), which supposedly indicated their over-all performance, would be considered seriously when they applied for admission to graduate programs or for jobs. A high GPA indicated that they had performed well in examinations, written excellent term papers, and rendered competent laboratory reports. For many years, I met many of our most successful students. I was in charge of the undergraduate Honors programs, both in the Political Science Department and in the degree program in Russian and East European Studies. In this capacity, I decided whom to admit to these Honors programs, functioned as their academic adviser, taught a special Honors seminar, and, in Political Science, chaired the sessions in which they had to defend their Honors theses. I also served for a number of years on a committee that screened applicants for Rhodes and Marshall scholarships. In order even to be considered for one of these awards, a student had to have an outstandingly brilliant academic record. Indeed, many of the young men and women we interviewed had received nothing but A's, and some of them had ten or more A+ grades on their transcripts. They were supposed to be the cream of the crop.

My colleagues on the committee and I were appalled at the deficiencies in these students' general knowledge, however. They often were ignorant about matters that in my youth every *Gymnasium* graduate was expected to know. They had received excellent pre-professional training, but knew nothing about history, geography, literature, art, or music, and if they had pursued studies in the social sciences or humanities, their ignorance of the natural sciences was profound. Whenever I tested the general knowledge of my Honors students in Political Science, I encountered the same deficiencies. Almost all would miserably fail whatever 'general knowledge' test I would ask them to take, and many of them reacted to such tests with indignation: "Why should we know such things?" they would ask. Or they would say: "We know all sorts of things that you don't know." That was true. I would have flunked any test that asked about baseball statistics, rock bands, and many other topics of concern to the younger generation, and I am sure most of them knew more than I about internal combustion engines, electronics, and computers.

For the lacunae in our students' general education, one could not only blame the de-emphasis on good college teaching, but also the poverty of the high school curriculum. Furthermore, the withering-away of general liberal-arts knowledge was a product of the knowledge explosion, which compelled all of us to specialize in forever narrowing sub-fields, so that there was no time for satisfying broader interests.

When I joined the University of Michigan in 1966, the school's drift toward corporate entrepreneurship was temporarily hidden from view, possibly slowed down, but ultimately accelerated, by the rise of the student counterculture. A fresh wind seemed to be blowing away a good deal of pretense, stuffiness, and needless authoritarianism. Students, especially undergraduates, renounced their previous passivity. They became rebellious and made demands, and the University responded by giving in to some of their demands.

My impression of our students in the 1950's had been that they were quite conventional. They held conventional views and sported conventional appearance: they were clean-shaven and had their hair cut short. The women were neatly coifed and dressed. I found nothing wrong with this general appearance. Indeed, I took it for granted. At Harvard, students were still subject to a dress code demanding that men were to wear jacket and necktie to class; and women had to wear skirts. When in the late 1940's a cousin of mine took me to a class he was taking at the University of Chicago, I was shocked to see students wear sweatshirts and other informal clothing. At Harvard, that would have been considered an insult to the professor.

Students in the 1950's also tended to be non-political. They seemed to accept the verities they had been offered in their high-school civics courses and did not question them. They lived by a code that rated some fraternities and sororities higher than others and all 'Greek' organization members over those not enrolled in any of these clubs.

Of course, a few mavericks refused to accept this order of things. The members of the Young Socialist club at Michigan State University obviously were dissenters—or at least some of them were. Others may have been super-conformists whom the police had urged to join the organization in order to inform on it. My courses dealing with Marxist ideology or Soviet politics always had some of these mavericks in them, but the majority of my students were people of conventionally conservative views who took these courses in order, as they said, to 'know the enemy.'

The student rebellion was, to some extent, a revolt against the University administration's assumption that they stood *in loco parentum* and had to guard their students against alcohol, sex, and violations of societal taboos concerning proper behavior, proper language, appearance and clothing. It was a revolt against the very notion of propriety, sexual and otherwise.

My first inkling that some cultural change was brewing among students came while I was at Michigan State University sometime in the mid-1960s. Some students had taken me out for a glass of beer. For that, one had to drive at least a mile beyond the city limits, because East Lansing was dry. The dive we visited had a dance floor. Rock music was blaring from loudspeakers, and young couples were gyrating in a style so orgiastic that I turned to one of the students in my group in astonishment and asked her, "Is this prelude or substitute?"

She grinned and said, "That depends."

University policies were quickly affected by this sea change. For instance, I was told that, shortly before I joined the faculty at the University of Michigan, the Dean of Women had alerted the parents of a female undergraduate student in a letter that their daughter was 'dating a Negro.' Whether the Dean of Women habitually wrote such letters or this was a unique occurrence, I do not know. In any event, the matter was made public in *The Michigan Daily*, the independent student paper. The Dean of Women resigned or was forced to resign. There was not a Dean of Women at the University of Michigan since then, and the special rules by which the lives of female students were previously controlled were relaxed or abolished. It did not take many years for the University to accept the notion that male and female undergraduates might live in one and the same dormitory floor in adjoining rooms.

A much more important beginning of the student counterculture could be seen in the freedom marches and freedom rides against Southern racism. Here was a movement that managed to mobilize the conscience of young Americans, especially when Southern sheriffs let their dogs loose on unarmed demonstrators within view of the TV cameras, when civil rights activists—black and white—were murdered, and Black churches were bombed. The shock produced by these acts of violence was intensified when John Kennedy, Robert Kennedy and Martin Luther King were assassinated. Politics in the United States had taken a murderous turn.

The central issue that engendered disgust and protest, however, was our involvement in the genocidal war in Vietnam, a conflict into which our political and military leadership had plunged us needlessly and recklessly, lying to themselves and to the citizenry about the rationale for this involvement.

The students, some of them dimly, others clearly, recognized the futility of this war. They saw the atrocities committed in its name and felt ashamed of their country. They fiercely fought against the threat of being drafted for service in a war that they considered criminal. They also came to reject some of the principal values or priorities of their parents and of the entire older generation, including individual careerism, material acquisition, competition for success, middle-class respectability, sobriety and rationality. They argued that genuine participation, free sharing, collective action, spirituality, and conservation of the Earth's limited resources were more important than acquiring wealth, competition, and the use of force to maintain power over others. To put it more simply: they thought that democracy was preferable to capitalism, and they took the incompatibility of the two for granted.

In the name of anti-communism, the Left in American politics had been destroyed or had destroyed itself. In the counterculture of the 1960's the Left was reborn, but in entirely new form, for it represented, among other things, a rebellion not only against the hated 'establishment,' but also a repudiation of communism.

The New Left criticized classical Marxism, as well as Russian communism and its client party in the U.S., on a variety of grounds. It found fault with economic determinism and with the fatalism that could be derived from it. It did not share Marx's faith in the industrial working class. Distrusting Lenin's dogmatism and bureaucratic style of Party leadership, it believed in spontaneity and free discussion. It thoroughly disliked the stuffiness and Puritanism of Soviet culture, as well as the humorlessness of communist discourse. Altogether, the New Left tended to regard Marxism-Leninism as part of the repressive bourgeois culture that they wanted to overthrow.

Of course, there were people whom they admired and whose ideas they echoed. One of them was Herbert Marcuse, whose original blend of unorthodox Marxism with a radical interpretation of Freud had wide appeal. Another hero of the New Left was the American sociologist C. Wright Mills. He described the U.S. political system as controlled by a wealthy and powerful elite of industrialists, military brass and professional politicians, who easily switched from one of these pursuits to another while justifying their rule by a tough Machiavellian ideology that Mills labeled 'crackpot realism.'

Upon reflection, Mills's thesis about a United States run by a self-perpetuating group of people in control of the wealth, the weapons and the communications media was not all that different from the pluralist model of American democracy to which many political scientists subscribed. Both Mills and the pluralists recognized the persuasiveness of elite rule and elite power. Both acknowledged a broad stratum of people who lacked the money and the power to participate in politics at all. By refusing to sell this system to his readers as a form of democracy, however, Mills was more honest than the pluralists were. At least, he recognized the permanent hold that a powerful and wealthy minority maintained over the vast disenfranchised majority.

If my radical students showed any interest in Marxist theories, they preferred to read unorthodox Marxists and left-wing communists. These included Karl Korsch, who preached revolution from the grass roots of workers' councils, and Rosa Luxemburg, who fought against Lenin's Machiavellian pragmatism, and argued that a revolution won by immoral and undemocratic means was condemned to failure. Also popular were the Berrigan brothers and other clerics, who interpreted Christian scripture as a command to work for social justice. That all or most of these ideas had been advanced in earlier decades or centuries was something the people of the New Left did not seem to know. That was a common phenomenon in the history of political ideas, especially radical ones, however. They arose, made a lot of noise, perhaps effected some changes, but then, having spent their force, died down, were suppressed and forgotten. Decades later, a new group of radicals would come along and re-invent them.

The New Left was highly critical of the role played by the United States and by worldwide corporate capitalism in the poorer counties of the world, and it sympathized with all movements and parties that attempted to liberate their countries from Western control and exploitation. CIA recruiters, ROTC programs, 'establishment' commencement speakers, and similar visible symbols of America's role in the world became favorite targets for harassment by radical students.

The counterculture was active on many college and university campuses, but the University of Michigan was one of its most important centers. I was here that SDS—Students for a Democratic Society—was born and drafted its programmatic statement, the Port Huron platform. Moreover, the first teach-in against the Vietnam War had taken place at Michigan the year before I joined the faculty. Thus, by moving to the University of Michigan I was plunged into one of the centers of the counterculture and personally became acquainted with many of its leaders, both among the students and faculty. Some of these students trusted me. Many others showed that they considered me an unreliable, wishy-washy liberal. Lively political discussion went on in classrooms, over cups of coffee in the Student Union, and in the dormitories.

The American counterculture was no isolated phenomenon. Similar movements sprang up in France and Poland, Germany, Czechoslovakia, and many other countries, and student protest movements continued to arise in various parts of the world. Occasionally such movements managed to link up with protest waves outside the campus, such as in Poland and France, where, in the 1960's, students, intellectuals and workers linked forces to agitate together. In the United States, however, the students remained more isolated. Some surveys conducted at the time suggested that neither their parents, nor the working class, and not even their age mates not attending college agreed with the views and the lifestyle of the radical students. In general, the student movement was confined to the so-called elite schools—Michigan, Wisconsin, Columbia, Antioch, Oberlin, and Berkeley. Once it spread to Kent State and Jackson State Colleges, troops were called in, and we had small American versions of the Tienanmen massacre. Even before that, TV viewers could observe the massacre that Mayor Richard Daley of Chicago unleashed on the protesters at the time of the 1968 Democratic convention.

This event showed that the student rebellion was not nearly as isolated a phenomenon as the media portrayed it. In those Democratic primaries of 1968 that had been open, the victory of delegates obviously sympathetic with the counterculture, and therefore supporting Eugene McCarthy or Robert Kennedy, showed considerable support for a politics of significant change. In many states, however, caucuses of professional politicians elected the convention delegates. Their overwhelming number brutally rolled over the reform delegates. Just as in Poland, Czechoslovakia and France, the protesters had no chance. "Fascism," said Huey Long, "will come to the United States, but we will call it 'democracy.'" The 1968 Democratic convention was a foretaste of how this prophecy might be fulfilled.

Given its narrow base and insufficient support in society, the New Left was impotent. For that reason, the only politics in which it could engage was symbolic politics, which at times took the form of repudiation of all politics. Symbolic politics included teach-ins, demonstrations, rallies and folk festivals, protest songs, radical theater and humor magazines. It also expressed itself in the deliberate defiance of middle-class conventions regarding clothing, hairstyle, food, and sexual relations. It included endless discussions and fights between different radical sects, and on the outer fringe of the student movement, it also brought with it small groups that were ready to express their protest by laying bombs, robbing banks, and similar acts of violence.

I knew some of the activists in the Weatherman faction of SDS who preached such tactics. One of my students, who idolized Patti Hearst and the Symbionese Liberation Army, later joined a Central American guerrilla movement and ultimately may have been murdered by some death squad or Contra squad. John Sinclair, whose ten-year sentence for possession of a single joint of *cannabis* became a national scandal, gave a guest lecture on anarchism in one of my political theory courses. In some marginal way, I was participating in the counterculture.

Endless debate and symbolic politics was the rational side of the counterculture. The dropouts, flower children, and young people from the affluent suburbs who manifested their rejection of bourgeois respectability and middle-class values by taking mind-altering substances other than alcohol represented its irrational, or Romantic, side. These young people fled into primitive agricultural communes, grew their food organically, and sang their mantras in the evening by the light of kerosene lamps. They grew beards and ponytails, discarded their brassieres, and wore outrageously outlandish rags, to the chagrin of their middle-class parents.

The relationship between the political and the anti-political wings of the movement, between its rational and Romantic factions, its radicals and yippies, was complex. They overlapped. They sympathized with one another in guarded fashion. In the final analysis, however, they agreed on little more than the rottenness of the 'establishment.' If one added to them the many different segments of the Black movement, the incipient feminist movement—itself split into mutually hostile factions—or even the motorcycle gangs, then the counterculture of the 1960's appeared as a crazy mosaic of rebellious manifestations. One could sympathize with the anger and despair that gave rise to this rebellion, but one could not help noticing the futility of the protests and the deliberate, provocative silliness, the infantile defiance, with which it expressed itself more often than not.

Some of the shenanigans that our students engaged in were self-serving, even while they were meant to undermine conventional politics and laws. For instance, some of my radical students at Michigan State University discovered that, for a small fee, they could purchase a mail order ordination as minister or priest in some phony church. Once they had their ordination, they were exempt from the draft as clerics. I remember the malicious grin of one of my students when he showed me a document that declared him a bishop.

I observed an even cleverer ploy a few years later, when I had joined the University of Michigan. Around nine o'clock one evening, one of my graduate students, an activist in the SDS, phoned me. "Al," he said, "I have got to talk to you." When I told him to make an appointment for the following week, he told me it was urgent and he wished to see me right away. So I asked him to come on over. Half an hour later he appeared, accompanied by his wife and several other people: an Episcopal priest who was the confidant of the SDS radicals, a young man whom I did not know, and a huge black man, also unknown to me. I asked them all in, offered them a beer, and asked what the problem was. In response, they asked the black man to tell his story.

That story, told in good English with an indefinable accent, was as follows: He was, he said, the eldest of twenty-five sons of the Paramount Chief of several tribes in Portuguese Angola, and he showed us photos of an African village where he said he had grown up. He had been studying anthropology at the University of Arizona on a fellowship given him by the Portuguese government. Recently, however, his father had begun to defy the colonial authorities and had "gone into the hills." Thereupon, officials from the Portuguese Embassy in Washington had asked him to renounce his father. He had refused, and then his fellowship had been canceled. U.S. authorities had detained him, pending deportation. Friends in the ACLU had bailed him out. He had jumped bail and was now being hunted by he FBI. He had flown into Detroit, made his way to Ypsilanti, and there, on the campus of Eastern Michigan University approached a student, who directed him to the Ann Arbor office of SDS, where my graduate student had received him.

There were three things this man asked for—quarters for the night, someone who on the next day might help him cross the border into Canada, and $300 so that he could buy an air ticket to London or Paris and from there make his way back to Angola. Our home could easily accommodate him for the night. That was no problem. Three hundred dollars were easily gathered together; the priest seems to have had a slush fund for just such emergencies. As for the border crossing from Detroit to Windsor, my graduate student made a quick phone call to some of his black friends in Detroit and then told the man not to worry. Someone would pick him up the next morning and know how to smuggle him across the border.

Indeed, around noon the next day I got a phone call from a colleague who taught at the University of Windsor. "Your friend has arrived," he said, "and we collected three hundred dollars for him." I told my colleague that we had already given him that much money. "I know," he said, "but with another $300 he told us he could fly as far as Dakar and then make his way into Angola more easily."

A few weeks later my colleague from Windsor called again. He had, he told me, inquired into the fugitive's story and found out that it was phony from beginning to end. We had been had by a clever con artist who sponged on radicals, knowing very well that they could not denounce him; for who would be fool enough to go to the authorities, confessing that he had harbored and abetted an alleged fugitive from the FBI? Six months later another phone call from Windsor told me that 'our Angolan friend' had been in town again and managed to con another group of sympathizers.

What became of the former activists of the student protest movement? Many of them became prosperous lawyers and physicians. Some may even have voted for Ronald Reagan or George Bush in presidential elections. I remember first visiting our son when he was studying at Oberlin, where the students demonstrated their rebellious spirit by their scruffy appearance—barefoot, bearded, and pony-tailed, in faded jeans with holes at the knee. In May, at the end of the spring term, I drove back to Oberlin to pick up our son, whose semester of studies was over. This time, I saw large numbers of students on campus who were neatly dressed in summer suits and ties and light dresses, their hair properly trimmed. "Who are these people?" I asked Stefan.

He looked at me condescendingly. "Don't be so dense," he told me.

"Those are the graduating seniors. Today they're kissing their freedom good-bye and preparing to join the establishment."

I write about the 1960's with a certain degree of nostalgia, but also with ambivalence. Our own two children became part of the counterculture, each in their own fashion, and it affected their lives permanently, for better or for worse. As I have suggested, the movement engaged in a great deal of silliness and self-defeating provocation. Symbolic politics itself was a confession of weakness and thus condemned to failure. So were reckless acts of violence, which also emphasized the deep ideological divisions within the movement. Despite its emphasis on participatory democracy, some elements within it were quite elitist and sexist. The rumor was that in the SDS, the men made the decisions and engaged in action, while the women served them coffee and slept with them. Asked what the position of women was in the Black movement, one of its leaders is said to have replied, "Flat on their backs."

Why then should I feel nostalgia for the sixties? Because these 'kids' tried to make people think of alternatives to politics-as-usual. Because they voiced much legitimate criticism, they were, for a moment, the conscience of America. Reluctantly, American society responded to some of their demands, though often in a manner that created as many problems as it solved. We learned to express collective sensitivity to some of the underprivileged segments of our society. In our litigious culture, however, that took the form of defining entitlements, which then come into conflict with existing laws and privileges. The resulting legal complications promoted the cancerous growth of administrative, legal, financial, and counseling services and thus contributed to the growth of universities into gigantic corporate structures that were no longer capable of being run in relaxed fashion by rotating faculty members. In addition, one of the legacies of the counterculture was the horrible mischief of 'political correctness' in all discourse.

Another result of the student protest movement was the practice of affirmative action in recruiting students. At the University of Michigan, this was practiced vigorously. All of a sudden, we had a fair number of black graduate students in the Department. Some were brilliant, having received their college education at the excellent University of the West Indies. Others came to us with barely adequate qualifications, victims of the woefully deficient training given to students in inner city high schools. Some of these people abandoned their doctoral program after a while. Affirmative action, for them, had become no more than the infamous revolving door.

Jointly with a black graduate student, I wrote a paper that suggested that affirmative action, in order to be effective, should be supplemented with remedial instruction, even though that had its drawbacks, too. The Department never responded to this, but the University as a whole, in later years, provided such service to any student who wanted it.

The Department also hired a number of black professors, including a colleague who chose to call himself black although he was of South Asian origin. These faculty members and a few of their white colleagues immediately constituted themselves as a radical caucus. One of their first actions was to attract to the Department a number of black graduate students, among them a few whose academic credentials were not up to the standard of their White fellow students. They also proposed that, in our doctoral program, where candidates must undergo examinations in several so-called sub-fields, the Department recognize a new sub-field, to be called Political Economy.

Political economy was an interesting term with a history of its own. In the 19th century, it denoted the economic theory of unrestricted free enterprise within a political system that existed primarily in order to defend private property. Political Economy, in short, was the ideology of capitalism. Hence, Karl Marx gave two of his major works the subtitle, "Critique of Political Economy." Political Economy, for him, was the enemy.

By a strange twist, however, radicals in the sixties and seventies used the term as a synonym for Marxism. It is easy to see why: they wished, in their teaching and writing, to bring out the economic roots of politics, to show the power of money hiding behind the front of constitutional democracy, just as Engels and Marx had done in their writings. Moreover, they must have sensed that their request for the recognition of a new sub-field would have been denied had they honestly called it 'Marxist studies.' Political Economy was a more harmless-sounding code name. That they chose this term, however, which Marx loathed perhaps more than any other, also showed that they themselves probably had not read much of his works. Many born-again Marxists had not read Marx. Just as many people confessing Christianity have never read the Bible.

The Department unhesitatingly agreed to recognize Political Economy as a new sub- field in its doctoral program, and then asked all colleagues who wished to be the sub-field's faculty to so indicate. Of course, our radical colleagues signed up, but so did a number of quite conventional political scientists who had not the slightest intention to write or teach any radical doctrine, Marxist or otherwise. They just wanted to mock their radical colleagues. I do not know of any graduate students who ever offered Political Economy as one of the sub-fields in which they wished to be examined.

Having succeeded, at least on paper, to insert Marxist studies in the departmental doctoral program, our new black colleagues proceeded to confront the Department with a broad set of additional demands, which they said were non-negotiable. These demands included recruiting so many more minority students, hiring so many more minority faculty— I don't remember the demands in detail. Of course, these peremptory demands were refused. Thereupon, the new black colleagues got themselves jobs in other universities and left us. Like their white colleagues, they were academic entrepreneurs on the make. In leaving us so abruptly, however, they abandoned the minority graduate students whom they had attracted to our Department, and who very much depended on the mentoring of these professors, and that was unforgivable. It suggested that their radicalism was phony.

In the spirit of affirmative action, or, perhaps, in an effort to look politically correct, the Department also added a Native American to its faculty. Her name was Susie. While her mother was of Scottish descent, her father had been a full-blooded Lakota Sioux. Born and raised on the Pine Ridge Indian Reservation, Susie had attended schools run by the U.S. Bureau of Indian Affairs, but eventually obtained her doctorate in

Political Theory. She had as sharp a mind as I have ever had the privilege of encountering, and we became good friends. She lived in two worlds at one and the same time, being quite at home in Anglo-American culture, but feeling most comfortable in periods when she was very self-consciously Indian. Disdaining 'politically correct' word usage, she did not mind referring to herself as an Indian. She discussed the plight of Native Americans on their reservations with considerable bitterness and was active in various organizations trying to alleviate their condition.

Susie did not suffer fools lightly and held a number of lightweights and mediocrities in our Department (every department has them) in contempt. Because she did not always conceal her negative opinion about others, however, she acquired a reputation as an abrasive personality, and there were people in the Department who resented her.

Once she and I were friends, she wanted to give me a Lakota name. "If you had to be an animal, what would you want to be?" she once asked me, and I told her I would want to be a bear. She then wrote to her grandmother, giving her a brief character description, and asking her to suggest a name for me. On the basis of the grandmother's response, she then named me Mato Witko. She told me it meant 'Crazy Bear', but added that 'crazy' was in fact a mistranslation of a Lakota word meaning someone who can be expected to act in unexpected or unconventional fashion.

Another legacy of the counterculture was the accumulation of slight changes in the purely academic aspects of how university students were treated. One of the most popular pamphlets produced in the 1960's was one with the title "The Student as Nigger," which lampooned the allegedly authoritarian style of instruction prevalent in universities. Arguing that the very architecture of the classroom was a barrier to genuine interchange, it denounced curricula with requirements that had become meaningless, or whose meanings were not explained to the students. It suggested that multiple-choice exams were intellectually insulting and that conventional methods of evaluating students' performance were mechanical and degrading.

To these entirely justified complaints, the universities responded, at times sensibly, at other times shortsightedly. For instance, in the late 1960's, the University of Michigan created the Residential College, an undergraduate institution combining living quarters with classrooms under one roof, where the students, faculty and administrative personnel formed a self-governing community, making its own rules. Soon after joining the University, I took charge of one of the core courses taught in the Residential College and became a member of this community, which was an interesting and, on the whole, successful experiment in academic democracy and, for me, an altogether pleasant experience.

Two decades after the high time of the counterculture, universities were confronted with a different set of accusations. The new bill of indictment criticized their offerings in the humanities and social studies for being imbued with cultural bias and patriarchy, and the demand now was for a Black, a Chicano, a native American, a feminist or a Lesbian approach to scholarship. For now, I will leave that can of worms unopened.

CHAPTER 8

MANCHESTER, 1850-1870

WHEN ENGELS DECIDED to go to Manchester, he was thirty years old, and still dependent on his parents for his livelihood. At the time he moved to England, a year earlier, he had had the gall—or the desperation—to ask his father for a renewal of the regular allowance he used to receive, but had been turned down. As his mother had explained it to him, his parents could not really be expected to support their son as long as he was going to go in a direction they could not possibly approve. She thought her son's principles a disaster for humanity, and sinful.[209]

There must have been anxious family councils in Barmen at the time, and one of the possibilities discussed was to send young Engels (not *that* young any longer) to America, the place where the European bourgeoisie was wont to send its black sheep.[2] The solution that was found mutually acceptable was for the young man to work for the family firm in Manchester. For his father and mother, this was obviously better than losing their son by totally repudiating him or sending him into exile across the Atlantic. For his part, in negotiating this solution, Engels staged a careful show of reluctance, and pretended to his father that he was making a great sacrifice. In fact, however, he was quite pleased once again to have preserved a tolerable relationship with his parents, and to have job security for a while. Not that it was much security. He was hired provisionally and was paid no salary, but was allowed to draw his living expenses from the firm. When he withdrew more than was thought appropriate, he was subject to questions and scrutiny.

For his parents, the solution was acceptable because work in Manchester kept heir son occupied with what they thought were solid

215

and respectable pursuits, and it removed him from the corrupting company of Marx and other radical émigrés in London. Besides, the Engels family very much wished to have its own representative in Manchester to safeguard its interest against those of their partners. Engels himself gained not only the means for survival, but also a respectable cover for other activities he might want to pursue, i.e. his political life, as well as his sex life. Most importantly, the job enabled him to give some financial support to Marx.

The relationship between father and son, having been stormy in the past, became cool and businesslike. Indeed, a certain grudging respect seems to have developed between the two. Engels obviously sought to make a good impression on his father by manifesting modesty, decency, and business acumen, and he seems to have succeeded in this. They met several times in Manchester and got along well, except when the conversation veered into politics. Then the differences erupted, and the relationship worsened. His father may have been disappointed at the continued stubbornness of his first-born son, and at the coolness between them. Engels confessed to Marx, however, that if it did not cost him any money, he preferred a cool business relationship with his father to any kind of sentimental humbug.[211] Yet, he had a portrait of his father in his soldier's uniform hanging in his house, and toward the end of his life he was proud that he had got along well with his "pious and arch-reactionary" family, despite his political differences with them.[212]

Later in life, Engels voiced the opinion that revolutionaries had to make themselves independent by acquiring some essential skill. Socialists, he wrote to a young correspondent, were outlaws politically and socially, and the entire bourgeoisie took pleasure in trying to starve them out, and indeed considered this its duty. The ones hardest hit by this were professional intellectuals, because the bourgeoisie considered them traitors to their own class. It would therefore have been better for him and Marx, he continued, if they had has some essential manual skill with which to make a living.[213] Engels did not have such a skill, however, and thus depended on his position in Manchester. When in the early months of 1851 his father asked him to stay on, he again played reluctant in order to have a bargaining position, but then agreed, reporting to Marx that his negotiations with his father had been successful.

Only now did he feel that he was going to be living in Manchester for some time to come, and he ordered his books shipped to him from Brussels, where they had been stored since before the revolution. In the summer of that year, his father came to Manchester for an inspection and further negotiations. Once again, after some bargaining, Engels agreed to stay on, this time for several years. His financial position immediately improved, with his annual living allowance fixed at two hundred pounds.[214] Business was bad that year, however, and in September his father proposed to diminish the allowance by one-fourth, a grave threat because Engels had already overspent the full allowance by a substantial sum. That danger passed him by, and in March 1851 his father was once again in Manchester to help reorganize the firm.

Under the new arrangement, Engels received more money and, equally important, complete freedom in spending it. He now received a salary of a hundred pounds a year, plus a five percent share of the firm's profits, which in 1859 was raised to $7\frac{1}{2}$ percent. Mayer reports that his total earnings in 1854 were 268 pounds, and only 263 pounds in 1855. They jumped to 508 pounds in 1856, however, and then to 937 pounds in 1857, 940 pounds in 1858, and 1,078 pounds in 1859, which at that time was a fairly substantial income.[215] The higher income, however, was accompanied by a greater workload. In 1854, Engels became a member of the Manchester Cotton Exchange, and he gradually assumed more responsibilities in handling the firm's correspondence and managing its office. By the fall of 1856, he was supervising three male clerks.

Peter Ermen, a merchant born in Holland and educated on the Continent, founded the firm of Ermen & Engels. He came to England in 1825 and first went into partnership with his brother Anton. The partnership was enlarged in 1837 when another brother, Gottfried (Godfrey) and Friedrich Engels, Sr., joined. The firm owned cotton-spinning mills in England and on the Continent.[216] The partnership between the two families was not free of friction. When Engels arrived in Manchester in 1850, he sensed that Peter Ermen regarded him as an unwelcome addition, wished to get rid of him, and would make life in the office unpleasant for him.[217]

To his brother-in-law, he reported that the Ermens made it hard for him to examine the accounts. The letter gives the impression that Engels was trying to spy on the account books for his father.[218] The following year, Peter Ermen retired from business, leaving Anton in charge of the family's interests in Germany while Gottfried took over the management of the Manchester firm.[219] Engels intensely disliked Gottfried Ermen. He saw him as a typical representative of the business class he hated so much, and often described him in nasty adjectives. In time, he also came to believe that Gottfried was cheating on his partnership contract with the Engels family by patenting inventions in his own name rather than the firm's, and pocketing the profits.

When his father died in the spring of 1860, Engels at first went to Barmen to participate in the funeral and in the settlement of the estate. Having only recently been tried in absentia and convicted of desertion from the army reserve, he was subject to arrest but was not touched by the authorities. He did not stay long, in any event, because he had to hurry back to Manchester for a serious conflict with Ermen concerning his future position in the firm. He was in fact in a difficult position. While to Mr. Ermen, he represented the heirs of his late partner he was in no position to make demands regarding his own personal position in the company. His financial security was thus at stake. Added to this, his own brothers were preparing to cheat him out of his paternal inheritance, and succeeded in withholding his share in the capital of the German firm.

In Manchester, Engels bargained with toughness, but then fell ill and would have fared badly if his younger brother Emil had not come to complete the negotiations.[220] In the end, he settled with his brothers as well as with Ermen. A new contract signed in May 1860 specified that he would remain with the company as a senior clerk, with firm assurance of becoming a partner in a few years. His brothers settled with him by depositing ten thousand pounds sterling in his account with the

Manchester firm. For Engels, this was a very unsatisfactory end to the struggle over his father's inheritance, and he signed with considerable bitterness. He said he did it for his mother, who was then sick with typhus, and whom he did not wish to sadden further by the spectacle of litigation among the brothers.[221]

In fact, however, he may have had no power to bargain for a better deal. Given his political past, his brothers might have gotten away with an even larger share. Emil's intervention on his behalf showed that they did not wish to break with him entirely. Whatever the motives among these fighting brothers, their relationship remained cool for many years. In subsequent years, when his brothers sought to cheat him financially in a variety of ways, he again settled with them for his mother's sake. His brothers were highly conservative businessmen, who obviously thought Engels had removed himself from the company of decent people. He resisted them only when they tried to involve him in intrigues against each other.[222]

Engels became a full partner in the firm as of September 1864, with one-fifth of the firm's capital in his name. He was now in charge of the office, an independent and wealthy business executive. It was an occasion for him to move into a larger and better home. The first years of his exile in Manchester were hard for Engels, however, he had little money, hated his work, loathed his boss (the feeling seems to have been mutual), missed the company of Marx, and found Manchester a boring place, in which it would be hard to entertain a visitor.[223] Much as he wished to continue his self-education, this was often difficult to do. In the office, he was kept busy, and since the place was locked up at night he had to work at home, where at first the only light he had was candles.[224]

Study conditions outside his home were poor. The libraries in Manchester were either not accessible, had inconvenient hours, or did not have the materials he wished to read.[225] To his friend Ernst Dronke he wrote with obvious envy, "Père Marx day after day goes to the library and increases not only his knowledge but also his family at an astonishing rate. I meanwhile drink rum and water, work like mad, deal, and twist in boredom."[226] A bad toothache troubled him much during the first bleak winter he spent in Manchester.[227] One of the few diversions he enjoyed was going into the countryside, he wrote to his sister, omitting to mention that the countryside he sought was the area where Mary and Lizzy Burns had their house.[228]

While Engels must have enjoyed, at times, the double life he led as a businessman and a communist, the sneakiness of his existence and the extra burdens it imposed on him were often hard to take, and in the first few years he seriously overtaxed himself, especially his weak eyes that often hurt from overstrain and made him think he was going blind.[229] In 1857, his health collapsed, and he came down with a serious respiratory infection. In the summer, he spent several months, first on the English coast, and then on the Isle of Wight, to recuperate.[230]

His personal time budget was tight. He tried to squeeze as much achievement out of every hour as possible, despite any and all conflicts. Uninterested in his commercial work, he often sought to "cheat the office," as he called it, although he did feel the compulsion to do his share for his father. Always complaining about the large amount of time had had to devote to this "shitty commerce" (*Scheisshandel*), he sometimes deplored the excessive requests from Marx to handle yet another correspondence chore or write yet another article. When indeed he neglected his office work, he sometimes made mistakes that took even longer to correct.[231] As a mere clerk, Engels had little freedom in the office. He was dependent on Ermen in many things. He had to account for absences, and since he did not get along with him well, he often was unable to ask for extraordinary favors.[232]

As he looked back on his first two years of exile in Manchester, he felt gloomy. When his favorite sister asked him what he wanted for his birthday, he replied that he had given up wishing for things, because that did not get one anything. He had no talent for wishing, anyway, he added, because every time he caught himself in the weakness of making a wish, it was always for something that he could not have anyway. Hence, it was better to stop wishing altogether. (He compared the mood of his letter with that of Ecclesiastes.)[233]

His life was embittered further by the unpleasant realities he and Marx had with most of their numerous fellow émigrés in England, including some of their former friends and comrades-in-arms. As Engels himself observed then and many times later, emigration for political activists was a thoroughly demoralizing experience, a school for scandal and meanness that transformed everyone in it into an ass, a fool, or a scoundrel, and the biggest ass was the one who thought himself the coming savior of the fatherland.[234] Political émigrés, he wrote many years later, were condemned to sit on the sidelines while history went on. They could do nothing but talk and dispute with each other, but in their self-importance they came to believe that the governing of the world depended on their conversations and their gossip.[235]

In a published article, he sneeringly described the impatience that took hold of such émigrés, their mania for conspiracy, and their dispositions that compelled them again and again to start revolutionary action regardless of the prevailing circumstances. "After every failed revolution or counter-revolution," he wrote, "a feverish activity develops among those who have managed to flee abroad. The different party shadings organize, accuse each other of having steered the cart in the mud, and indict each other for treason and all other mortal sins possible. At the same time, they stay in vivid touch with the home country. They organize, conspire, print circulars and newspapers, swear that within twenty-four hours things will get going again, that victory is certain, and in the expectation of this they already distribute government offices.

"Of course," he added, "one disappointment follows another, and since these are attributed to accidental mistakes by individuals, rather than to unavoidable historical circumstances (that they do not wish to understand), the mutual accusations are heaped high, and the whole thing ends in general bedlam. This is the history of all refugee groups from the royalist émigrés of 1792 down to our own day, and he among the refugees who has understanding and insight will withdraw from the infertile bickering as soon as it can be done decently, and will do something better."[236] Here, Engels was obviously describing the situation in which he found himself in the early 1850s.

As we have seen, he and Marx had decided by the end of 1850 that the revolution was over and lost for the time being. To be sure, during his first year in Manchester he continued his contacts with his Chartist friends, contributed to a Chartist journal, and went to meetings of the Manchester Chartist committee, although he was careful not to become a member,[237] and he tried to spread his views among them through the study of the Communist Manifesto.[238] He had been heartened to learn that on the basis of the Manifesto a number of small communist cliques had formed in various places, whose members would become the cadres of the next revolution. Staff personnel, he wrote to Marx, was what had to be recruited. Once the revolutionaries were there, the soldiers would join by themselves, but a cadre of somewhat educated people was needed now.

Engels at this time was still optimistic enough to think of the revolution as only a few years away. He hoped that commercial employees might be recruited into such study groups. They would be ideal in case he and Marx would have to organize a government administration. "They are used to hard work and neat bookkeeping," he wrote, "and commerce is the only practical school for useful office clerks. Our lawyers, etc., are no good for that. With clerks for bookkeeping and accountability, talented ex-students for editing dispatches, letters, and reports, *voilá ce qu'il faut*. With six clerks I will organize an administrative branch a thousand times more simply, more clearly, and more practically than with sixty senior government officials and cameralists... Besides, these clerks are used to long hours of routine work, they are less demanding, can be kept from goofing off more easily, and in case of unreliability are more easily removed."[239]

While Engels thus daydreamed about coming to power, Marx, in London, remained active in the League of Communists. By 1852, however, we hear nothing further about contacts with Chartists, and the League dissolved itself on Marx's motion in the fall of 1852. Meanwhile, Engels and Marx made it quite clear to their fellow émigrés what they thought about the chances of reviving the revolution. For their former associates, this "cool interpretation of the situation," as Engels later

called it, was unacceptable, and the two friends found themselves
denounced as traitors to the cause of the revolution.[240] By the summer of
1851, they had become almost totally isolated within the émigré colony,
subjected to "countless acts of personal meanness," denounced as police
spies, and ridiculed for their beliefs. There was a period in 1852 during
which Engels and Marx could not go into the pubs frequented by the
émigrés without being physically assaulted. In letter after letter, Engels
and Marx complained to each other and to the few friends who still
talked to them, reassuring each other that the people who had followed
them in past years had been a pack of contemptible, confused, and
impotent petty-bourgeois loudmouths. "We have always been superior
to this riff-raff," Engels wrote to Dronke, "and have always dominated
them in every serious moment."[241]

To Marx he wrote, defiantly, that the two of them really had no need
for popularity or support. Indeed, they did not want it. "When the time
comes that we are needed, they will beg us, and we can make our own
conditions. Meanwhile, let us do our homework. As for our
achievements so far—the *Neue Rheinische Zeitung*, the *Manifesto*—they
cannot take those away from us. They can make a lot of noise, but they
would not have the courage to kill us, and after all we will never be *loved*
by the democratic, red, or even the communist mob."[242] By 1853, the
two friends agreed that their following had shrunk to half a dozen
people, and that they could not be called a 'party.' One year later, Engels
came to the conclusion that "we cannot rely on anybody in that whole
gang, except you and I on each other."[243] Thus, in his Manchester exile,
Engels was doubly miserable, feeling cramped by his work for the
despised Gottfried Ermen and totally isolated from his former
revolutionary associates.

If this suggests that Engels and Marx suffered the insults and attacks
of their former friends like patient lambs, that impression is false.
Despite the assertion Engels frequently made that it was best to maintain
oneself aloof from émigré squabbles, he and Marx were quite in the thick
of them, dishing out as much dirt as they had heaped on them, and their
work on these polemics offered them occasions for more glee and

merriment than anything else in their bleak existence could.

All their lives, they bitterly and sharply fought their political antagonists, and their targets were always fellow-socialists or fellow-radicals, hardly ever spokesmen for the upper classes, for with the bourgeoisie and the aristocracy, they felt no need to argue over anything. Much of what they wrote took the form of polemics against former friends and associates, and in these they never minced words, but on the contrary sought to destroy their rivals. Ruthlessly, mercilessly, they lampooned their antagonists' lack of information, fantastic premises, and faulty logic, as well as their inadequate writing style and their sordid private lives. They never shrank from *ad hominem* arguments, and work on these polemics gave them much glee and merriment.

The two friends kept an archive that contained all their published writings, unpublished drafts, and correspondence, as well as a wealth of other material about the revolutionary movement, including material about their associates and enemies.[244] They kept their own material because they knew themselves to be historic personalities, and they kept other material quite clearly for the purpose of having confidential information that they might some day use against their enemies. When Ferdinand Freiligrath refused to support Marx in his nasty squabble with Karl Vogt, Marx angrily asked, "Has he forgotten that I possess more than a hundred letters from him?"[245] The material was never used against Freiligrath, but on several occasions the two friends dipped deeply into their archive.

In early 1852, Janos Bangya introduced himself to Marx. He was a Hungarian officer who had participated in the revolution of 1848-9 and came with recommendations from Hungarian revolutionaries whom Marx trusted. Having gained Marx's trust as well, Bangya expressed an interest in material about some of their antagonists among the émigrés, and when Marx gave him a few brief character sketches, he proposed that Marx write a book-length expose of the whole lot of their enemies. He asserted that he had a publisher who would be interested in printing such a book, and he pledged to pay twenty-five pounds on delivery of the finished manuscript. Marx and Engels quickly agreed with each other that it would be good politically and financially to do this work. They could each contribute whatever material they had collected, write for additional material to the few friends they still trusted, and then write the book together. Engels did voice some political reservations, but dismissed them, writing that twenty-five pounds were worth a little scandal.[246]

Marx traveled to Manchester in the early summer, and there, with much merriment, the two friends drafted the manuscript. What they produced in a few weeks of collaboration was a hundred pages of petty, low gossip that lampooned the sordid private lives and puerile ideas of their rivals. Their targets consisted primarily of people who would be totally forgotten today had not Marx and Engels honored them with this 'book.' Most of them had been comrades-in-arms—Gottfried Kinkel, one of the few men whose bravery had impressed Engels during the 1849 campaign in Baden, Arnold Ruge, Marx's former co-editor on the *Deutsch-Französische Jahrbücher*, Karl Heinzen, another participant in the 1849 campaign, August Willich, whom Engels now described with malicious brilliance as a typical partisan leader, a Don Quixote and Sancho Panza rolled into one, Eduard Meyen, a former friend of theirs from the Berlin 'Doctor's Club,' Carl Schurz, who had helped Kinkel escape from prison, and some others.

The manuscript was delivered to Bangya in July. The money, paid promptly, was alas insufficient to cover Marx's debts. Several months then went by, and the brochure did not appear in print. After Bangya replied evasively to his anxious inquiries, Engels finally decided that it must have fallen into the wrong hands. Finally, the truth dawned on him that Bangya had been a police agent.[247] The experience of unwittingly collaborating with the police seems to have left a bad taste in his mouth. In fact, however, they were both lucky that Kindel and Co. did not get wind of this episode, for it would have confirmed their worst suspicions about Marx and Engels. The experience may have been one of the reasons that Engels did not contribute much to the petty and sordid campaign that Marx waged seven years later, at great cost in time and money, against Karl Vogt, an affair that is not worthy of further discussion at this point.

In time, Engels began to feel a bit more comfortable in his double life. When he departed for Manchester in 1850, Jenny Marx had congratulated him because he was now on his way to becoming a cotton lord, and she added the wish that this would not alienate him from the cause.[248] We cannot know whether she was serious, joking, or merely envious, but she must have been as aware as anyone that he was a middle-class man with middle-class tastes, and that he would always be tempted by the comforts of bourgeois life to which he was hopelessly addicted. He liked his wines and his beer, jokingly defining his conception of happiness by his favorite vintage (Chateau Margaux 1848).[249] He was habituated to smoking,[250] enjoyed his books, his travels, his dogs and his horse, and was somewhat of a gourmet who insisted on preparing his lobster salad all by himself. In later years, the parties he gave for his friends were famous for the vast quantities of wine, beer, champagne, oysters, and other delicacies that were consumed in one evening. When he was in Barmen after his first important meeting with Marx, he wrote that it was high time for him to get away from his home and its debilitating influence, lest he become a Philistine himself.[251] This was the same letter in which he declared it impossible to be both a businessman and an active communist.[252]

By now he was in fact both, and discovering that it was indeed possible and enjoyable to lead a double life. He was by no means untypical in this. Many of his associates in the movement were, at one time or another, communists and businessmen simultaneously. His good friend George Weerth combined subversive politics with his career as a commercial agent. Freiligrath, who wrote revolutionary poems for the *Neue Rheinische Zeitung*, earned a good living as a banker. August Bebel, the militant leader of the German Socialist Party, was a manufacturer. Wilhelm Bracke, another early leader of the German party, was a grain merchant. Many names could be added to this list. Yet, Engels remained aware that many socialists, and especially workers, distrusted him for being in business, a distrust that might have deepened had they known how wealthy he eventually became.

He seems to have thought about his double life a great deal, and toward the end of his life he more than once asserted that it was not at all impossible—one could very well be a socialist and a member of the Manchester Cotton Exchange at the same time, getting along quite nicely with the individuals one had to deal with, even while hating and despising the *class* of people who frequented the Exchange. "Will it ever enter my head," he wrote, "to apologize for having been the part-owner of a factory? Anyone wishing to make an issue of that would get a really nice response from me. If I were sure that tomorrow I could make a million in profit at the Exchange and thus be able to furnish ample means to the Party in Europe and America, I would go to the Exchange at once."[253]

Apparently, his conduct as a businessman was in no way affected by his communist convictions. As a member of the world of commerce and industry, he was just as much interested in profit as any of his "Philistine" colleagues, the difference between him and them being that he was fully aware where these profits came from—i.e. from the exploitation of his workers. Engels knew that his wealth was gained at the expense of the workers' health, welfare, and human dignity. Writing about the capitalist's struggle against the workers' interests, he said, "Incidentally, it does not depend on the good will of the individual capitalists whether or not they want to engage in this struggle, since competition compels even the most philanthropic individuals among them to join his colleagues and establish the same work period as a regulation that they do."[254]

He lived a double life in two respects: as a businessman and socialist who worked for the firm during business hours and for the movement in his spare time, and as a member of the 'respectable' class who kept two living quarters—his 'official' bachelor apartment where an elderly housekeeper kept things in order for him and where he could see his business acquaintances, and his real home, which was the house of his lover and her younger sister. Only his best friends and probably the police knew all aspects of his life, although in time he became bolder about his relationship with Mary Burns. As early as 1854, he reported to

Marx that his business acquaintances had learned about it, but at that time their knowledge still caused him concern and embarrassment.[255]

Already in 1846, in a letter to his brother-in-law, Engels had referred to Mary Burns as his wife.[256] Her home on the outskirts of town where she lived with Lizzy became his refuge from the annoyances of the commercial life and "respectability,"[257] a place where he could be himself in the company of the woman he loved. Except for his escapades in France, he must have been faithful to her, just as he expected her (and later her sister) to be faithful to him. It will forever remain unknown what role Lizzy played in this *ménage* while Mary was still alive. The few hints we have suggest that she did not share his bed until her sister's death. Philosophically a libertine, Engels was strangely monogamous in practice, whereas Marx, who in his outward behavior was committed to bourgeois morality, in fact had an affair with his wife's lifelong servant, who bore him a son, as well as a serious flirtation with his cousin, a young woman he described as gracious, witty, and equipped with dangerous black eyes.[258] If on occasion Engels complained to Marx about his bachelor loneliness, or even about a period of enforced celibacy that got him so aroused that he could not sit at his desk, we must assume that these problems occurred when Mary was absent or ill.[259] Another period of celibacy Engels mentioned was probably caused by his own serious illness.[260]

When Mary died suddenly in January 1863, Lizzy stayed in the home the sisters had occupied and became Engels's life companion. Although to his friends and relatives he referred to her as his wife, they were not legally married until one day before her death, when in order to grant her a last wish he called in an Anglican priest for the bedside ceremony. When traveling with Lizzy, he registered as Mr. Frederick Burns,[261] and to fool the police he had much of his mail sent to 'Mr. Burns.' A photo taken of Lizzy Burns near the end of her life shows a sturdy, rather stout body obscured by the wide folds of her plain, dark, Victorian dress, and a rather severe peasant face hardened by years of care and hardship. Engels described her as a revolutionary Irish woman and a genuine proletarian.[262] Both sisters were fierce Irish nationalists and may have had personal links with revolutionary Feinians. They introduced Engels to the study of Ireland and gave him a feeling of lasting sympathy for their nation. Incurably romantic as he was in some matters, he tried all his life without success to verify his assumption that they were related to Robert Burns.

How much the two sisters were able to participate in other aspects of Engels's political and intellectual life is obscure. Lizzy was illiterate,[263] Mary probably also. It is unlikely that either of them learned German or any other of the many languages Engels read and wrote. The kind of free secretarial service or even the passionate and knowledgeable partisanship that Marx got from his wife and daughters were things Engels could not have expected from his companions. Mary and Lizzy provided a comfortable home for him, conjugal love, and competent management of a household in which a great number of people were entertained. Aided by a maid, they were in charge of smoothing his life by keeping the house in good shape and providing meals at the appointed times.

They even managed to provide him with a child, Mary-Ellen ("Pumps") Burns, daughter of one of their brothers, who moved in with her Aunt Lizzy about the time of Mary's death or shortly thereafter, and whom Engels and Lizzy reared as if she was their daughter. Engels carefully supervised her education, saw to it that she learned German, tried to teach her manners, and spoiled her in many ways. After Lizzy's death, she took command of the Engels household—Marx sardonically labeled her the "reigning princess"—and continued living with Engels. She was around twenty years old at the time, perhaps a bit younger. Even after she married Percy Rosher in the early 1880s, she spent much of the time with Engels, continued to act as the mistress of the house, and for many years still accompanied him to the seashore when he went for his summer vacations. To Engels, her children were very much like his own grandchildren.

Pumps must have been a disappointment to him. An Irish beauty with black hair, blue eyes, and a full figure, she could be jolly and charming. She was neither very bright, however, nor very reliable. She was flirtatious and pleasure seeking, and liked to flaunt her belongings.

In many respects she seems to have been an example of the type of person Engels hated most—the upstart. Her education was not a great success. Much of what she learned was forgotten quickly. She apparently had no interest in the movement. For Engels, she was simply a member of the family.

She was a troublesome member, however. She had a hot temper and at times was rude to his friends. She was demanding, and forever imposed her presence on others, interfering with Engels's work and social life. Her husband, too, was a disappointment to Engels. Percy Rosher was an inept, mediocre person engaged in small business dealings at which he failed repeatedly. Engels more than once bailed him out with large amounts of cash. He did it out of family loyalty, but nonetheless resented the imposition because he believed that his money should be spent only for the sake of the movement.[264]

Engels also expressed his family loyalties by acting as a fatherly friend to a distant relative, sixteen years his junior. If the letters he wrote to Marx tell us more about this obscure cousin, Carl Siebel,[265] than about Mary or Lizzy Burns, it was because he kept his private life hidden not only from the "Philistines," but also from the Marxes. Ever since he had shown Mary off to his friends in Brussels in 1845, it had been clear to Engels that most of his friends, including the Marx family, disapproved of the liaison either because, as workers, they suspected him—rich bourgeois that he was—of exploiting this working class woman, or because it offended their Victorian sense of propriety.

The latter reason applied in the case of Karl and Jenny Marx. "Herr Dr. Karl Marx and Mrs. Marx *née* Baroness von Westphalen" (this was the way Marx would register in a hotel, even though Jenny had never been a baroness) were outraged enough to decide not to acknowledge Mary's existence. In Marx's letter to Engels, I found only one leering reference to her, which Engels left unanswered. Where Mary was concerned, Engels kept even Marx at arm's length, even though he cannot have known the sardonic comments the Marxes and their daughters exchanged about him and his women. Karl and Jenny did likewise, although shortly before Mary's death Marx visited Engels in

Manchester, renewed his acquaintance with her, and met her sister Lizzy. When he and Jenny had spent some time in Manchester for a much-needed vacation a few years before, however, they went, of course, to a hotel. The thought of lodging under the same roof with Mary was apparently not acceptable to Mrs. Marx.

Marx's cynical reaction to Mary's death in early 1863 almost caused a break in his friendship with Engels, but they weathered the crisis and in time the relations between the women of the two families became somewhat warmer, although it took many more years after Mary's death before Marx managed to refer to Engels's family in the second person plural.[266] In retrospect, this seems a fantastic snub. Engels's closest friend refused to enter his home because his wife disapproved of his companion. What a remarkable friendship this must have been to last in the face of such rudeness! Or should we conclude that Mary was less important to Engels than is usually assumed—that she was his faithful bedmate and housekeeper but essentially a convenience, and in no way a full partner in his life?

As a family man, Engels thus lived in isolation both from his friends and his business associates. Partly because of his wives, whom he could not easily have taken to the social functions of his class peers, and partly because of his own disinclinations, he took little part in the social life of the business community, although he did belong something called the Albert Club. For most people in the business world he professed contempt, while to them he may have appeared as a quiet, retiring, and possibly colorless foreigner interested only in business, sports, and perhaps some strange pursuits that one might expect a foreigner to engage in. They may also have been puzzled by his seeming reluctance to discuss his church affiliation.

Engels expressed impatience with the social conventions of his class—silly rules of etiquette, as he called them. He thought himself too bohemian to conform to them, and also observed that for someone in the movement it was simply not feasible to do so. He tried to stay out of the social treadmill where one party led to another, each entailing a whole chain of further obligations. This, he thought, was something for people who did not have enough serious work to do.[267] He did not succeed entirely at this. In time, he did develop a social life with merchants, factory owners, cotton printers, and other bourgeois, most of them Tories by party affiliation, and during the Christmas season in particular, he was drawn into the whirl of parties, reminding him that with one foot he stood within the bourgeoisie. Moreover, as long as he remained in Manchester, he took his Club activities seriously.[268] On the whole, however, outside the office and the Exchange Engels tended to avoid his business colleagues. When he took a vacation, he preferred the lower-class beaches like Ramsgate, with its Coney Island-like amusement area. It was a place, he wrote, that was neither fashionable nor expensive.[269] It is possible that either he or his wife would have felt uncomfortable at a resort more appropriate to his standing in the community.

The cultural life of Manchester interested him somewhat more. He went to concerts of the Hallé Orchestra and became a member of the Athenaeum, serving for a while as on its circulation committee. The large colony of German businessmen and professionals sought his participation, at times successfully. He himself cultivated friendships only with the scientists among them. When Germans all over the world celebrated Schiller's 100th birthday in 1859, however, the newly founded Schiller Institute in Manchester solicited his membership. At first, he dismissed it as not worthy of his attention, as a place for gossip and self-advertisement, run by obscure German doctors and aesthetic Jews,[270] but when the Institute organized a Schiller festival, he participated by helping in the staging of a performance of "Wallenstein's Lager," and after the performance he went to a "very jolly" drinking party that lasted until four in the morning.[271] Eventually, he did join the Institute, going to its meetings rarely at first because, he wrote, there were so many Jews in it that he took to calling it the Jerusalem Club.[272] By 1864, however, he was President of the Institute, and soon complained about the amount of time he spent in its committee meetings.[273]

What Engels liked most about being a member of the Manchester business class was the opportunity this gave him to practice his favorite sport, riding, as a member of the Cheshire Hunt. Engels believed physical exercise to be good medicine for physical and psychic ailments, and among all sports, he much preferred riding.[274] He sometimes chided Marx for his physical laziness, which he said Marx masked by pretending that he was too busy with work,[275] and when Marx was in Manchester after completing the *Grundrisse* in 1858, he took him riding every day. "Last Saturday I went fox hunting," he wrote to Marx during the Christmas season of 1857, not long after his serious illness. "Seven hours in the saddle. Such a thing always excites me hellishly for several days. It is the most magnificent physical pleasure I know. In the entire field, I saw only two that rode better than I did, but they had better horses. That will get my health back to normal, for sure. At least twenty men fell off their horses, or fell with them. Two horses were ruined, and one killed (I was present at its death). Otherwise, no disaster occurred."[276]

The sport so obsessed Engels that he used its imagery in his serious writings, as in a passage in which he compared the economic crisis generated by capitalism to a wild steeplechase that finally comes to rest in a ditch.[277] His mother worried about his escapades on horseback, wondering whether they might not be too expensive or too dangerous, but he tried to reassure her.[278] Nonetheless, in the late 1860s, he had a bad fall from a horse during a foxhunt and suffered some damage in his groin region. Through neglect or, as he himself put it, through excess, the injury caused him very serious trouble fifteen years later. Excess of any sort, incidentally, was the one vice that Engels was most ready to excuse in own self and others.[279]

Everything he did he did energetically and often to excess, including his efforts to relax. When his office duties were done and his studies or his political work at home could be interrupted, he liked nothing better than to drink, talk, and sing in the company of the few like-minded friends he had in Manchester, or of friends who came in for an occasional visit. Some of these parties turned into heavy and prolonged binges followed by nasty hangovers.[280] In the summer of 1859, he got into a brawl with an inebriated bourgeois who had insulted him. Engels, apparently not sober himself, had struck at the man with his umbrella and hit him in the eye.

The affair cost him fifty-five pounds and a great deal of anxiety because it could have become a public scandal or even led to his expulsion from England. Engels, Marx, and most of their close friends apparently were heavy drinkers. That included Marx's daughters, who Marx thought had gotten their drinking talent from him.[281] Engels evidently could hold his liquor better than Marx, however. After a binge in which the two friends went to London during a Christmas vacation in 1851-2, Marx had to stay in bed for several weeks to recover.

Keeping his persona as a communist apart from that as a businessman was not always easy. There were conflict situations every day, with most of which he learned to live. In despising the class of people who were members of the Cotton Exchange, he may have despised the bourgeois in himself, but he had the inner satisfaction of having transcended that inner bourgeois. There were countless minor matters, nonetheless, which reminded him that he lived according to two conflicting social and moral codes. Occasionally he voiced his consciousness of this with a curious mixture of tact and defiance. He sent Christmas cards to his friends and went to hear performances of Handel's "Messiah" without thinking twice about it.

Attending the religious rite at the funeral of a close friend, however, made him feel uncomfortable. During the ceremony, he was aware that the bright red ribbon on the wreath he had deposited was a shocking offense against English middle-class sensibilities. Yet, while the preacher's presence at the event made him feel queasy, he was even more opposed to the notion of using his friend's funeral for the sake of a political demonstration.[282] Again, for many years he owned shares in the Evangelical Community Center of Barmen. It was only when one of his nephews tried to dun him for a Christmas contribution to this church-affiliated institution that he gave the shares away.[283]

In the final analysis, Engels consoled himself about his exile and rationalized his middle-class existence by telling himself that his principal function was that of providing for Marx and his family.

Besides, he was confident that a new crisis would come in due time, and with it not only the end of capitalism but also his own release from penal servitude to hateful commerce. On numerous occasions, he and Marx reassured each other that the crash was approaching. Sometimes he, and at other times Marx, was more optimistic than the other, but every time he convinced himself of the approach of a new revolution he became cheerful, even though a business crisis meant a decrease in his income and additional work for him in the office.[284] With glee he reported sudden drops in stock prices, crises in the cotton market, or wholesale bankruptcies in the business world, and as his business friends became despondent he felt a new bounciness.

Both friends expected a sharp crisis in the mid-1850s,[285] and when he thought it was about to break, Engels described its expected consequences in a letter to Marx, adopting the tone of Biblical prophecy: "This time there will be a *Dies Irae* as never before, the entire European industry kaput, all possessing classes deeply involved, total bankruptcy of the bourgeoisie, war and dissoluteness to the highest degree. I also believe that all this will be fulfilled in the year of the Lord 1857, and when I saw you buying furniture again I immediately declared the matter a sure thing and laid bets on it."[286]

When the crisis did break out in the summer of 1857, he was jubilant. It was, he wrote, washing seven years of bourgeois dirt off him, and was acting on his physical well being like a bath in the sea. "In 1848 we said our time was coming, and it did come in a certain sense. This time, however, it is coming completely. It is now a matter of life and death," he wrote to Marx, and in his New Year's greetings six weeks later predicted that 1858 would be a riotous year.[287] Curiously, once Engels had retired from business and become dependent on the interest from his investments, he became much more nervous whenever the market went down. Thus, in July 1870 he wrote to Marx, "I wish that damned panic would abate a bit. I have got to sell more shares."[288]

To be sure, both Marx and Engels were often cautious. For Marx, the Polish uprising of 1863 signaled the beginning of a new era of revolution in Europe, but in stating this he added that the cozy delusions and childish enthusiasm that he and Engels had shared in 1848 were now gone to the devil. "We are more alone now than we were then," he said, "and also we now know what role stupidity plays in revolutions and how revolutions are exploited by scoundrels."[289] Yet four years later, he too was cheerful once again. The International he had helped organize was making satisfactory progress. "*Les choses marchent,*" he wrote. "And in the next revolution, which perhaps is closer than it looks, we (i.e. you and I) will have this mighty engine in our hand."[290]

If we wanted to draw a portrait of Engels in his middle age, we would have to depict an erect and vigorous man, tall enough to have been accepted into a Guards regiment, with a disproportionately small head and a rather ordinary face framed in his well-known full beard, appearing in public in conservative business attire. Although he physically overtaxed himself, writing so much that at times his arm and fingers were paralyzed with pain, and suffering from recurrent eye trouble, he was in general of robust health. Among his enemies, he had the reputation of being a ruthless antagonist who, like Marx, could not distinguish between political or ideological and personal differences. His friends knew him as a man with an unfailing sense of humor, attested by the "good-natured and frivolous twinkle" in his eye.[291] His own favorite virtue, he stated in a questionnaire submitted to him by Marx's oldest daughter Jenny in August 1868, was "jollity."[292]

His friends also knew him for his loyalty, generosity, hospitality, and as a marvelous host and entertainer with a great talent for telling jokes and stories, for imitating many dialects, and for conviviality and practical jokes. He himself stated his favorite occupation to be "chaffing and being chaffed."[293] When he sent Christmas packages abroad, with greeting cards, plum puddings, and the obligatory red-berried holly, he packed the holly on top "so that the customs agents prick their fingers on it."[294] Naggingly aware of his lack of formal education and his dilettantism, he modestly described his main character trait as "knowing everything by halves." Yet others were struck by his encyclopedic knowledge. Marx's black son-in-law, Paul Lafargue, who became a warm friend of Engels, asked himself with some wonder how a man who for twenty years had worked in the business world could have found time to cram all that knowledge into his head.[295]

His conviviality notwithstanding, Engels was in many ways a very private person. In Jenny Marx's questionnaire, he states that his favorite trait in men was to mind their own business, and in women not to mislay things.[296] In both cases, these responses express his wish to be left undisturbed. Other qualities he praised on various occasions included decisiveness,[297] courage in the face of death,[298] and the ability to hold one's liquor.[299] He liked Carl Siebel because he had talents, was good-natured, not at all stuck-up, and very straightforward, frank, and open.[300] His heroes were the men of the Renaissance, those "giants of intellect, passion and character, diversity and learning," who he thought had been "everything but limited in the bourgeois sense." On the contrary, they all breathed the adventurous spirit of their time. They traveled far and wide, spoke four or five languages, and were brilliant in their fields—Leonardo in painting, mathematics, mechanics, engineering, and physics; Dürer as a painter, engraver, sculptor, architect, and fortifications engineer; Machiavelli as a statesman, historian, poet, playwright, and military writer; Luther as a church reformer, language reformer, and poet-composer of the 16th century Marseillaise (this was Engels's characterization of the chorale, "A Mighty Fortress is Our God").

Not yet constrained by the division of labor, these men were active, fighting partisans, wielding pen and sword, no cautious types among them.[301] Perhaps above all, Engels was forever enthusiastic about people who were fighters. Whoever did not fight for his rights, he more than once declared, deserved to be oppressed,[302] and there was nothing, he believed, that built character so much as having worthy opponents. "The misery is that our people in Germany have such pitiful antagonists," he wrote to Marx. "If the bourgeoisie had only one single capable and economically trained leader, he would very soon set those gentlemen on a potty and give them clarity about their own confusion. But what can be the result from a conflict where on both sides only commonplaces and Philistine's baloney are used as weapons? In the face of the higher bourgeois mug in Germany, a new vulgar German socialism is developing…"[303]

While most of his favorite character traits were the virtues of soldiers and revolutionaries, Engels also very much believed in certain virtues usually associated with business people. The most important one for him was honesty. Many times he complained about the alleged failings of German business people abroad, whom he accused of dishonesty, sneakiness, trickery, and the sale of shoddy merchandise. When his nephew Emil asked him for help in his effort to visit textile plants in England so he could learn more about his competitors, Engels advised him that honesty was always the best policy. "It works best," he wrote, "if you honestly tell people to whom you have been recommended what you are up to and who you are. To try it with tricks, as many German textile manufacturers have done, almost always has led to people being discovered and denounced to the others at the Exchange, so that they got to see nothing more. The way of competing here is, after all, on a more generous scale than in Germany, and the little tricks often used there don't work here at all."[304]

This dig at German cotton spinners is curious, but hardly seems a case of Oedipal rebellion because in all his critical remarks about his father Engels never even hinted that he might have been tricky or dishonest. He seems simply to have been scrupulous in his business ethics. For instance, much as he hated Gottfried Ermen, when his brothers asked him for information that might have enabled them to compete better against him, he refused, saying that he had a moral obligation not to harm his former partner and associate.[305] Of course, in this particular case, his feeling that he owed his brothers no favors of any kind may also have been a motive. Still, in money matters, he was careful to the point of finickiness.

Marx was well aware of this trait in him, and at times other friends and Party associates felt it, too. Engels himself once wrote to some German workers who had asked him to help them finance a cooperative venture that friendship and Party loyalty should never prevent caution in money matters.[306] In general, he seems to have felt that the practices and habits of the business world might be applied fruitfully to socialist politics. He once compared propaganda and parliamentary work with the duties of the traveling salesman or the advertiser. "They are boring and tedious," he wrote. "Success comes slowly or not at all, and yet there is no other way, and once a person has committed himself, he must go through with it or lose his entire investment."[307]

Although Engels often expressed contempt for his business associates in Manchester and sometimes wished he had time to write an expose of the whole class called "The Woes and Joys of the English Bourgeoisie,"[308] he also expressed admiration for some of its traits and achievements. For him, England was the classical bourgeois country, and he believed the English capitalists to be the only bourgeoisie that knew its class interests and had both the political skills and the political courage required to work for those interests. He grudgingly admired the success of the English system in co-opting a portion of the working class, although, optimist to the last, he regarded this as a form of abdication, demonstrating that the bourgeoisie was compelled to call in the workers to fight for bourgeois interests. In the same breath, however, he would complain that the workers of England did not take advantage of this opportunity to oust the bourgeoisie.[309]

Although at first puzzled by the medieval forms still adhering to British laws and institutions, he acquired admiration for their flexibility and efficiency and high respect for the political and personal freedoms granted in England (although not in Ireland). "The English jurist," he wrote, "has his feet implanted in a legal history that has managed to save a goodly portion of old-German freedom through the Middle Ages, that does not know the police state because it was nipped in the bud during the two revolutions of the 17th century, and that has culminated in two centuries of steady development of bourgeois freedom."[310]

On the whole, however, most bourgeois traits were abhorrent to him. He saw the bourgeoisie as a class devoted entirely to filthy self-interest, measuring everything by its monetary value. "There is only one way in which the bourgeoisie expresses its confidence in any form of government," he and Marx wrote in one of the reviews of events in 1850, "and that is its standing on the stock exchange."[311] When the two friends, in their scurrilous manuscripts about their fellow émigrés, wanted to describe Arnold Ruge as a typical bourgeois, they called him a coward and a scoundrel, stupid, sly, avaricious, servile, arrogant, and of gross, insistent peasant manners.[312]

With unconcealed contempt, Engels later characterized Bismarck and Napoleon III as typically bourgeois: "The bourgeoisie may indeed admire the great men of today. It sees itself mirrored in them. All the qualities through which Bonaparte and Bismarck achieved successes are businessmen's qualities—pursuing a specific goal by waiting and experimenting until the right moment has been found, the diplomacy of the back door that is always left open, making accords and bargains, taking insults when one's interest demands it, the slogan *'Ne soyons pas larrons'* (We are not crooks)—in short, everywhere the businessman.[313]

"Gottfried Ermen," he added, "in his way is as great a statesman as Bismarck, and when one follows the wiles of these great men, he again and again finds himself at the Manchester Exchange. Bismarck thinks, 'If only I continue to knock at Marx's door, I will some time find the right moment, and then we will do a little business together. Just like Gottfried Ermen."[314] (Bismarck had made an approach to Marx, through intermediaries, offering him employment).

What these and many other ironic characterization show is that in his general theory of capitalism Engels was motivated by an aesthetic and moral revulsion against the entire world of commerce and its consequences—the inequalities of social stratification, poverty, squalor, criminality, prostitution, the sexual bondage of the bourgeois marriage, bourgeois politics including its injustices, corruption, and violence, ideology as the reign of stupidity, and the inauthenticity of an alienated life, pursuing false needs and values.

Because he thought of himself as a cool scientist and was afraid of being a sentimental phrasemaker, he often hesitated to express his moral and aesthetic revulsion directly, but had to personalize it by lampooning the ruling classes. His inverted Hegelianism, which stressed revolutionary action according to a script written by history, and which consciousness could only recognize but not change, acted as an intellectual straightjacket. For this reason, among others, Engels could not possibly understand that conservative thinkers some decades previously, had described capitalism and the bourgeoisie in terms almost identical with his.

Of course, Engels was aware, and often said so, that the rage and revulsion he felt were necessary preconditions for the development of true consciousness of capitalism and other systems of exploitation.[315] Indeed, at times he sought deliberately to rekindle the flames of these emotions. "The other day," he told Marx, "in order to stimulate my old indignation once again a bit, I read the book by the Dresden prisoner Röckel, from the year '49, about his treatment in the penitentiary. The infamy of the Saxons goes beyond anything I have ever experienced. There will have to be a severe reckoning over very many scoundrels."[316] And to his friend Bebel he gave the advice, "Don't under any circumstances forget any dirt done to you and to all our people. The time for vengeance will come and will have to be exploited thoroughly."[317]

The aestheticism hidden beneath this wrath is revealed most clearly, perhaps, in Engels's biting observations of upstarts, about whom he always wrote with venom and a dash of snobbism. Listen to his comment on the vine-louse *(phylloxera)* plague in France: "It is very gratifying to know that in these last days of capitalist production this *phylloxera* has wiped out the Chateau Lafitte, Lagrange, and other *grand crus*, since we who know how to appreciate them don't get to drink them anyway, and the Jews and parvenus who do get them do not know how to appreciate them. Hence, since they have no further mission to carry out, they might as well perish. Our progeny will rapidly create them anew when they are needed for great people's festivals."[318]

Here he is describing the nouveau-riche public on the Isle of Jersey: "Public: *Spiessbürger*, clerk, apprentice clerk, and snob, giving occasions for much amusement and some annoyance. On such trips, the true Briton, as soon as he is in Jersey, throws off that domestication that he has acquired so painfully, only to assume it again all the more consciously at the *table d'hôte*. The increasing distribution of financial means to certain upstart individuals—one can hardly call them strata— of the English lower middle class, and the spread of luxuries and of the affected respectability connected with it, was nice to observe in Jersey, precisely because Jersey still has the reputation of being a cheaper and therefore unfashionable little isle. The respectability standard of Jersey travelers seems to get lower with every year…"[319]

"*Spiessbürger.*" Everything Engels hated is concentrated in this word, one of the two favorite terms of contempt in his vocabulary. The other one was "Philistine." *Spiessbürger* literally means a townsman armed with a pikestaff and moving on foot, hence a piker or pedestrian. As a term of contempt it originated in the Late Middle Ages, when the nobility fought on horses, with spear-carrying burghers fighting as an auxiliary infantry. It became a term of contempt for ordinary townsmen not rich enough to own horses and armor, and in the seventeenth century it came to be used by students as a word for burghers who acted, thought, behaved, dressed and spoke in old-fashioned ways, for people of narrow horizon, petty interests, and little wealth, and people who preferred a cozy, unperturbed life of small comforts to any kind of adventure.

The *Spiessbürger* thus was not very wise to the world. He was submissive and cowardly, a bit self-important, somewhat good-natured, and rather stupid. Living in tiny, insignificant towns, he was disinterested in the grand historic process going on around and over him. Engels used the term figuratively for any people who could thus be described, so that he could, for instance, assert that Prussia's nobility and German princes, too, were nothing but a bunch of *Spiessbürger.*[320] To the German *Spiessbürger* he also attributed not only a general lack of manliness, initiative, and independence, but also that bureaucratic rudeness, that barracks tone of discourse that he thought was a particular German failing.[321]

If *Spiessbürger* originated in aristocratic contempt for petty townspeople, "Philistine" was the German intellectual's sneer at the solid citizen. Originally used by theologians against non-theologians or dissenters, in the seventeenth century it became another word used by students to denote the town guards, later the town merchants and landlords, and in the end all people not in the academic world. Hence, it came to mean people interested in the prosaic affairs of the world, sober and wooden, and lacking the sense for higher things, conformists and conventional people without spiritual or intellectual needs or the need for a feeling of freedom. Against the Philistines stood the artists, intellectuals, scholars, and cultured persons, the sons of the Muses, as they liked to call themselves in Germany, indignant at the Philistine's belief that he, too, was cultured.

If the word *Spiessbürger* was uttered with a faint sense of condescending amusement, the term "Philistine" was said with greater hostility. The former was an enemy by default, merely because of his stupidity and limitations. The latter was the active enemy. He was the member of the ruling class, who sought to transform the entire society in his image. Engels pointed out that the English equivalent of the Philistines was that section of society associated with the word "respectability,"[322] and this was typical again of his essentially aesthetic disapproval of this class that he blamed them particularly for being stuck-up and aspiring toward a higher culture for which by education and intellectual horizon they were unfit. About one such person he wrote that she would doubtless feel uncomfortable in the undignified atmosphere of his house and his friends.[323] Ironically, Engels's two pet terms of contempt came from the vocabulary of German students, yet apart from *Spiessbürger* and Philistines, there was hardly a group among the population of which he was as suspicious as students and self-proclaimed intellectuals who flocked to the socialist movement.

All his life, Engels fought against the Philistine in himself, i.e. against his paternal heritage. Already as an adolescent he wanted to become a son of the Muses, in accordance with his maternal heritage. The Philistine, we have seen, was the man of respectability, of the Victorian establishment. Yet, one could argue that Engels's remarkable combination of qualities and talents, habits and preferences, made him an eminent representative precisely of the Victorian Age and its respectable leaders—his preference for neat, punctual, businesslike behavior, his sobriety and reverence for science and industry, his attitude toward work and his remarkable faith in progress, not least, in fact, his moral convictions and his radicalism, and indeed including his lustiness, his secret family life, and his love of alcohol. Thus, Engels in Manchester could justly be described as a representative (though radical) Victorian.

CHAPTER 9

TEACHING AND COUNSELING

THE WORD "SCHOOL" derives from a Greek word meaning leisure, spare time, idleness, or absence of useful work. Learning, for the Greeks, was a leisure-time pursuit, something to be done idly, unhurriedly, and playfully, which is why they were so good at it. School, then, is the use of leisure for the pursuit of knowledge, the acquisition of skills, and the cultivation of judgment. These are all special ways of relating to the world. At bottom, the relationship sought is analogous to an erotic relationship: the knowledge-seeker wishes to explore, embrace, or penetrate reality. In school, we learn the proper techniques. That is the function of the teacher. The other function is to arouse the student's interest; and the good student, in turn, starts by being curious.

All learning is conversation—conversation with teachers, fellow-students, books, and the world outside. What did the Greeks do when they had leisure? They exercised their bodies in athletics and their minds by arguing and conversing, the way Socrates gabbed and conversed with his young lovers. Dialectics, in its original meaning, is ability to converse, or the art of argument.

The ideal teacher, from kindergarten to graduate school, arouses students and shows them the way to learn. Professors thus function as stepping-stones for their students. Conversely, students also perform the same function their teachers, for the good teacher learns from his students, even from the so-called poor ones. I have always liked the Latin proverb, *docendo discimus*—we learn by teaching.

Albert Einstein, in secondary school, was a poor student. He hated the arid academic learning his teachers fed him and refused to absorb it. He almost flunked. Later, he barely made it through his doctorate and, once he had his Ph.D., could not find a job, even as a secondary school teacher. He was fired quickly from his first job as a private tutor. In the end, he doubtless was a brilliantly successful student, one of the best in history. Good students often rebel against their teachers.

When Max Planck was ready to enter a university, he wished to study physics, but a senior professor in that field discouraged him. "We know all there is to know in physics," he asserted. "There are no more great discoveries to be made, only details to be filled in. It's a boring, arid field." This was in 1875. Max Planck disregarded the advice of this smug academic, and lived to open a new universe of knowledge. The moral of this story: Don't trust people who are self-assured in their knowledge. They may have stopped thinking. Another Latin proverb applies here: *De omnibus dubitandum*—one must doubt everything.

Fields of knowledge have a tendency to fossilize, as do patterns of doing things. This is true particularly of the social sciences, the humanities, and the arts. This process of institutionalization is called academicism. Academicism discourages and frustrates innovation. Hence, the innovator in these fields more often than not is an outsider. Some of the most interesting social science ideas, for insistence, seem to have been generated by novelists and poets. In fact, I am tempted to say that one of the greatest political scientists of all time may have been William Shakespeare. We must therefore beware of the idiocy of specialization.

Technology has opened the world for us by making us see the invisible and measure the unfathomable. Alas, however, in our reliance on these tools for perception, many of us have forgotten to use our own eyes and ears. Having refined our instrument of measurement, we no longer know how to observe. In contemporary political science, observation is regarded scornfully: The scientist is supposed to measure, to think in terms of quantities that can be put into mathematical formulas. Observation that falls short of that is called impressionistic or anecdotal.

University professors are supposed to teach and to counsel, to engage in research and to publish its results, and to help administer their university, college, department, and professional associations. Like most other professors, I performed my share of such administrative duties. I served as Director of the University of Michigan Center for Russian & East European Studies, and sat on the editorial board of the University of Michigan Press. For one term, I was on the Board of Directors of the American Political Science Association, and, for several years, I was with the National Committee for Soviet and East European Research. In my professional association, the American Association for the Advancement of Slavic Studies, I served for several years on the board of directors of its women's affiliate—the Association for Women in Slavic Studies. I also served on the editorial boards of several professional journals.

Within my Department, I always preferred assignments that caused me to deal with students, especially undergraduates. In a department with thirty or forty faculty members, I was often the only professor who volunteered for these assignments, which were time-consuming for anyone who took them seriously, and I took them seriously. I always defined myself as a teacher first, and a scholar second. I also spent a substantial part of my time in counseling students, especially since I felt that, at the University of Michigan and especially in my own department, that function was badly neglected.

Concentration counseling meant assisting students in choosing courses, declaring concentrations, contemplating careers, and making other important decisions affecting their lives. It also entailed authorizing some of these decisions and certifying that departmental rules have been complied with. Because these rules, in turn, were confusing and subject to change, counseling always began with the job of explaining these rules to the student.

Success in counseling remained elusive because these different tasks interfered with each other. Discussing career choices and course offerings, stimulating students to enrich their curriculum, guiding them through the resources that the university has to offer—these tasks were challenging and made counseling interesting. They taxed a professor's ingenuity, imagination, knowledge of the university, and other powers. Wielding authority, deciding to make exemptions, and dealing with borderline cases could pose dilemmas for the counselor that could be petty or aggravating, and monitoring adherence to college or departmental regulations could be an unwelcome bureaucratic chore.

The mixture of tasks involved made it easy for a counselor to opt for carrying out only some and neglecting others. Many professors shirked counseling altogether, often on the pretense that the bureaucratic monitoring was a waste of their precious time. Others seemed to believe that counseling only involved monitoring adherence to formal rules, and therefore assumed that no student ever needed more than ten or fifteen minutes of their time. In fact, however, effective counseling required time and effort, and by shirking their responsibility, many professors cheated the students and the taxpayers.

Teaching was a profession fraught with grave responsibility. How one should discharge one's responsibility as a teacher (and counselor, since the two functions cannot be separated) was by no means clear. For one thing, our students themselves were by no means certain what they wanted to accomplish in the course of their four years of undergraduate study. Obviously, they wished to acquire the kind of knowledge, skills, and methods that they could later use to earn a decent living or that would qualify them for more advanced study on the graduate level. Many students, of course, did not know toward what profession they were headed. For them, college was an opportunity to shop around, to explore new fields of learning, to open themselves up for new experiences and interests.

While engaged in their studies, students also needed feedback from their instructors about how they were doing and whether their performance indicated hitherto undiscovered talents and abilities. They needed counseling about choices open to them regarding fields of study, careers, and course selections for the next semester. In their classes, they wanted to be stimulated, perhaps entertained, and surely not bored. They did not wish merely to be entertained, however. I have known professors who degenerated into clowns and whose students held them in profound disrespect.

The conventional style of college teaching, by lecture, is very difficult, and may well be on its way out—to be replaced by the workshop, the seminar, or the TV set. I once gave a lecture to a group of graduate students who were preparing for their role as graduate students. The title of the lecture was "The Lecture." I used the following notes in presenting this talk:

By and large, the lecture is a rash undertaking and its true aims are unattainable. Perhaps I ought to express the hope that by giving a successful lecture, I might prove my thesis wrong. I suggest that you do two things while I talk: First, listen to what I am trying to say, try to determine whether or not that makes sense to you, and then, later, communicate these reactions to me. Second, I would like you to observe HOW I say it.

Through teaching, we hope to affect the way in which our students relate to reality. Let me suggest to you, in profound seriousness, that this is indeed an OUTRAGEOUS enterprise—a shocking invasion of privacy—an irresponsible meddling with other people's lives.

To accuse teachers of irresponsibility is a grave thing. Yet, consider the effects of teaching: If it is done poorly, it is no more than a waste of everyone's time and a lot of parents' money. If done well, however, the results are quite unpredictable. Good, effective teachers affect their students in a great variety of ways, but they can never know or even guess what their students will do with whatever they have given them.

I am tempted to offer a daring analogy: At its best, effective teaching is a form of seduction. At its worst, it can be akin to rape. The principal role models that teachers recognize support the views I am presenting here. I can think of two important ones: One is Socrates, who taught his young lovers in a setting, which in its ideal form is described in the "Symposium." The other is the medieval apprenticeship in which, for several years, the apprentice became a member of the master's family.

To be sure, we no longer live in the age of Pericles, and the good old days of feudalism are long gone. In some rare interstices, the apprenticeship relationship between teachers and students persists: some laboratory research, the clinical part of medical school, and the teaching of musical performance, to name a few. Music seems to be one of the few skills where a performer will sum up his training and credentials by saying, "I studied with Nadia

Boulanger."

My point is that the age-old prevalence of the lecture as the standard form of academic teaching suggests that there is more to teaching and learning than what electronic programs can convey. Put yourself in the position of a professor on stage. Across from you, across a veritable abyss, are between 20 and 400 young women and men sitting there more or less captive. How do you affect their minds?

One way that you will not be able to do it is with showmanship. Entertaining them with jokes, with stories and anecdotes will keep some of them awake. It will keep others coming back to class sessions, but it will not teach them anything. We do not want to rape our students' intellects. We want to seduce them, to open them up for intellectual experience and intellectual activity. We want to show them that these are pleasurable activities.

To do this across the abyss between their seats and the podium in Auditorium B is terribly—terrifyingly—difficult. Because I know that, I am indeed terrified before every lecture, or at least jittery. Here is the teacher. There are the students. Between them is the abyss. The basic purpose is the same: An invasion of their intellectual privacy.

Consider the difficulties under which this attempt is made—the severe restrictions: You have got fifty minutes for it; not a minute more and not many minutes less. Teaching means giving away intimate glimpses into your own mind, stripping away its outer covers in the hope that the students will get hold of some of that mind's workings or contents. A lecture, in short, is the shameless display of thought processes.

I give some of my more successful lectures while pacing up and down, not looking at anyone in particular except when I want to emphasize a point. I am, rather, looking into myself, thinking out loud, talking to myself, or seeming to do so, groping for the right word, inviting the students to watch and hear me think, and trying to coax them into joining me in this enterprise. This usually approaches the IDEAL of education no closer than a striptease does to actual sexual intercourse.

Let me now turn to some techniques that may make a lecture effective. Here again, I will start with some similarities it may have with striptease, that is, with the art of arousing across an abyss by artfully shedding one's coverings. Success here depends on the performer's belief that she is beautiful, sexy, desirable, or, in the case of the lecturer, as intellectually interesting. Lecturers, in short, must be enthusiastic about their subject, believe it worth presenting, and be convinced of its inherent ability, and their own, to turn the students on.

It may be useful to give the students an outline of what you are going to say. But that involves a risk: Too much guidance beforehand might kill their interest. It is better to let the structure of your ideas shine through the performance so that the outline is revealed in all its clarity and complexity at the end—the way you understand the structure of a sonata only after you have heard it.

Like a musical composition, a lecture has themes and counter themes that are developed and interweave. It might have a recapitulation and a coda in which you might come back to the original theme. There should also be a lot of repetition. Repetition is a didactic device. Its effect is to drum ideas into the listeners' minds. Of course, drumming becomes monotonous, and repetition easily gets boring. You must therefore enliven it the way composers do, by presenting variations on your themes.

If you become an artist in this sort of composition, you might some day give lectures such as those I remember from one of my professors, which were composed so lucidly that often I would write down the conclusion even before he said it. An important device for reaching your students is simplicity, especially simplicity of language. Everything worth saying can be said simply.

In saying this, I disagree with a certain philosophic tradition that equates simplicity of language with simple-mindedness—arguing that reality is complex, and we must express that complexity. True enough. The intellectual's task is to make simple things look complicated and to make the complicated appear simple.

We must also shock our students by making what is unfamiliar familiar, and what is familiar, unfamiliar. Bertolt Brecht called this device "alienating" his audience. One can compare the government of, say, Ghana, with an old-fashioned urban American political machine, Joseph Stalin to Henry Ford, or the Communist youth organization to Greek-letter fraternities, as I have done. In this lecture, I have compared something you know very well, namely, education, with something unfamiliar to some of you, which is sexual flirtation—alienating you further by illustrating something sublime with something ridiculous.

Just now, I expected my listeners to laugh. The first time I gave this lecture they did. That makes the audience feel good because it is a release of tension. It makes the speaker feel good because it confirms his power over his audience, his control over their reflexes. The second time I gave this lecture I did not get a laugh. My excessive seriousness may have scared the audience into repressing their spontaneous reaction, or my deadpan delivery fooled them, or perhaps they were not paying attention.

Some jokes will test your audience's knowledge. For instance, I often tell a story about a student of mine who told me she wanted to study Russian. "What for?" I asked. She replied by saying she wanted to be able to read Marx in the original. The laughs I do not get for that indicate a specific level of ignorance, which is important for me to know.

At this point, I explained to my listeners that I had paced my delivery of this lecture with the help of carefully prepared notes. I was aware that some of my listeners may have been offended by the sexual imagery I used. I did want to convey that there might indeed be something akin to erotic tension in the intellectual intercourse between teacher and student. Today, many would condemn that statement as sexist.

Once I had begun to consider myself a feminist, I learned to guard my tongue against even the slightest lapse of this sort. When re-reading a letter of recommendation I wrote for one of our graduate students, about 1970, I was appalled to note that I had written as follows:

A nice Jewish girl from a Music and Arts High School, Debby performs as well as any of our male graduate students without losing any of her feminine charm. She is an extremely attractive woman who can think like a man.

Today I would not dare write that way, but I am glad, in any event, that a good university hired her.

All students certainly want to pass and to graduate. Today, however, a college degree alone carries little weight. In order to count, it has to be backed up by a brilliant record that is expressed in grades. The resulting pressure felt by the students has been passed on to the faculty and has led to the grade inflation of the last few decades. We can distinguish an excellent student from a poor one with just a glance at their GPA. What exactly are we measuring or evaluating in slapping a letter grade on students' work, however? Do we measure the amount of facts they might have absorbed or their memorization ability, their skill in handling complex information, their style of presentation, or the originality of their analysis?

I once participated in a seminar-workshop on problems of grading students' essays organized by the English department, and learned very quickly that standards of evaluation are fluid, subjective, and unpredictable--so much so that students often did not know what kind of performance would give them favorable or unfavorable evaluations. Despairing of my own authority to evaluate my students' performance, I once asked the students in one of my classes to grade themselves, or at least suggest to me what grade I should give them. I found that the best students gave themselves nothing better than B, while the poorer students gave themselves A's. A colleague in another department told me that he, too, let his students give themselves grades. He knew that he couldn't trust them to do this honestly, but believed the entire evaluation system was so tainted that he might as well let it be undermined that way.

According to the Catalog of the University of Michigan, various departments of the Liberal Arts College offered Honors programs to qualified undergraduates, and each department listed criteria for being admitted to any of these programs. Each department also designated one of its professors as director of its own Honors program. My own department chair once appointed a young colleague who had just joined us to do this job. I do not know whether they discussed what might be expected of him in this role, or whether he was pleased to be given this assignment. It seems, however, that this brilliant and imaginative young man was given no directions or ideas about what he should do as director of the Honors program. After his first year in the department, our Honors students were in an uproar of dissatisfaction.

I was asked to take over his job and to rescue the program. I accepted readily, since I enjoyed working with very bright and promising undergraduate students. One of my duties now was to admit applicants to this program. To be admitted, a student's grades up to the end of the sophomore year had to good enough to yield a certain grade point average. In order to prevent overcrowding, I could, of course, apply this rule very harshly, but I could also apply it leniently. A large number of sophomores usually applied for admission, and there was a time when I admitted as many as thirty. Once accepted into the Honors concentration program, Honors Juniors had to enroll in the special course that I was expected to teach them. In the fall term of their junior year, they all assembled for this Junior Honors Seminar.

"How many of you are headed for law school?" I asked them, and all the thirty students raised their hands. "I see I asked the wrong question," I said and this time asked, "How many of you intend to go on to Harvard Law School?" Fifteen or twenty hands went up. Obviously, our students were eager to be admitted to an Honors program because they regarded graduation With Honors as an essential step in the pursuit of their career.

The questions of how to organize the Honors Seminar, and what content to give it, were left entirely up to me. I therefore wrote a note to all my departmental colleagues asking them to send me any article or conference paper of which they were very proud. I would let my Honors students read the article and then invite its author to appear before them to discuss it with the Honors students or 'defend' it before them.

Very few of my colleagues at first responded to this invitation, but after I had sent out another note shaming the reluctant ones, I had enough articles and could schedule the appearance of the authors before my class. The purpose of the entire exercise was to give these students a broad overview of current research in Political Science as it was practiced in our own department. Some of the pieces they were asked to read were brilliant and interesting; others were less impressive, not to say shoddy. These Honors Juniors were not bashful in criticizing some of the professors' work, and many of them appreciated excellent scholarship. Thus, I tried to develop their critical faculty. My experiment in role reversal seemed to me to have been a success.

Through their junior year, I functioned as concentration adviser to all the Honors students. This took up a lot of my time, but I enjoyed dealing with them. Once they entered the fourth year of their studies, they had to devote their efforts to the preparation of an Honors thesis under the guidance of a faculty member who specialized in the subject matter that the thesis would deal with. It was up to me to refer each student to the most suitable colleague, and here, too, I found that many professors were extremely reluctant to assume that kind of mentoring relationship with an undergraduate student. In time, however, most seniors writing Honors theses found some faculty member willing to help and advise them.

I asked all students who had written an Honors thesis to submit it to a faculty committee, including their thesis adviser and me, as chairman, and then appear before that committee to 'defend' their thesis. The committee would evaluate their overall performance in courses, their thesis, and their skill in responding to questions about it, and on this basis decide whether they should be graduated With Honors, With High Honors, or even With Highest Honors. The ceremonial valedictory performance that I instituted was seen by many of these students as a pleasant climax to their undergraduate years.

A second-year student once came to me asking to be admitted to the Honors concentration program. Her grades during her first two years had been so mediocre that I was compelled to refuse her, however. She did not take 'No' for an answer, but rather pleaded with me, promising to work hard and to justify my leniency by excellent performance. Ultimately, she convinced me that she had the potential to become a late bloomer, and, with some reluctance, I admitted her to the Honors program. Two years later, her Honors thesis was completed, and she appeared before her committee to defend it. The thesis was a brilliant and mature work of scholarship, which could easily have served as a Master's thesis, and in the defense she fielded our questions with such elegance and self-confidence that it was a delight, and I congratulated myself for having recognized her potential.

When the exam was over, we asked her to leave the room so that we could come to a decision about her. My colleagues on the committee unanimously suggested that she be given an A+ for the thesis and that we graduate her with highest honors. I demurred, however. With grades as mediocre as hers, we could not confer highest honors on this student, I argued, for what would the graduate admissions people in any prestige graduate or professional school think about our standards? Let us compromise, I suggested, by giving her high honors and promising to write very positive letters of recommendation for her. We then called her in, told her our verdict and congratulated her. When I asked her to explain the unimpressive grade record accumulated in her first two years, she grinned and said, "I had a good time."

I remember a counseling session with a bright junior who came to me for advice on two matters: what field of concentration should she choose, and for what courses should she sign up in the coming semester? I talked with her for almost an hour, went though the entire impressive list of interesting courses available, but nothing interested her. In the end, I told her in a very friendly manner that she was wasting her time, and mine, and her parents' money, as well. She obviously did not wish to be in college at all, at least not for the time being, and therefore she ought to drop out, get herself a job, live for a while in the real world; and, after a few years she might be eager to return to school. She thanked me and left. A few days later, I received a phone call from her father, a mathematics professor at some other school. I felt some apprehension: Had I overstepped my authority as a counselor when I advised his daughter to drop out? Was he going to give me 'holy hell' for it?" I need not have panicked. All he said was that he wanted to thank me for telling his daughter something he had not had the courage to tell her.

Students entering a large institution like the University of Michigan found themselves in an academic cafeteria that offered a bewildering surfeit of interesting courses to pursue. They had to learn to find their way through this richly laden table with the help of printed guidelines and regulations about how to construct an academic program. These rules were themselves a bureaucratic maze through which most students needed to be guided by counselors. Those students who were too timid or too brash to seek such guidance might never learn how to structure their coursework so that at the end of four years they could receive their degree. Others might get counseling that was so mechanical and soulless that it became an aggravation in itself. Many professors had a fabulous talent for eluding students who wanted to consult with them, and when students wished to receive some feedback on their performance, they sometimes got no more than a letter grade without any further comment.

This description might be dismissed as a caricature, but certainly enough of it corresponded to the perception of many students that the four years of college were akin to an obstacle course devised by some sadistic demon. Obstacle courses, as is well known, are themselves good educational devices. They test the runner's courage, skill, and energy and fill those that have run them successfully with pride. The academic and bureaucratic obstacles of the undergraduate years, however, could also be overcome by running around instead of over them. Thus, not all those who went through college got themselves a good education. Whenever I functioned as a counselor to undergraduates, I encouraged them to take on the academic obstacles with courage, and at the same time, I tried to steer them around the purely bureaucratic ones.

At the University of Michigan, this latter task was not very difficult. There were rules on how to break rules, and, ultimately, every student, with the help of some sympathetic faculty member, could write his or her own concentration program. Some of my most promising students took that road with alacrity, once they had been told it was possible.

I distinguished between two aims of the undergraduate education in the humanities and in social studies. One aim was to prepare students for a professional or academic career in the field—in my case, political science. The other aim was to treat undergraduate courses in politics as part of a general citizen's education. Some of my colleagues considered that an unprofessional or even anti-professional attitude. That did not prevent me, however, from teaching political subjects in the general education mode.

Professors at the University of Michigan could choose to teach whatever they knew well, and I certainly did that. The could also decide to teach subjects that they didn't know well, but about which they wished to learn more, thus learning with the students. I certainly taught such courses also. In fact, I went beyond that in my teaching, venturing into areas that had only the remotest relation to politics or history, in which I had some knowledge beyond that of my students, but certainly no expertise. If they were subjects of interest to me, I simply wished to share my fascination with my students and thus broaden their intellectual horizon.

In all my teaching, I tried to use the material discussed in class in order to arouse interests and stimulate wide-ranging discussions. Whenever I taught political theory, I treated that genre as a special form of problem solving. All people writing theoretically or philosophically about politics did so because something problematic in their society prompted them to do so. Hence, the writings of political theorists had to be studied within their contexts. Written words, however, then had histories of their own, so that, having explored the origins of political ideas, one could then trace the uses made of these theories and their transformation into ideologies and dogmas, their adoption by revolutionaries or conservatives, their adaptability to justify both charity and genocide. At the same time, one could observe how one and the same political system could be justified by diametrically opposite principles and attitudes. For instance, I gave lectures on Machiavelli and Luther, two men who held totally divergent views and who, had they known each other, would have loathed one another; and yet, the practical lessons to be drawn from their writings in the field of politics and statecraft were remarkably similar.

In teaching political theory, we assigned writings that had stood the test of time, that students and scholars had read for many centuries. Today these are often dismissed as the writings of "dead white men," which should be rejected in favor of those by those speaking for oppressed minorities. It was these writers of the age-old "canon," however, whose books had shaped and misshapen the minds of our civilization, for better and for worse. If they had survived into the canon, it was always because the winners in history adopted them. At the same time, there was no reason why, when reading Plato, we could not suggest to our students that the Sophists might have right against Socrates; or that Arias might not have been right against Athanasius; or Lily Braun against Karl Kautsky. By encouraging criticism of the acknowledged great luminaries in intellectual history, I encouraged my students to be suspicious of whatever ideologies they had been fed throughout their short lives. Thinking starts with criticism. It is, therefore, an essentially subversive activity.

When winners adopted theories of protest and rebellion, as they often did, or when people preaching theories of change, reform, or revolution, radical theories could miraculously be turned into conservative ideologies. It was generally accepted that those theories then served to keep the masses obedient, but what was often overlooked was that leaders needed theory much more than the masses did. Elites, in order to remain in control, had to apply rough methods. They could easily develop troubling consciences if they did not have elaborate self-legitimating devices—political theories reassuring them that they had a right to rule and were doing the proper things—otherwise, they might not be able to sleep at night.

All politics is anchored in history. The two are inseparable because historic events, situation, and conflicts are the raw material that generate politics, and are in turn shaped by it. In political "science," we studied how human communities were governed. Government has often been regarded as the noblest of all human pursuits; but with equal frequency, and with equal justice, it has been denounced as the arena in which the basest, the most murderous human passions contend with each other, to almost everyone's detriment. The genres involved in teaching about politics are tragedy, comedy, melodrama, irony, and theater of the absurd.

Politics is problem solving. In my courses, I defined the human being as a problem-solving animal. Individually and collectively, we are endowed with perceptual and intellectual tools to recognize problems facing us. We are also marvelously endowed with the ability to devise material means, human organizations, and action programs to cope with recognized problems. There is only one hitch—every solution generates new and unanticipated problems. Every policy has unforeseen consequences. Every organization, every institution, sooner or later develops its own serious pathology. In politics, no solutions work for a very long time. Murphy's law bedevils politics much more than engineering, because human beings are a much trickier material to work with than concrete or steel.

Murphy's law can be seen at work when we consider the so-called great men of history, those political leaders who have managed to destroy great empires and erect new ones. They have usually done this with blood and iron, by winning wars. The great men have often been the great murderers of history. Many times, the great empires they built have lasted only a short time, suggesting that they wasted countless lives and rich resources for nothing.

We can observe Murphy's Law best, however, in complex organizations that are popularly known as bureaucracies. In some of the older textbooks in political science, bureaucracy appears as one of the prevalent utopias of our century. The classic definition of bureaucracy is "the imposition of rationality on human affairs through complex organization and scientific management." What could be more ideal than to see rationality rule human affairs? Isn't it nice that some brilliant theorists have worked out blueprints for complex organizations and patterns of decision-making that ensure the formulation of correct policies? Alas, however, while in theory bureaucracy solves the problems created by human irrationality, in real life it creates pesky irrationalities of its own. Theoretically a utopia, in real life it often is a nightmare.

My approach to teaching about politics, then, always stressed ambiguities and ambivalence of this kind. I tried to demystify politics and the persons who engage in it. I sought to stress not only the ingenuity of this pursuit, but also the human failings that bedevil it. I wanted to develop in my students a healthy skepticism regarding conventional verities about history and politics, and awareness that the winners usually write history, shape laws, and staff institutions. I wanted to show them that both in politics and in ideological conflict, the losers often have been, if not the worthier, then at least the most interesting people.

I never expected my students to adopt my own views and judgments, but, at the least, I wished to open their minds to the possibility that some conventional assumptions deserved to be questioned. Sometime in the sixties, a church minister wrote an angry letter to the editors of his local newspaper. In it, he argued that students were questioning too much, and he suggested that asking too many questions was a destructive activity, and a sign of immaturity. You kids, he wrote, in effect, need to realize that there are tried and true answers that mature people know, which give them their security. Once you have his security, you will stop asking so many disruptive and corrosive questions.

Ever since reading that letter, I tended to divide humanity into those who think they have answers and those who still ask questions. I prefer the latter group, for those who are satisfied with answers have stopped using their minds. I myself never felt that I had answers. I did not give answers to my students and did not expect them to give me any. I was satisfied if they asked questions, and I then tried to give them a variety of answers. I never tried to indoctrinate any of my students, but never concealed my opinions.

Beyond skepticism, I have tried to convey something much more important through my teaching. I tried to introduce my students to the sheer joy of learning, to the pleasure derived from using one's mind, which is similar to the athlete's pleasure of using her body or the artisan's pleasure in the creative use of his hands. I encouraged them to use their minds while giving them no answers. I urged them to question, while allowing them to come up with their own answers. Plato, I think, compared the philosopher with a road sign: the sign indicated the direction of the road, but did not go along with the wayfarer. I employed the opposite strategy, refusing to indicate the direction in which the students were to go, but accompanying them on their journey.

I once encountered a young man who reminded me that, some years ago, he had been enrolled in one of my classes. "You changed my life," he said to me, expressing gratitude. I asked him how, although I did not remember him at all, I had changed his life, and he reminded me that one sunny spring day I had entered the classroom wearing a dandelion in my buttonhole. Some student then made a mocking remark about this, to which I had replied, "It doesn't have to be expensive to be pretty." These words, said my former student, had stirred up some deep reflection in him, which had changed his life.

O my goodness! If a flippant observation tossed out to counter some silly criticism could have such grave consequences, teachers should be aware of the heavy responsibility they are shouldering when they say anything at all. It was a frightening realization that by merely opening our mouths we could 'change lives' in directions of which we had no inkling.

My goal as a teacher was to contribute to the students' intellectual awakening. How could one do that? One way of defining the method would be to say that one should place the students into an environment that promoted intellectual exploration. This environment, of course, was the college. Colleges could function as cultural oases within the arid world of mundane pursuits. I often compared my work as a teacher to that of a gardener. Our students were tender plants. We sought to plant them in fertile soil, provide them with sunshine, water and nutrients, weed out those that despite our efforts did not thrive, and hoped to see them sprout and blossom and ultimately bear lush fruit. In this image, the entire college could be seen as analogous to a nursery or hothouse, and the individual teacher as one of many members of a gardening team.

Regarding the role of the individual teacher, I liked to use an image taken from "The Lecture," arguing that the teacher's job was to introduce students to a pleasurable activity in which they were as yet insufficiently experienced—the use and development of their intellects. Introducing innocent young people to pleasures that they have not yet experienced is called seduction; it seemed to me that good teaching was a form of seduction.

How did one seduce students into using and developing their intellects? By displaying one's own pleasure in doing it. Professors needed to open up the workings of their own minds for inspection. In my case, this meant that I display my intellectual self as seductively as possible. I did this by engaging students in my own thinking processes, by thinking and puzzling and doubting in front of them.

Prior to my retirement from active service on the faculty, I spent much of my working time in my office. The door would always be open. My office hours would be posted at the door—usually about five hours a week (most of my colleagues would post one or two hours a week). Students were free to walk in any time. Their reasons for coming to see me were diverse. They might wish to discuss the term paper they were preparing in one of my courses, they might have questions about things discussed in class, seek some general counseling about their academic program, or just want to come in for a chat. If I happened to be busy with something else, and they had come in outside of posted office hours, I might give the visitor short shrift—though with apologies—and with an indication when they might see me at a more convenient time. In general, however, I thought it my duty and my privilege to be there for them.

Something unexpected by me, and unplanned by the students, occurred a few times during such visits: The student might look subdued or depressed and speak in a low monotone. "You seem to be in a blue mood today," I might say, noticing this. More than once, such a simple observation opened the floodgates of words or even tears in the student sitting opposite me, and I then heard their stories of woe: a recent death in the family, a painful breakup with a lover, a variety of academic difficulties—whatever.

Why did these students burst into tears when all I did was to take note of their melancholy mien? Because in the entire university I may have been the only one who has taken the trouble to make that observation. For these distressed students, the university—despite its fellow students, professors, teaching assistants, counselors, and administrators—was a faceless bureaucracy, a monstrous machine that treated its students administratively. On the basis of rules, regulations, and routines, students were reduced to a set of categories that could be recorded in the computer. I elicited a river of tears or an avalanche of words because I was the first person in a long time that treated the student with compassion, as a human being.

When the students' distress was due to academic difficulties, I usually tried to show them how to overcome these, if only by suggesting that, for the time being, they lighten their course load. Beyond that, I rarely did more than to listen to their tales of woe. I did that patiently, however, generous of my time. There was not all that much advice an untrained counselor could give. Although I have had no training in clinical psychology, I was a human being—old enough to have seen much of the human comedy, hence in possession of a certain amount of common sense or even wisdom. If I could pass any of this on to a troubled student, I would do so.

Although this attitude of mine was often appreciated, I was aware that this was not always the case. Once, a student told me she had been given poor counseling by an advisor who had not the slightest understanding of her spiritual or intellectual needs, and that she now hated the University of Michigan and hoped to transfer somewhere else. My compassion with her caused me to let go of my common sense, and I gave her a hug before she left my office. This show of physical affection frightened or offended the student. Weighed against such incidents, however, many of my students became lifelong and loyal friends.

Some years ago a student came to me, already in tears. She told me she was a senior enrolled in some other department. Two months before graduation, she said, she had suddenly been informed by her advisor, or by some credit auditor, that she would not be receiving her degree in May because she was two course credits shy of the minimum required for graduation. She then told me a story of negligent counseling, contradictory advice given her by her professors, and a merciless bureaucratic run-around, so that my anger was aroused. I asked her why she had come to me with this story, and she told me that I had been recommended to her as someone who would at least listen to her complaint

I then phoned the Dean of Students, a kind and patient man. "I have a graduating senior in my office," I told him, "who has consistently been given wrong advice and suddenly is being asked to take additional course work on which she had not felt the need to plan. I am tempted to refer her to an attorney, but want to check with you beforehand to see what can be done for her." In response, the Dean invited me to sit in on a committee meeting that was about to examine her record and discuss her case. In the meeting I had a chance to peruse her transcript and found out that she was not two credits short of fulfilling graduation requirements: she was 35 or 45 credits short. She had failed a few courses and had withdrawn from others. In some of her courses, she had not delivered the required work or had neglected to take the exams. They all counted as failures. Nobody in her department, however, warned her that she was in deep trouble, or if she had been counseled correctly, she had neither understood nor heeded it. The entire structure of the curriculum had remained a mystery to her for more than three years, and she obviously was bureaucratically accident-prone. That such a ludicrous thing could happen demonstrated the loneliness and facelessness that a very large university could assume for a very shy and perhaps dreamy student.

In my field of studies, students are usually graded on the basis of written work they submit—final exams, essays, term papers or theses. Evaluating such work really is an impossible task. The learner wants to be evaluated, but also fears it because the grade may be poor. Yet, regardless of the grade, we must assume that the student also wishes to learn something.

The teacher's aim is, or ought to be, to share with students some knowledge, technique, skill, intellectual qualities or character traits and, by helping students to acquire them, allow them to develop their potential. Learning, then, could be defined as the process in which the student acquires what the teacher has to offer. At its best, the learning process is one of self-development or self-generation and self-birthing.

The ideal teacher would function both as an inseminator and as a midwife.

In order for learning to take place at all, the teacher may have to make the very leaning process or the subject matter attractive and interesting to the students. Hence, before insemination or midwifery can be practiced, the teacher will have to arouse the students' desire to learn. The more the teacher succeeds in this, the less evaluation is needed. For, to be honest about this, one of the chief functions of evaluation in our educational institutions is to serve as a stimulus, as a goad to learning. The promise of a good grade (or the threat of a poor one) is the principal reason why many students study. To the extent that we can awaken and foster genuine interest, we can dispense with this goad and use it constructively, as feedback. Conversely, the more we rely on the grading system as a goad, the less care we give to the quality of our teaching effort. The existence of the evaluation system may, therefore, function as a substitute for good teaching.

Evaluation is a feedback device. Feedback means constructive criticism: students need to be told what they are doing right and what they are doing wrong, where they have talent and promise and where their performance suggests insufficient aptitude. Academic promise and performance can take a variety of forms, however. No individual teacher masters all of them or finds all of them congenial. Ultimately, in fact, the teacher's aim should be to help students gain intellectual independence including independence from the teacher. The ideal student is one who goes beyond and repudiates the teacher, so that teachers serve as a stepping-stone for their students. How many of us, however, have the character strength to give recognition for this type of intellectual independence to our students?

What do we measure in evaluating written work? Learning done in a course is the difference between the knowledge, skill, and qualities students had at the beginning of the term and those they have at the end. In order to accurately measure this, we would have to know our students much better than we do. Moreover, learning often is a dialectical process in which the student goes off in one direction by detours or by seemingly going off the opposite way. Intellectual order at times comes out of a period of confusion. We often learn by unlearning things and may attain wisdom through various stages of ignorance. For observing this process, one semester is insufficient. Ideas need time to germinate, and the best ones ripen very slowly.

Hence the practice of taking an entire class of students, looking at their performance during a brief semester, and then ranking them on a scale from A to E is ludicrous. While, at the end of the term, I have had to give each student a letter grade, I did this most reluctantly. What I would have preferred would have been to tell the student in words what I thought of the work he or she had done. Written work done by students should be seen as exercise analogous to exercises done under teachers in other fields—learning to play an instrument or train one's voice, as well as athletics, acting, dancing, carpentry, and other crafts. In all such exercises students combine a multiplicity of skills with the eventual aim of performing on the level of the teacher, or better. All that the teacher can do is to tell the student whether he or she is exercising well and how the work might be improved. That is always a highly subjective judgment and should not be made lightly. Excessive rigor in holding students to the teacher's standards can be stifling. Excessive openness can turn into dishonesty or intellectual sloppiness.

A complicating factor is the divergence of attitudes and aptitudes among the students. In every class there are some eager learners and some who have enrolled for bureaucratic reasons, such as distribution requirements, or to get a so-called 'easy A'. Every class contains some students who are reasonably well familiar with some of the material covered and others to whom it is altogether new. Some already are brilliant essayists and others have never been taught how to write well. Some of the most brilliant students may not know how to spell. Some have been reading books all their lives while others are only beginning.

Because teachers cannot know all these complications, some make assumptions about their students. When I was a student in the *Gymnasium*, my Latin teacher assumed that all of us were decent, eager, hard-working boys. It was difficult to convince him of the opposite, yet once a student had so convinced him, the teacher henceforth treated him like an enemy. Our Greek teacher, conversely, assumed that we all were lazy good-for-nothings. Once a boy showed him he was serious about his studies, however, he went out of his way to encourage and inspire him further. He was by far the better teacher of the two, and the fairer.

Some of the assumptions made by those two gentlemen may spook every teacher. I always tried to view students as young plants: tender shoots that want proper soil, adequate nutrients, appropriate climate and moisture to sprout into mature plants and bring forth beautiful blossoms and luscious fruit. There are times, however, when the teachers think they are wasting their trying to educate. Whenever we feel that way, reading term papers, exams and other student work become a demeaning chore. Sometimes students' essays can appear like flower buds; other times, like so much excrement.

Around 1970 a group of students who had taken course work with me, or for whom I had served as their advisor, approached me with a proposal to join with them in an informal learning community. These young men and women—ten or twelve of them—suggested that they all rent a small house where they could live together and, under my guidance, study any topic that interested them. They planned to read books and devote afternoons, evenings, or any other regular period to discussions of what they had learned.

I was going to be on leave during the coming academic year and intended to do research for a major work, but thought it would be easy to fit in time for this learning commune, and so it was. They did, indeed, rent a small house close to the campus, settled in its rooms, took turns cooking and cleaning, and began to read and come together for discussions. The entire scheme at first seemed to work quite well, but there were snags. First, a significant number of commune members were also undergraduates. As such, they were under pressure to do their assigned course work, and this interfered with their contributing as much as they wished to our joint studies. In the end, this weakened the impact of our experiment. In addition, some serious personality conflicts disrupted the comradeship that had, at first, prevailed among the participants. The enmity that developed between two members, in particular, became too disruptive. The experiment failed.

CHAPTER 10

ENGELS AND MARX

THE TIME HAS come to discuss the remarkable relationship of Engels and Marx, as it developed through the decades since their first important meeting in 1844. From that time until March 1883, when Marx's death parted them, these two men were a team, almost closer to each other than brothers, as similar to one another in thinking as any two such different personalities could be. We have many touching statements from both, attesting to the closeness of their friendship and to the high regard each had for the other. Amazing examples exist, also, of how even when they were hundreds of miles apart they had similar ideas, conceived identical plans, reacted in complete unison to certain stimuli, and gave entirely identical responses to questions. The first such item comes from the year 1845, a few months after their friendship was formed, and the last comes from the year of Marx's death.[324]

And yet, their personalities are a study in contrasts. Marx could be described as a totally alienated person. He was a Lutheran Jew raised in a Catholic province, a profound scholar who had developed a philosophy of action in a world in which the time for action always seemed to fade away, and a man of boundless interests obsessed for more than thirty years with one topic, which he hated with every fiber of his being. He was a family man, married to the most prized noblewoman in his town, who was profoundly uncomfortable in his marriage and often cursed himself for having married at all, a good father who loved his daughters dearly but never stopped wishing they had been boys, and a man forever incapacitated by painful ailments that he himself knew to be of psychic etiology, as well as by a persistent talent for wasting both time and money.

271

In every respect, Engels was the opposite. He was totally organized in his daily life, maintaining self-discipline without depriving himself of wine, women, song, scholarship, and vigorous physical exercise. The same talent for organization characterized his intellectual life. He knew how to pursue a surprising variety of interests and managed to do quite well in many of them, even though his formal education had stopped short of graduation from secondary school. Remarkably liberated from prevailing sexual morality, he nonetheless lived in what seem to have been happy, mutually satisfactory, monogamous common-law marriages.

For almost forty years, Marx and Engels shared ideas, interests, and projects. For about twenty-five of these years, they lived apart and, except for their recurrent visits to each other, corresponded with never diminishing frequency. Even after 1870, when Engels moved to London and settled in a house within ten minutes' walking distance from the Marxes, both of them traveled a great deal and in these periods had to correspond with each other. Being relatively lonely, at least for considerable periods, they strongly felt the need for extensive communication with one another. Their correspondence is therefore a vast and rich source of knowledge about their relationship.

Late in his life, Marx once wrote to Engels that he was always following the latter's lead in taking up new subjects of inquiry.[325] This was, perhaps, an exaggeration. In certain important areas, Marx gave the cues and Engels followed, for instance in the incorporation of Lewis Morgan's work into their doctrine. It is certainly, however, a correct statement of the lead that Engels gave to Marx in the study of economics. Marx's intense interest in this field dates from his reading of Engels's 1844 essay. It led him to write the unfinished and unpublished economic-philosophic manuscript of 1844, which was meant to be the beginning of a major work. Ever since 1844, Marx gave highest priority to the task of completing this work. His intent was to uncover the regularities or 'laws' governing the workings of capitalist economies, which he and Engels regarded as the key to the understanding of bourgeois society. He and Engels saw this as providing the necessary theoretical groundwork for their common views.

Thus, among the two, Marx saw himself as the theorist. Engels, meanwhile, by joint consent, was regarded as the man with the practical knowledge, whose many talents might be used more suitably for a variety of scholarly and political tasks of a less abstract nature, especially the preparation of works falling more properly within the realm of political journalism—i.e., promotional, agitating, and popularizing work. Although this was how they defined the division of labor between them, things did not always work that way. To be sure, Engels left the elaboration of economic theory entirely to Marx, at times arguing that the material Marx sent him for comment was too deep for him, or too difficult to comment upon quickly—and if a quick response did not come from Engels, it was likely that he would not respond at all.

Engels also made theoretical contributions, however. Furthermore, Marx, in turn, was forced to do far more journalistic work than he liked, while Engels often despised the journalism he was doing and hoped he might find time for more theoretical work—although not in the field of economics. Marx, too, had to function as a popularizer, and in the First International the political work had to be done almost exclusively by him, since Engels until 1870 was prevented from participating in it. Similarly, until 1870, Marx far more than Engels was engaged in the interminable infighting with rival émigré groups.

Linked with the problem of dividing tasks between them was the problem of securing their physical survival. That meant not only exile in England or the United States, since on the Continent they would have been jailed or deported, but also the necessity for both of them to make a living. Of the two, Marx was poorly equipped for survival in a hostile world. His knowledge of German, French, and Roman law was worthless to him in England. His philosophic views would have made it difficult or impossible for him to find academic employment in any English university. There were many possible menial tasks that he would not have wished to undertake, for the sake of his wife and daughters for whom he desired to provide a middle-class environment. As for his political journalism, no periodicals on the Continent would have been open to him after 1849. Marx and his family faced starvation unless he hired himself out as a tutor to a wealthy family. This, however, he does not seem to have contemplated. Years after settling in London, in an hour of total desperation, he once applied for a job as a clerk with a railroad company, but was rejected because of his poor handwriting.[326]

Engels, with his commercial training and experience, was better equipped for survival in a capitalist world. Indeed, through his family he had privileged access to the firm of Ermen & Engels, and to the respectability of commercial work in Manchester. If Friedrich Engels hated one thing more than bourgeois respectability, however, it was the professional life of a businessman. Any time spent in it was penal servitude. Why, then, did he submit to it for twenty years? The answer lies not only in his attachment to his family and in his need for a livelihood. His principal motive in enduring this twenty-year sentence was the opportunity it afforded him to support Marx.

In his student days, Marx had hoped to become a professor. Because he was too radical, however, and because his academic sponsor was himself dismissed from his academic post, Marx did not secure an appointment. Having no income, he tried repeatedly to obtain part of his father's estate, but his mother refused, sensing perhaps that the money would be gone quickly. Before meeting Engels, Marx had already developed the habit of sponging on friends and supporters, taking advances from publishers for books that were never finished or not even begun, and in other ways living on other people's money. Shortly after their meeting in Paris, in September 1844, Engels became his chief financier. Beginning in the winter of 1844-5, their correspondence includes numerous requests for money by Marx, and equally numerous exhortations by Engels not to be bashful in asking.

Regular remittances began as soon as Engels had been installed in his commercial job in Manchester. At first, it took the form of a few pounds—one, two, four, never more than five—whatever he could spare, the notes torn or cut in half and sent in two envelopes, their serial numbers carefully noted. If pound notes were not available, Engels would send postage stamps from the office or cotton thread for Jenny

Marx from the textile factory. In later years, there were food baskets and crates of wine, especially around Christmas, not to mention foreign postage stamps for Tussy Marx's collection.

The idea that Engels was a potentially rich source of money seems to have come to Marx early in their relationship. After all, he knew about the economic status of Engels's parents. The desperate need Marx felt for exploiting this source is apparent in a rather insidious plan not far short of blackmail by which in 1848 he proposed to utilize Engels's mother to press a substantial sum out of his father. Engels apparently did not give his consent to this, but there is not evidence, either, that he allowed the suggestion to warn him about the relationship to come.

What ensued was a relationship based on Marx's seemingly inexhaustible needs for money. He was unemployed and penniless. His family was large. Six children were born into it between 1844 and 1851, of whom three died between 1850 and 1855. For the sake of his highborn wife and his daughters, Marx sought to live in bourgeois style. Only once, when his financial house of cards had totally collapsed and he had to confess to be totally at his wit's end, did he propose to give up the last show of respectability, take his daughters out of their schools, find a proletarian dwelling, live on potatoes, and get rid of the maids.[327] Most of the time, however, they maintained a front of respectability— frantically so whenever outsiders came into the household, and most frantically in front of the man who courted the daughters.[328] Thus not only did the butcher, the baker, and the landlord have to be paid, but also piano teachers, schools, wine merchants, dressmakers, the tax collector, doctors, and pharmacists.

Marx was totally unable to manage finances, and his wife often spent money recklessly. He was embarrassed by money matters and irritated by them to the point of near-madness. Both he and Engels were aware that his recurrent bouts of severe carbunculosis were caused in part by financial worries.[329] His eldest daughter so associated sickness with social misery that she was confident that physicians would no longer be necessary after the revolution. In "our new society..." she wrote, "there will be less need for priests of the body. They will all go bankrupt together with their brethren, the physicians of the soul…"[330]

Because Marx was always deeply in debt, a substantial portion of his budget (supported by remittances from Engels) went for the payment of discounts and interest to pawnbrokers and moneylenders. On some loans, interest was as high as fifty percent.[331] In his desperation, he became reckless. He wrote threatening letters to his mother, to no avail while Jenny, without telling him, turned for help to her step-brother, the Prussian Minister of the Interior, also in vain.[332] Marx let promissory notes go, in protest, or paid them with yet new promissory notes. Always impatient with actual calculations, he miscalculated his indebtedness when making occasional reports to Engels. Once, he omitted a bill of exchange and then forgot the amount, so that when it was presented for payment he was caught by surprise and had to send Jenny to the merchants around the corner to scrape the amount due together by hasty borrowing.[333]

In short, Marx made debts carelessly, and then had to ask Engels to bail him out.[334] The fact that he and Jenny tried to hide the facts from each other complicated matters, because the debts were often larger than they both suspected. Add to all this the truly astonishing fact that Marx indulged in what he himself called high-risk stock speculations, even while confessing to be a pauper. How often he did this, and how much he gained or lost in the long run, I don't know, since all the evidence I have seen amounts to just one letter to his uncle in which he boasts about a four hundred-pound profit he made on one such speculation.[335] Engels probably did not know about this venture, and perhaps the letter was a lie, but he, the businessman, nonetheless asked Marx's advice on when to sell or not to sell papers from his own portfolio.[336]

The growing needs for cash were met by increased remittances. One- or two-pound gifts gave way to ten-, fifteen-, and twenty-five pound remittances, and sometimes more. The larger gifts came in response to the most desperate letters describing tragic-comic scenes of Marx hiding or running away from his creditors[337] or scenes of unmitigated tragedy. "A week ago," wrote Marx in one such letter, "I reached the pleasant point where I can no longer go out because I lack the coats that have been taken to the pawnbroker, and I cannot eat any more meat because I lack the credit. Now all this is but shit, but I am afraid that this mess will end in a scandal. The only good news we got was from my ministerial sister-in-law about the illness of my wife's indestructible uncle. If that dog dies now, I am out of the worst."[338] The tragedy of the letter lies not only in the actual situation described, but also in the depth of dehumanization that it caused in Marx. The rich old uncle lived on for another three years, and when he died he left them about a hundred pounds.

Marx's cynicism was his defense against despair, but at times he also became desperate. The knowledge that he was ruining his beloved wife and mercilessly exploiting his best friend racked him with guilt. Having to reveal the mess of his affairs to Engels and to Jenny filled him with shame. And the more guilt, shame, and financial disaster overwhelmed him, the more he felt that his intellect was being destroyed and his ability to work broken.[339] His wife Jenny, however, did not even possess the ability to use cynicism as a defense mechanism. Hence, the letters in which she describes the humiliations to which the family was subject are perhaps the most heart-rending of all.[340]

At times, Jenny did not even have the consolation that it was all for a good cause. Once the revolution came, she said to her husband, it would be even worse, and with bitterness she added her opinion that all the windbags among the political émigrés would then get to the top and would be sitting pretty.[341] Marx, in turn, came to resent his family and to regret that he had ever married. He expressed this most clearly in a famous long letter to his future son-in-law, Paul Lafargue, and more briefly in many other statements. "There is no greater jackass stupidity for people with general ambitions that to marry at all, and thus to betray themselves into the *petites misères de la vie domestique* and *privée*,"[342] he confessed to Engels.

In 1864, when Engels improved his own financial situation significantly by becoming a full partner in the firm in which he heretofore he had been a clerk and correspondent, his payments to the Marx family increased. Sums of twenty-five or even fifty pounds were sent from Manchester, at times in rapid succession. Marx's indebtedness, however, seemed to increase proportionately. He or his wife inherited various substantial sums—a hundred pounds from her uncle in 1856, another 120 pounds from her mother that same year, and another 150 to 200 pounds from a distant Scottish relative. Marx's mother, in 1863, left them an estate of about 750 pounds, and in late 1864, Marx inherited the substantial sum of 825 pounds Sterling from an old comrade-in-arms, Wilhelm Wolff. That was quite a large amount of money in 1864.

By July of the following year, however, he had to confess to Engels not only that the money was gone, but also that the debts had again become overwhelming. For the last two months, he wrote, he had been living off the pawnbroker and was facing a mounting storm of creditors. The mere payments of old debts amounted to 500 pounds. "I would rather let my thumb be hacked off than write this letter to you. It is truly devastating to remain dependent half one's life."[343] He then apologized for maintaining so bourgeois a household, but added that it was the only means by which he could ensure a future for his children, i.e. by enabling them to enter into suitable relationships and conditions. If the children were all male, he added, the whole family could have lived in proletarian style.

Engels's total payments to Marx in 1866 seem to have amounted to 240 pounds. In 1867, the sum was 350 pounds. In the summer of 1869, Engels was able to leave the firm in which he had been a partner. He settled with his former partner for a very substantial sum that according to Henderson amounted to about 1,250 pounds. Engels could live from the interest to be gained by reinvesting the settlement sum, and he offered Marx an annual allowance of 350 pounds for the next few years. At that time, Marx's debts amounted to 365 pounds, so that even while expressing his boundless gratitude to Engels for this magnanimous offer, he had to indicate it was not enough.[344]

Nevertheless, from the moment of Engels's settlement with his former partner, Marx's financial situation became secure. However dire the emergency, Engels could always sell a few shares if necessary. The two eldest daughters married. The worst was over. To the last moments of Marx's life, however, Engels remained aware of his importance as a financial mainstay, and because he wanted to make sure that the fiscal order underneath his partner would not be disturbed, he became more than normally solicitous for his own physical well-being. Thus, in the fall of 1882, a few months before Marx's death, Engels wanted to visit him on the Continent, but forbade himself the pleasure lest something might happen to him on the trip. Wrote Marx, "Your self-sacrificing care for me is unbelievable, and deep down I often am ashamed—but I do not want to discuss this topic now."[345]

When this relationship began, Engels was not the rich man he became in late life, but a poorly paid commercial employee occupying a tenuous and insecure position within his family and his firm. He felt himself observed in his spending and living habits. He knew that he was expected to maintain certain standards of bourgeois decency in his lifestyle, and yet was also expected to live within his meager salary. He very often was short of cash, but nonetheless urged Marx to ask him for it, and Marx really did not require such urging. His entire relationship with Marx was a source of embarrassment to him with his employer, with whom he did not get along well to begin with. If he dipped deeply into his own cash or credit reserves, it was often in great fear of being discovered and being asked the purpose of these withdrawals. By early 1853, he himself was in debt and was forced to move into cheaper quarters and drink less expensive wines. He moved back into more pretentious quarters only when his father came for his next visit, so as to forestall embarrassing questions about how he was spending his money.[346]

Here was a curious paradox. Marx, the pauper, always tried to live so that it seemed he had an income. The houses he occupied, once he was out of the Soho slum, were large and pretentious. Every move the family made was expensive. So was the education of his two elder daughters. Marx was so successful with his bourgeois pretense that in 1868 he was elected, much to his dismay and amusement, Constable of the Vestry of St. Pancras, at the very same time his creditors were about to sue him.

Marx ignored the election, did not go to the swearing-in, and was thereupon summoned before the Vestry in legal language that seemed quite threatening. An English friend whom he consulted advised him to tell the Vestry that he was a foreigner and they could kiss his ass.[347]

Meanwhile, Engels, at least at the beginning, had to try hard to make it appear that he was living within his modest income, which he was not.[348] When it was a matter of choice, moreover, he preferred to skimp on himself and restrict his own lifestyle rather than deprive Marx. If disaster struck in the Marx home just after he had indulged in some pleasure, he felt guilty, as in 1857, when he bought himself a horse with the Christmas money his father had sent him, thinking that all was well with Marx, and then learned that things were worse than before.[349]

Again, when he lent his name as guarantor of major loans that Marx obtained, this too had to be done behind the back of his business associate.[350] When things became more desperate than usual, he even considered deals and maneuvers that were on the boundary of legality or business propriety—asking Marx to provide him with forged receipts for payment of non-existent debts, dipping into his partner's account, remitting bills of exchange without sufficient coverage, etc.[351] For a mid-nineteenth century businessman with Engels's almost exaggerated sense of probity and responsibility in financial matters, the mere consideration of these steps was absolute recklessness and a token of the self-sacrificing nature of his relationship with Marx.

If Marx thanked Engels only rarely, and then in words that seemed grudgingly curt, this was partly because of his eternal embarrassment at being so dependent on his friend. On the few occasions when he allowed his emotions of gratitude to be expressed, the embarrassment, shame, and guilt all came out at the same time, and crowded out the gratitude. Besides, on the non-emotional plane of politics and practicality, the two friends regarded the relationship as perfectly proper—not pleasant, perhaps, but in no way objectionable, because it was all for the sake of the movement, which demanded Marx's survival and health so that he could devote his full efforts to the theoretical work that would inspire the working class. If Engels got irritated, he showed it rarely. His insistence on having prompt acknowledgment of every remittance, however small, seems to have irritated Marx, and especially his wife, as much as their occasional failure to comply with it irked Engels. The fact that he kept careful account of every payment he made to them may seem strange among two men who were such close friends, but was no more than the reflex action of a careful business manager.

Once, in the spring of 1863, Engels got into an ugly discussion about money matters with a mutual friend of theirs, Ernst Dronke, after which he got drunk, and in his drunkenness wrote an angry letter to Marx. After his hangover had cleared, he wrote another letter to Marx in which he professed not to remember what he had written earlier, but in a fashion he apologized for whatever he might have written. *In vino veritas:* the letter written while under the influence of alcohol may have been hard-hitting, because it is not available to us, possibly simply because it is hidden in some archive, but more likely, perhaps, because either Marx or Engels destroyed it.[352]

However lopsided their financial relationship, their intellectual and political partnership was a relationship of equals. Each regarded the other as his alter ego and looked up to him with respect. Each felt entitled to give peremptory orders to the other on a variety of occasions.[353] Both took it for granted that they could make full and unrestricted use of each other's writings, and this freedom they granted each other as a matter of course was in sharp contrast with the touchiness they felt about the unauthorized use of their ideas by third persons, as well as about the possibility that others might come up with similar ideas before them. For the entire duration of their partnership, they never ceased furnishing each other materials and ideas. Indeed, they functioned as ghostwriters for each other. This, however, was rather one-sided, since very little that was written by Marx appeared under Engels's name—the major exception is one chapter in *Anti-Dühring*, which was entirely written by Marx—whereas there is a mass of material written by Engels but publicly attributed to Marx.

In this regard, financial and political considerations exerted an influence. Politically, it was important for Engels to keep his communist activities secret from his family and his employer, indeed from the entire business community to which he belonged. In the earlier years of his work in Manchester, he might have jeopardized his position by any outside journalistic activities, whether revolutionary or not. Marx, having severed all his ties with the bourgeois world except in his appearance and lifestyle, could afford to publish under his name. Not only that, for financial reasons he was desperately dependent on any journalistic work he might find.

Not long after settling in England, Marx had become acquainted with Charles A. Dana, then editor of the left-of-center *New York Daily Tribune*, and had impressed him with his sharp mind and his knowledge of world affairs. In the summer of 1851, Dana approached Marx with a proposal to write a number of articles on recent German politics for the *Tribune*. In effect, he was suggesting that Marx become the European correspondent for the paper. He offered good pay for articles on a variety of subjects and wished to begin at once with a series of articles on the course of the 1848 revolution in Germany. He asked that the first such piece be delivered in a very short time.

For Marx, this was a golden opportunity to earn some cash through the use of some of his best talents. Bur there were difficulties. He did not write English well. Indeed, it was not until 1856 that he proudly showed Engels the first English-language article he had written all by himself, and was relieved by Engels's approval, although irritated at the same time that his friend felt the need to proofread it.[354] Indeed, he never learned to speak English without an accent, and his writing was still unidiomatic at times, even after he had been in England for thirty years.[355] Further, even though this journalistic work might be pleasant, Marx regarded it as an intrusion into his concerns with economic theory. Other interferences were provided by his domestic misery and by the recurrent conflicts within the socialist émigré community. Thus, Marx had no sooner received Dana's offer, and accepted it, than he turned to Engels with the request to write an article on Germany for the *Tribune* and deliver it within a week. Dana, he added, need never know who wrote it.[356]

Engels had no idea what kind of paper the *Tribune* was. Marx's letter also left him in the dark whether he should write one article or several, and whether there might be other topics on which they might write contributions to the paper.[357] Nevertheless, he sat down at once to the work and began to produce articles for the New York paper in almost assembly-line fashion. The contributions he made ranged over an impressive variety of topics. First came a book-length series of articles on German politics from 1848 to 1850, which was published as a book under Marx's name, and for which Marx continued to claim authorship all his life, even in letters to his friends.[358] Engels did not reveal his own authorship until almost ten years after Marx's death.[359] After that came a long series of articles by Marx, dealing with English politics and international affairs, as well as a few articles on international politics by Engels, and an occasional piece written jointly. A steady stream of contributions crossed the Atlantic for about ten years, each article channeling much-needed money into Marx's pocket.

Although Engels made this work possible by quickly coming up with the first series of articles, the number of contributions written by Marx is a multiple of what Engels wrote. Still, some of Engels's work is hidden in them, if only because in the first years he had to translate every one of Marx's pieces into English.[360] To this one might add the observation that in the second half of the 1850s, a German-language outlet became open to Marx through the good offices of Ferdinand Lassalle. This was the *Neue Oder-Zeitung*, which also paid well for contributions. Many of the articles Marx placed there were nothing less than the translations of articles written by Engels and published in the *New York Daily Tribune*.[361]

For Engels, this work was a hated chore. He thought poorly of his contributions, believing them to be journalistic hackwork written under the most unfavorable conditions, so that from one week to the next he forgot what he had written. He complained that this quickie journalism had a dehumanizing effect on him, and expressed contempt for a paper that would print such stuff.[362] In America, however, they were exceedingly successful and were regarded as some of the best journalism that had ever been published there. Articles by Marx and Engels published in the *Tribune* were widely reprinted or quoted in other papers, and the editors of the *Tribune* were so proud of their European correspondent that they repeatedly congratulated themselves—and him—in their editorials.

Dana's pleasure with his European correspondent (he did not suspect that there was an alter ego in Manchester) was so great that in 1854 he asked Marx to write a series of magazine articles on the history of German philosophy from Kant to the present. An honorarium of fifty to sixty pounds Sterling beckoned Marx, who immediately turned to his friend with the suggestion that they do these articles together, because all by himself he would not have the courage.[363] Apparently Engels did not have it either, for nothing came of this proposal. Three years later, however, Dana came up with another project. He had just then consented to become editor of an ambitious encyclopedia work, the *New American Cyclopedia*, and suggested that Marx, whom he knew (or thought he knew) as a brilliant writer on military, political, philosophical, and economic matters, write a large number of encyclopedia articles for this new venture.

Again the money was alluring, and this time Engels was so enthusiastic that he suggested to Marx that they do the entire encyclopedia all by themselves.[364] Nothing came of this bold proposal, and indeed the onset of the American Civil War interrupted the publication of the reference work after only a few volumes had come out. Yet, the articles on military history, technology, organization, and leaders that Marx did submit to Dana, and for which he received pay, fill 380 closely printed pages in the *Collected Works*. Almost every word was written by Engels, most of it under much pressure and in a great hurry. Marx was anxious to keep his connection with Dana, while Engels was at that time very busy in his firm. His father had just died, and there were tedious negotiations with Gottfried Ermen. Late in his life, Engels dismissed these articles as pure hackwork not worth republishing.[365]

Engels helped Marx not only by contributing hastily written moneymakers. He also provided him with ideas—sometimes, crucial ones. I have already pointed out how much Engels had contributed toward the formulation of their common doctrine between 1844 and 1848, including the form and contents of as important a work as the Communist Manifesto. Henceforth, their exchange of ideas concerned details far more than grand design, but some of these details were important. Thus, Engels was the one who initiated an exchange of ideas between them about the nature of Oriental despotism and the Asian mode of production.[366] In the first version of his major work, the *Grundrisse*, Marx took over the ideas Engels had given him—lock, stock, and barrel.

Similarly, the judgment Marx expressed on the work of Darwin was copied almost word for word from a letter Engels had sent him some months before.[367] And it obviously was Engels who inspired Marx to write his first important work of political analysis, *The 18th Brumaire of Louis Bonaparte*. He not only gave Marx the general idea about which the book should be written, but also suggested the title, and the introductory page, in which the entire work is neatly and pungently summarized, is only a rephrasing of the letter from Engels.[368] Apparently, Marx soon forgot how much he owed his friend in the case of this book. In a letter to Engels he patted himself on the back for having come up with the ironic observation in its first sentence.[369]

When the two friends moved to England in 1850, their common resolve was that Marx should resume the study of political economy, which Engels's work had first stimulated him to do in 1844, so that he might develop the theoretical underpinning for the theory of capitalism, which again Engels had developed in his economic essay of 1844 and in his book on the English working class. The task was nothing less than the critical examination of all past and present economic theories and their replacement by a new theory that would analyze the development, working, and impending collapse of capitalism. This would be the theoretical capstone of their joint work. Having determined the economic workings of society to be the base on which all other social institutions and relations rested, and having observed those regularities in economic life that could be described as the laws of capitalist development, the principal theoretical task remaining for them was to find the explanation for these laws. Cornerstones are laid first. Capstones come last. Searching for the explanation of phenomena observed and described quite properly comes after the presentation of these general laws.

All socialist economics, Engels wrote in later life, was derived from Ricardo's theory of value, according to which labor was the sole measure of value, and from his division of society into three classes, which led to the classification of all products into the three categories of rent, profit, and wages.[370] It could be plausibly argued that Marx's contribution to socialist economic theory consisted in the inversion of these Ricardoan doctrines. He inverted the labor theory of value by treating labor itself as a commodity with very peculiar qualities. This in turn led to the ingenious distinction between labor and labor power, the latter being the one commodity that, by being used, creates value.[372] He also devised the theory of surplus value, which in his opinion rendered much of the writings of the classical economists like Ricardo, with their puzzlement over the differences between rent, profit, and wage, superfluous.[372]

From the beginning of their joint endeavors, it was Marx's aim to arrive at these theoretical formulas. Then, of course, he faced the task of depicting the entire capitalist production process and its development in a vast, all-encompassing panorama, for the purpose of verifying his theory. Marx had first planned to do this work in 1844. Engels urged his friend to complete it quickly so it could be "hurled into the world." Soon, he showed impatience at Marx's failure to produce a manuscript and began to give him some good advice on work discipline. He would do this many times in subsequent decades.[373] But all that Marx got done, in addition to accumulating a mass of notes, was the unpublished (and unpublishable) fragments known today as the Economic-Philosophic Manuscripts of 1844.

Now, in the fall of 1850, Marx again set out briskly to familiarize himself with all pertinent material, most of which was totally new to him. He found out fairly quickly that he disliked economics, and that the project was like a millstone around his neck. "I will be done with the entire economic shit in another five weeks," he wrote to Engels on April 2, 1851. "Once that is done, I will work this economics out at home, and in the Museum throw myself on another branch of learning. It is beginning to irk me." Engels agreed with him. "I am glad that you are at last done with the book on economics," her wrote Marx. "Really, that thing took much too long, and as long as you still have a book in front of you that you consider important but have not read, you won't get down to writing anyway."[374]

Three months later, however, Marx was still collecting material and now thought he needed two months more, since the material was terribly complicated. The misery of his domestic life weighed upon him and prevented him from working. "I would long ago have been finished at the library," he wrote to Engels at the end of July 1851, "but the interruptions and interferences are too great, and at home, where everyone always sits in a state of siege, and rivers of tears annoy and enrage me through entire nights, I cannot do much, of course. I pity my wife. She bears the brunt of the pressure and *au fond* she is right. *Il faut que l'industrie soit plus productive que le mariage.* Despite it all, you will remember that I am *trés peu endurant* and indeed *quelque peu dur*, so that from time to time my equanimity is lost."[375] Still, despite all sorts of annoyances, he wrote to a friend in America that the thing was rushing toward its conclusion, and one had to call a decisive halt at some point.[376]

Four months later, Marx was quite deeply bogged down in economic matters and began to look for help from Engels. Thus, in late October he asked him to give him his critique of a new book by Proudhon, and when Engels sent him a lengthy critique the following month, he liked it so much he thought it ought to be published. "Too bad," he wrote, "we do not have the means for putting it out. Otherwise I would have added my own crap (*meinen Seich*), and it could appear under our joint authorship, provided this did not get you into trouble with your firm."[377] Engels answered by dismissing his critique as insignificant. In addition, he did not wish to see another book-writing project like that which produced *The Holy Family*, where Marx wrote fifteen pages for every page by Engels. "Your heavy artillery," he replied, "would make my portion disappear."[378] Nonetheless, he accompanied this refusal with a plan for a publication on economics, to be prepared by Marx and to be published in several volumes, which in effect proposed the format and rough outlines of what was to become Marx's principal contribution. Engels thus suggested the outline of *Das Kapital.*

Bogged down by domestic misery, by illness, by the never ceasing activity of grinding out article after article for the *New York Daily Tribune* and other papers, by nasty squabbles within the émigré community that ate up time and emotional energy, by the immensity of the task, by his own perfectionism, as well as by the revulsion which this material induced in him—bogged down by a myriad of obstacles and hindrances, Marx nonetheless continued working on his project, and the mass of material grew enormously. The accumulating work was rarely discussed between the two friends—in fact, hardly mentioned—with no indication that Engels had even a remote idea of what had or had not been done. With a few exceptions, Marx seldom if ever consulted him on any theoretical questions.

What boosted the work more than any other factor was the brief but severe economic crash of late 1857. Marx and Engels, a year after moving to England, had convinced themselves that Europe had settled down to temporary stability in a conservative order that would be shaken only during the next economic decline. They had predicted that this decline would begin in 1857. And, in 1857, it came, and with it the expectation of a new revolution. Here Marx did not wish to be caught theoretically unprepared. He now worked feverishly through the nights like a madman (to use his own words) to get the work together so that at least the outlines of the theory would be clear before the revolution began, and also, he said, "for me, personally, to get rid of this nightmare."[379]

Indeed, between November 1857 and March 1858 he produced a gigantic manuscript. Filling more than a thousand printed pages, this was in effect the first draft of *Das Kapital.* He knew even while writing this massive draft that it was not publishable in its present form, and would have to be rewritten. Even before the draft was finished, he began inquiries into the possibility of publishing the revised version in installments.[380] Six weeks later, he sent a rather brief outline of the total work to Engels, together with an abstract of the first installment planned for publication. This first installment appeared one year later under the title *Critique of Political Economy*. Engels found the abstract hard to understand, partly because it was too brief and cryptic, but also, he thought, because he was no longer used to abstract reasoning, and he expressed confidence that in the fully worked-out version the abstract, dialectical tone would disappear.[381] Almost eight years later, Marx reported to Engels that "this cursed book" had now been rewritten, but was still too unwieldy to be publishable. So now, on the first of January 1866, he had begun to rewrite it once more, volume by volume.[382]

I have related the genesis of *Das Kapital*, as it presented itself to Engels, in some detail in order to show the human side of this remarkable relationship, in which for two decades these two men did something they hated with a vengeance—Engels his penal servitude with his firm, and Marx his labors on what again and again he called "that shit." Engels made his sacrifice for Marx, but he also goaded Marx into making his own, and Marx must have felt a compelling obligation to finish the work, if only for the sake of his partner. This mutual sacrifice must have been emotional dynamite. The goading was painful for both, and so was the work itself, which Marx came to hate with increasing passion. The delay irked both of them, especially when they sensed that some other writer might anticipate their work. When J. K. Rodbertus, a German economist of socialist leanings, came out with a critique of Ricardo's theory of rent, something on which Marx had been working and would be working until the end of his life, Engels could not conceal his anger at the delay in the work, and Marx was so threatened by the news that he did not even acknowledge it.[383]

More than once, Marx wrote to friends that he really would like to devote himself to quite different themes. For instance, in a letter to Joseph Dietzgen dated May 9, 1868, he described himself foremost as a philosopher who wished he had time to write a new Dialectic. Yet the work obsessed him, so much so that even on his daughter Laura's honeymoon, he asked her to obtain books for him. "You will surely imagine, my dear child," he wrote her, "that I love books very much, because I am troubling you with this at such an inopportune time. But you would be very much mistaken. I am a machine condemned to devour them and then throw them, in a changed form, onto the dung heap of history."[384]

Totally absorbed in this work, he turned quite anti-social at times.[385] And still he worked on. "Why don't I answer you?" he wrote to a friend in the United States. "Because I am constantly hovering on the edge of the grave. Hence I must use *every* day on which I can work in order to complete a work to which I have sacrificed my health, my happiness, and my family... I laugh at the so-called 'practical' men and their wisdom. If one wanted to be an ox, he could, of course, turn his back on the torments of humanity and care for his own skin. But I really would have considered myself unpractical if I had croaked without completely finishing my book, at least in manuscript form."[386]

To this, finally, was added his perfectionism, which would not allow him to do anything by half, or to publish a line before every possible source of evidence had been examined. "I cannot," he wrote letter to Engels, "get myself to send away anything before the total work is in front of me. Whatever shortcomings they may have, that is the virtue of my writings—that they are an artistic whole—and that is attainable only in my manner, never to have them printed before they lie in front of me in their entirety. With the method of Jacob Grimm this is impossible, and in any event it is more feasible for writings that are not structured dialectically."[387] In a subsequent letter, he added, "You understand, dear fellow, that in a work such as mine there must be many shortcomings in details. But the composition, the coherence, is a triumph of German science, which an individual is allowed to acknowledge because it is in no way *his* merit, but rather belongs to the nation. This is even more enjoyable because otherwise it is the silliest nation under the sun!"[388]

Engels obviously got as obsessed with the work as Marx himself did. "On the day on which the manuscript is sent out, I will get mercilessly drunk," he wrote, "except if you come the next day and we can do it together."[389] When the first volume was finally ready for print, and Marx reported this in a deceptively casual note, Engels replied with a shout of hurrah that he said was irrepressible.[390] Only when the proofs had been read and had gone back to the printer did Marx allow his emotions to be expressed. "So this volume is done," he wrote. Only *you* deserve my thanks for making this possible! Without your self-sacrifice for me I could not possibly have done the tremendous amounts of work for the three volumes. I embrace you, full of thanks! *Salut*, my dear, beloved friend!"[391]

Engels gave more to this book than his impetus, prodding, and support. The most important additional contributions he made to it consisted of practical information about commerce and industry. This was a world that Marx knew from several points of view—those of a lawyer, a well-read social scientist, and a pauper-victim—while Engels, by contrast, knew it more first-hand as a manufacturer, businessman, and member of the Cotton Exchange. Through him, Marx therefore had access of a special kind to the business world, and he made much use of it, asking Engels a wealth of questions dealing with such practical matters as depreciation accounting and other bookkeeping matters, currency exchange problems, production techniques, the English and German names for machine parts, the circulation of capital in various branches of industry, and the proportion of variable to constant capital within them.

In addition to furnishing large amounts of such information, Engels also gave Marx access to figures on building costs, machinery turnover, and other technical matter through another firm owned by the Ermen brothers.[392] Later, when Marx was collecting additional material for Volumes II and III of the work, Engels provided information about land tenure laws and customs in Ireland and Scotland, especially the method by which landlords could evict their peasants and tenants.[393] Marx also consulted him on more theoretical questions and submitted ideas, drafts, and outlines to him for judgment. In sending him the proofs for *The Critique of Political Economy* for comment he pointed out that Engels's judgment alone was important to him and that he was awaiting his opinion with some anxiety—to the great amusement of his wife, he added.[394] And in fact, Engels gave criticism and advice not only in this case, but also when he received the first proofs of *Das Kapital*.[395]

Consultations of this kind occurred from the beginning to the end of Marx's work on this book, starting in early 1851, when he submitted for Engels's criticism an elaborate theory of money circulation and its relationship to the business cycle, to which Engels responded with care.[396] For forty years, Marx wrestled with the problem of how to deal with Ricardo's theory of rent. In 1851, he sent an early attempt to solve the puzzle to Engels, who this time took his time replying. Eventually, he wrote that he thought Marx had arrived at a brilliant solution that he, given his weakness in theory, would never have been able to devise, yet at the same time pointed out that some references to the puzzle could already be found in his own 1844 article on political economy.[397] The problem continued to trouble Marx, and after Volume I had come out, the two had a lengthy correspondence about it, during which Engels furnished Marx with an entire little treatise on the history and origins of rent.[398] On the whole however, it is even more striking how few such inquiries Marx made, how solitary was the work of this man, and how reluctant he must have been to enlist help and advice, even from his friend, his partner, and his alter ego.

Engels, in turn, seems to have been reluctant, overall, to get involved in this theoretical enterprise. We have already seen how decisively he rejected Marx's proposal that they publish some work on economic theory jointly, and how hesitant he was to discuss theory with Marx. As for Marx's inquiries, some were not answered at all, or at least we have no record of any answers. One example is a letter in which Marx sent Engels his modification of Quesnay's *Tableau Economique* in July 1863, followed six weeks later by additional reports of progress on this work. In another case, Marx communicated to Engels some important ideas concerning profit rate. When Engels replied with some minor criticism, he sent a long reply that went entirely unanswered.[399] At times, Engels apologized for not answering such inquiries, pleading that he took them too seriously to venture hasty comments, or that at the moment he was too busy in the firm. He also claimed that the day-to-day concern with business matters rendered him incapable of dealing with abstract theoretical material.[400] One gets the impression that Engels was as bored with economic theory as Marx himself, or at least that he was quite satisfied with the division of labor between them, which left this area to be worked out by Marx.

Of course, once Volume I was published, Engels studied it carefully and made copious notes, which, however, do not go to the end of the book.[401] After reading the first few chapters in proof, he expressed general satisfaction, even though he found the structure of the work obscure, the dialectical transitions slurred over, and the style in places marked by "a melancholy carbuncle imprint" (*ein gedrücktes Karbunkelgepräge*). Marx replied by assuring him that his satisfaction with this first batch of proofs was "more important to me than anything the rest of the world may say of it. In any event I hope that the bourgeoisie will think of my carbuncles as long as it lives."[402]

As he read additional chapters, Engels became more critical. The structure of the book, he said, was impossible. One chapter was two hundred pages long and had almost no subdivisions. The argument was constantly interrupted by the interjection of illustrative materials. Once the illustrations were presented, no resume of the main point was offered. Instead, all of a sudden, the reader found himself in the midst of a discussion of a new point. He found the task of reading this work terribly fatiguing and confusing, and confessed that there were some things he did not fully understand.[403] He was enthusiastic about the final chapters, however, especially the description of the formation of capital and the origins of surplus value. Clear as sunlight, he called these sections,[404] and his final verdict was that the book would have a sensational effect.

Engels had the idea of heightening this effect by promoting the sale of the book and calling attention to it in the German press. For this purpose, he proposed to employ what he called "little maneuvers." This meant that he would write reviews of the book from the bourgeois point of view and plant them, anonymously and through intermediaries, in the bourgeois press,[405] a scheme with which Marx agreed enthusiastically.[406] Engels even suggested attacking the book in reactionary papers[407] or making so much noise about it in some fashion or other that the authorities would denounce it.[408] "In this case," he wrote to Dr. Kugelmann, "we must, to speak with our old friend Jesus Christ, be innocent as doves and sly as snakes."[409] Since Marx himself refused to write these reviews, and the two friends did not trust Kugelmann, their front man in this case, to do them properly, Engels wrote them, and he must have had much fun posing as a manufacturer for a manufacturer's paper, as a Prussian Liberal for a Prussian Liberal paper, as an anti-Prussian for a Southwestern bourgeois paper, and so forth.

Writing these reviews was not the last work this "cursed book" caused him. Years later, after Marx's death, he would have to spend tremendous amounts of time and skill for the preparation of English- and French-language editions. There would also be many years of hard work on Volumes II and III. I will conclude my account of the relationship between Marx and Engels with some observations about these two volumes, but before I do that, it seems proper to present some generalization about how they themselves thought about each other.

In many ways and to many people Marx described Engels as his best friend, his alter ego, a man on whose judgment he relied absolutely, on whose approval he depended, and whose company he needed for relief from his darkest moods or just for the warmth of his friendship. To the pretty cousin with whom he flirted in Holland, he described their friendship as like that of Orestes and Plyades. When Engels was about to move to London, Marx wrote to his daughter and son-in-law, "That will be a great joy for me."[410] In times of great distress, he was moved to confess his friendship also to the friend himself.

There is a letter in which he describes his carbuncles in detail, and how he lanced one of them himself because he could not tolerate physicians touching him near the more sensitive parts of his anatomy. "Dear boy," he then adds, "under all these circumstances one feels more than ever the happiness of the kind of friendship existing between us.

You in your turn know that there is no other relationship that I value as highly."[411] That there were factors straining the friendship is obvious. Guilt, shame, and the never-ending need to be grateful must have been hard to bear. If Marx ever expressed other feelings of resentment or criticism, the evidence was destroyed after his death, when his daughters went through his private correspondence.[412] Heaven only knows what they might have contained. From what we know about Marx, he was quite capable of prolonged duplicity, especially in his relations with people from whom he hoped to receive financial and political aid. Thus his letters to Lassalle abounded with expressions of friendship, esteem, and approbation at the very same time when to Engels he indulged in vicious slurs about him.

As it is, therefore, we have only occasional glimpses at irritations over his friend's interference in his own affairs. H. M. Hyndman, who was by no means an unbiased observer, asserts that Jenny Marx openly deplored her husband's dependence on Engels and that she bitterly called him Marx's evil genius.[413] The poor woman may in fact have vented her chronic desperation in this fashion, but she also often turned to Engels as to a friend in whom she could confide and from whom she could expect more than just financial help. Marx himself, in the last months of his life, when he was physically and emotionally spent, expressed irritation over Engels's solicitude: "Sanguine, good old Fred, who, I repeat it, I say it amongst you and myself, will easily kill someone out of love."[414] Both he and Jenny at times seem to have resented the jolly middle-class life they thought Engels was leading in Manchester, and Marx may have resented even the time that Engels devoted to other friends.[415]

That Marx thought highly of Engels's work is quite obvious from their entire relationship, and was stated strongly to many people.[416] He did not, of course, indulge in the hero worship that Engels had developed toward him. For Engels, the older friend was the Copernicus or the Newton of social science, the man who had discovered the developmental law of human history and the special laws of movement governing contemporary bourgeois society, whose work constituted a revolution in historical understanding.[417] But he was also a friend, a brilliant conversation partner, and—important for Engels—a worthy drinking companion.[418] Engels felt at home with him and his family. He may have been a bit reserved with Jenny Marx, but he was very close to the Marx daughters and was their fatherly friend. Laura refused to reply to Paul Lafargue's marriage proposal before Engels had been consulted. Whenever Engels could get away from Manchester during his twenty years there he tended to go to London to visit Marx.

In the face of his friend's chronic inability to get work done, even when timely delivery was essential, Engels's patience at times wore thin.[419] Other causes for irritation were Marx's financial irresponsibility, his slow progress in learning to speak English well, and his messy filing system, in which once in a while a book or document got lost.[420] Despite such strains, the friendship was threatened seriously only once, at the time Mary Burns died. She passed away suddenly at the age of about forty, in January 1863. She and Engels had known and loved each other for twenty years, and had lived together for about fifteen. The letter in which Engels notified his friend was short and curiously unemotional. "I cannot tell you how I feel," he did say, but then added only once sentence: "The poor girl loved me with all her heart." Did he wish to imply, consciously or not, that he had not loved her? To be sure, in a later letter to Marx he confessed that in burying her, he had felt he was burying the last piece of his youth.[421]

Marx's letter of condolence was far more remarkable. It must be compared with the warm and sensitive letters Engels wrote on such occasions. The news, wrote Marx, had surprised and shaken him. "She was very good-natured, witty, and very much attached to you," he said. This was followed by a long Jeremiad, several pages long, about his own financial troubles, and finally a postscript: "How will you rearrange your own establishment now? It is extraordinarily hard for you, since at Mary's place you had a home that was free and withdrawn from all human dirt, as often as you wanted."[422] Engels was at first too hurt to reply at all. When he did reply, he struck out the most offensive passages from his first draft, but felt bitter enough to point out that his bourgeois friends in Manchester had behaved more decently than Marx had. In time, Marx apologized, pointing out that cynicism was the only remedy he had against his own and other people's suffering. Engels accepted this apology with alacrity, and the rift was healed.

To round out the story of this remarkable friendship, we must now turn our attention to Volumes II and III of *Das Kapital* (forgetting about the projected Volume IV). Volume I had been finished and published in 1867. The source material for the subsequent volumes had been collected. The total work existed in draft form—but then various drafts had existed for many years, yet had been deemed unsuitable for publication. Still, this time Marx seemed to feel that the bulk of the work had been accomplished. Even while Volume I was being printed, he and his publisher worked out a schedule for publishing the other two volumes. Volume II was to be in the hands of the publisher six months after the delivery of the manuscript for Volume I (i.e., late summer or early fall of 1867), and Volume III was to be written during the next winter, so that by the spring of 1868 Marx was scheduled to have completed the entire work. Things did not, however, go quite that smoothly. Nonetheless, in August 1868 Marx hoped to have it all done by September 1869,[423] and two months later he was even more optimistic, expressing confidence that he would finish it by the spring of 1869.[424]

The spring came, and Marx wrote to his friend Kugelmann that he expected to have the work finished that summer and would then come to Germany with the manuscript, presumably to deliver it to the publisher.[425] From this trip he returned irritable, sick, and plagued with a new outburst of carbuncles, but eager to throw himself into the intensive study of Russian.[426] He had decided that his study of the problem of ground rent would not be complete without data about land tenure patterns in Russia. Indeed, from then on until his death, he remained preoccupied with this problem and collected masses of material that he read, but without transforming his notes into anything more organized. In December he wrote to one of his Russian friends that Volume II would contain a detailed discussion of the Russian form of landed property, but that work was never even begun.[427]

After 1869, work on Volumes II and III was rarely mentioned, most rarely, it seems, to Engels. The only indications Engels received that Marx was working on his economic theory came from occasional requests for some books or journals, and even these came seldom. Engels, in turn, does not seem to have discussed the matter with Marx very much, except for recurrent admonitions that he take better care of himself, cure his ailments, and get well again so that he might be able to resume his work.[428] After he moved to London, he would force Marx to take vigorous walks with him. He himself craved the exercise as well as the company, and he told himself that it was good medicine for his friend.[429] It is unlikely that Volumes II and III were discussed on such occasions. Indeed, it seems they were not discussed at all between 1870 and Marx's death in 1883, or most rarely and indirectly.

Marx occasionally discussed the progress of his work with others. In the spring of 1871, his friend German Aleksandrovich Lopatin was spreading the rumor that the manuscript for Volume II had been finished, but that the publisher did not want to print it until all the remaining copies of Volume I had been sold. This, wrote Marx, was based on a misunderstanding. "I have deemed a thorough revision of the manuscript to be necessary," he stated in a letter to Nikolai Danielson, another correspondent.[430] The implication that indeed there was a ready manuscript escaped the recipient, and Engels did not get to see this letter until many years later. To Kugelmann he wrote in May 1874 that he had collected much more material but still had had no time to work on it.[431]

The year before, he had been experimenting with attempts to treat the business cycle econometrically by devising a mathematical model of it—whether this interest had any connection with work on Volumes II and III is not entirely clear.[432] Toward the end of 1880 he was still collecting new material, this time on the economics of California. "California," he wrote to yet another correspondent, "is very important to me because there is no other place in which the revolution through capitalist centralization has proceeded in this most shameless fashion— in such haste."[433] Why all this procrastination?

One could imagine a long list of things that prevented Marx from working on the completion of his magnum opus—the state of his health and the declining health of his wife, excitement over the war of 1870, the Paris Commune, and the misery of the Commune refugees who fled to England, as well as the necessity to write about the events, the interminable squabble with rival émigré groups within the International Workingmen's Association, which culminated in the Hague congress of this First International, work on the second edition of Volume I, intensive preoccupation with the study of Russian and of such disparate fields as natural science, anthropology, and Russian, and work on the translation of the *Manifesto* and Volume I of *Das Kapital* into French. The list is sufficient to explain Marx's inability to finish the work. But did he really mean to finish it?

As early as 1872, Marx spoke about *Das Kapital* in a letter to an American friend as if no further volumes would be forthcoming—as if it were a finished work.[434] Seven years later, when the anti-socialist law passed in Germany made it impossible for Marx to publish anything further in that country, he expressed satisfaction over the long, perhaps indefinite, delay caused by this, obviously pleased to have an excuse for not finishing. The reasons he gave at this time were not only the state of his health and his desire to incorporate material dealing with Russia and America into the work, but also the then current economic crisis in England. This crisis, Marx wrote, had many unusual and unprecedented features, and therefore had to be studied so that these novel developments could be incorporated into the theoretical work.[435] One gets the feeling here that Marx had undertaken the impossible task of writing a definitive work about something forever in motion—the capitalist system—a Sisyphean labor that could not possibly be completed because despite the perpetual incorporation of new materials it would always be obsolete. By the mid-seventies, Marx was no longer seriously attempting this inhuman labor.

By that time, Marx had become a prematurely old man who still observed the world around him with a penetrating eye and described it with sardonic wit, who received visitors with impressive dignity, scrutinizing them sharply through his monocle, and who still read prodigious amounts of material in half a dozen languages. He was rarely well enough for sustained work, however, and from the point of view of his work most of the time during the last eight or nine years of his life was lost in an attempt to regain his strength. This therefore became Engels's preoccupation, too, and it is expressed again and again not only in his correspondence but even in an occasional published piece.[436]

After Marx was dead and buried, Engels's immediate concern was to investigate the state of the manuscripts for Volumes II and III. Nine days after Marx's passing, Helen Demuth, his old housekeeper, found them, neatly tied together in a huge package. Engels examined these during the next few weeks and was astonished by what he found. He seemed to have a finished manuscript on his hands, and it had been completed before 1870. It was written totally in the Gothic script that Marx had given up around that year.[437] Closer examination revealed that Volume II had indeed been drafted around 1870, except that its middle part had been written earlier, and there were four different versions of this. For the beginning and the end, all that remained to be done was to put in quotations and notes. As for Volume III, there were two versions, both dating from the middle or late 1860s, besides this only some notes and mathematical calculations, in which Marx had tried to render the transformation of the rate of surplus value into the rate of profit, and then a mass of undigested notes about Russia and the United States, plus a scattering of notes on various other topics.[438]

In a letter to Marx's daughter Laura, Engels was more precise. What the package contained were the following: (1) the first draft, today known as the *Grundrisse*, which was finished in early 1858, (2) manuscripts entitled *Theories on Surplus Value*, written in 1861-63, but not completed, (3) Volume II of *Das Kapital*, completed in 1868 or 1869, i.e. before Marx's trip to Germany, but obviously not considered fit for publication, since there were three or four manuscripts in which Marx had attempted to revise the book, and (4) Volume III of *Das Kapital*, completed in 1869 or 1879 and never touched again, although it was obvious that the mass of undigested material on Russia and

American was intended to be integrated into this volume.[439]

In August of 1883, Engels began to work on the task of preparing Volume II for publication. He found that he had overestimated somewhat its state of readiness. Some sections he found incomplete, others only sketched, and the whole manuscript, he thought, with the exception of two chapters, was no more than drafts, with the notes in a hopeless mess, haphazardly thrown together for selection of suitable ones at a later time, all of this in a handwriting hardly legible even to Engels himself.[440] Nonetheless, the amazing fact remained that all that was there had been lying around without being touched for ten to fifteen years, and that Marx had let not a single person have an inkling of how close the work was to being completed.

"It is hardly comprehensible," wrote Engels to Laura in 1885, "how a man who had such powerful discoveries in his head, such an all-embracing and complete revolution of knowledge, could keep them to himself for twenty years. For the manuscript on which I am working now (Engels was by this time working on Volume III) was written either before, or together with, Volume I, and the most substantial part of it is contained already in the old 1860-62 manuscript. The fact is that he first of all was delayed by the difficulties of Volume II (which he wrote last, and which is the only one on which he still worked after 1870), since, of course, he wished to publish his three volumes in the correct sequence. Furthermore, his Russian and American material for the history of ground rent should still have been worked into the old manuscript, and that would probably have nearly doubled its dimensions."[441]

Later in the same year, Danielson sent him copies of his correspondence with Marx, which included some of his explanations for not having completed the work, which by now appeared transparent. Engels confessed that he could not read these letters without a painful smile. "Yes, indeed," he wrote Danielson, "we are so used to these excuses for the non-completion of the work! Whenever his state of health did not permit him to work on his project he was very depressed, and was only too glad to find some theoretical excuse for the fact that the work was not then being completed. In the course of time he used all these arguments *vis-à-vis de moi.* They seemed to calm his conscience."[442]

Two questions nonetheless remain. First, why did Marx, if he was so bogged down by theoretical questions, not consult his partner? Why are there no letters in which he shares his agonies over these problems, why no evidence that they ever discussed these matters? Here Engels may have indicated to him sufficiently often that he did not care to be consulted, although that is at best a partial explanation. The second question is equally puzzling: Why did Marx hide from his partner the true state of the manuscripts? Why did he not even give a hint as to how close he was to completing them? To this question, Engels suggested an answer. "Very simple," he wrote. "If I had known, I would not have given him any rest by day or by night until it would have been totally completed and published, and that is something Marx knew better than anyone else. He also knew that, in the worst possible case, which has happened now, I could edit the manuscript in his spirit, and he said so to Tussy."[443] Tussy was Marx's youngest daughter, Eleanor, and what he actually said to her, with surprising nonchalance, was that unfinished manuscripts for the remaining volumes of *Das Kapital* existed. They would find them after his death, and perhaps Engels might be able to make something out of them.

Marx had become tired of being goaded. He wanted his peace, and he kept Engels at arm's length. At the same time, he trusted him to complete the work—or else he no longer cared. In sharpest contrast to Engels, he may also have become a pessimist, or at least succumbed to bouts of pessimism, and if this is true, he may on occasions have questioned the meaningfulness of his entire life's work. Earlier, I quoted his letter of praise for Engels's *The Condition of the Working Class in England.* How unpleasant, he wrote at that time was the contrast between the exuberance, directness, and optimism of this book and the later "gray-in-gray." Among scholars, only Steven Marcus has picked up this allusion to the famous passage in Hegel's *Philosophy of Right*, where the great philosopher makes clear that philosophy can never prescribe but only explain—and then only after it is too late.[444] "When philosophy paints its gray-in-gray," wrote Hegel, "then has the shape of life grown old. By philosophy's gray-in-gray, it cannot be rejuvenated, but only understood. The owl Minerva spreads its wings only with the falling of dusk."[445] Having pointed this out, what Marcus omits to state is that Marx here expressed his sense of despair. He intimated that he no longer was confident that he could help change the world. Instead, all he could do was to interpret it.

Indeed, even when observing revolutionary stirrings, Marx by this time no longer believed that all this might be for the good. Thus, the Polish uprising of 1863 seemed to him to signal the beginning of a new era of revolutions in Europe. In stating this, however, he added that the cozy delusions and childish enthusiasm he and Engels shared in 1848 had now gone to the Devil. "We are more alone now than we were then," he wrote, "and also we now know what role stupidity plays in revolutions and how revolutions are exploited by scoundrels.[446] Similar notes of skepticism and near-despair are not found in the writings of Engels. For this, quite possibly, Marx in his gloomier moments thought him naïve.

CONCLUSION

PORTRAITURE IS NOT only a genre of pictorial art but, as well, of historiography. The painter, sculptor, historian, and photographer all face analogous problems. Wishing to render a recognizable image, a true likeness of their subject, they must study the person as carefully as possible. But that has its obvious limitations. Exhaustive study is out of the question. At some point of saturation, they must stop observing and start painting, writing, or whatever their medium may be. This is true especially because faithful portraiture demands careful study of far more than the subject. The study must include the entire world in which the subject lives or lived. Deftly suggesting this *milieu* with sparing means on a limited canvas is part of the art.

Moreover, because the medium necessarily is limited, every portrait must omit some traits of the subject and his or her environment. If everything one knew were to be included, the portrait would be too cluttered. It would be without structure, hence uninteresting, boring, and artistically unappealing. Indeed, while omitting some of the traits observed, the artist, in order to render a likeness worth our attention, must feel free to bring out, if not exaggerate, those features he or she finds most striking. The historian must do this no less than the photographer, painter, or sculptor, and all of them purchase their license to do so by careful study of their subject, as well as by their honesty in rendering what they see.

Since no two portraits of the same person can ever be alike, there is no such thing as a definitive portrait. Nor should the existence of other artists' renditions discourage anyone from attempting his or her own. The more controversial the subject, the less thinkable is a definite biography. "What a wee little part of a person's life are his acts and his

305

words," wrote Mark Twain. "His real life is led in his head, and is known to none but himself."[447] In an intellectual biography, the person's words and how later generations have perceived them, may be more interesting than his 'real' life.

One fact that has emboldened me to write a life of Friedrich Engels is that he has 'sat' for a surprisingly small number of portrait artists. I have profited greatly from reading them, especially two massive works that are likely to be considered standard biographies—Gustav Mayer's *Friedrich Engels* and W. O. Henderson's *The Life of Friedrich Engels*—but I hope my own much less ambitious work furnishes glimpses of the subject that they have not provided.

My principal source has been the excellent edition of the collected works and correspondence of Marx and Engels prepared in the German Democratic Republic and published in 39 volumes (Volume 26 comes in three volumes of its own), plus two supplements. The only major inadequacy of this edition is that while it contains virtually everything Marx and Engels wrote, it presents it in German, disregarding the language in which it was originally written. Only the correspondence preserves the polyglot émigré jargon—a mixture of German, English, French, Latin, and other languages—that the two friends used.

Unless otherwise specified, all translations are my own. They often diverge from translations with which a reader might be familiar, though I have refrained, more often than not, from entering into arguments with other renditions of the suggestive prose of the two friends. The intensive use I have made of the correspondence is justified not only because in it they exchanged their thoughts frankly and revealingly, but also because they often wrote to each other and to third persons in the awareness or hope that some day these letters would be published. Hence, the letters are, as it were, official statements of their views.[448]

The book is based on published sources. I have not sought to uncover new information about Engels, but rather to reinterpret the information already available. Trying to unearth hitherto unpublished material on Engels might have been possible, but it would have cost vast amounts of money and time, and the results would most likely have been disappointing. Anyone steeping himself in the available materials would get to know the man quite well, including the names of his dogs, his physicians, his lovers, his toothaches, his favorite dishes, and the tone of voice he adopted in a variety of situations.

I would be faithless to Engels if I did not point out what a great delight it has been to thus get to know this charming, talented, hard-working man. At the same time, I must ask the reader to judge whether, with all his personal gifts and grace, Engels has taken me in and made me transform this biography into a hagiography. If he has charmed me, it is because very often I have found myself in agreement with him—and one point of this agreement lies in his refusal to recognize heroes, his realization that even the most admirable persons are human. Engels, in a joint work with Marx, aptly described what happens when this is forgotten. "The most trivial things that occur to all trivial people," he wrote, "become all-important events. The petty pains and joys that every student of theology experiences in a more interesting form, the conflicts with bourgeois conditions that can be found by the dozens in every convent and every consistory in Germany, are turned into fateful world events." Thus, the impression is created that the subject of the biography was a great man from the time he was an embryo.[449]

The reason why it has been delightful to write about Engels is that, on the whole, he led a happy life. If I had to pick a single short sentence of his to sum up his character and to serve as a motto for this book, I would choose the end of a speech he made to a workers' meeting in Vienna on 14 September 1893, less than two years before his death. *"Wir haben nicht umsonst gelebt!"* (We have not lived in vain) he said, at a very satisfying moment in his life, while making a triumphal tour through Europe as the acknowledged founding father of the burgeoning workers' movement.

In writing about Engels, I have sometimes mused about the ingredients of this rare state of mind called happiness, and in putting together a recipe for this elusive condition one cannot help drawing an abstract portrait of him. Happiness seems to consist, first, of a sense of oneness with the cosmos, an intellectual feeling that one understands reality, an aesthetic enjoyment of what nature and man have wrought, and a readiness to accept the facts of life and death with serenity. Second, happiness is promoted by a sense of independence, autonomy, or freedom, which may come from being wealthy or privileged, or from living in a permissive environment, or by having a personal spirit of independence that does not recognize the boundaries most people take for granted.

Further, since civilized people have developed a talent for boredom, happiness may require that variety of experiences which comes to people of polymorphous personal development—people of many different inclinations, talents, tastes, and activities, such as Engels. He possessed an agile mind in a robust body, and could have been described as a sportsman, amateur artist, man of affairs, and a scientist. He was a dabbler in a great variety of endeavors and quite good at many of them, a person with many friends from various walks of life, and a polyglot. In many of the things he did he was successful—in business, in politics, as a writer, and in acquiring friends and lovers. He was a thoroughly decent person with high moral sensibilities. Aware that he was living as an exploiter in an exploitative society, as a man in a sexist society, and as a European in the age of colonialism, he coped with the resulting moral dilemmas by directing his moral indignation at the system that produced them, and by exhibiting an unshakeable faith in the dawning of a better world. A handsome and energetic man, he had a fighting spirit, courage, dash, and persistence.

Did the Victorian Age in which he lived tend to produce people of such qualities, or must we explain his personality as an accident of heredity and psychological conditioning? As for the first hypothesis, it is true that Engels lived in an age that seems to have promoted optimistic views about inevitable progress. Engels could well be called the last great optimist among the major contributors to social theory. About the time of his death, this mood was beginning to dissolve, at least in the Western world, and it is questionable whether anyone has recaptured it. The psychological hypothesis cannot be answered, but it does suggest one puzzle. We often seem to take it for granted that people whom we consider great—the outstanding philosophers, artists, teachers, or leaders—have been shaped and conditioned by a more than ordinary degree of alienation, since by definition they are atypical. Suffering and sickness, in the minds of many people, are the Devil's price for outstanding achievement.[450] If we agree that Engels belongs among the great, he is clearly an exception to this rule, and this, too makes it a pleasure to write about him.

Nevertheless, Engels had his share of ordeals and inner conflicts. He had a tense Oedipal relationship with his father. After his father's death, he was stricken with an illness that today would be described as a nervous breakdown—a textbook example of the symptoms indicating an unresolved father-son relationship. He went through a profound religious crisis and always felt the intense discomfort former believers often suffer in the presence of manifestations of religious faith. He suffered exile and political reverses. He worked at times to the point of exhaustion, and did so in partnership and friendship with a dominating, if not domineering, figure of titanic proportions—Karl Marx.

Yet, while millions of others succumb to such trials, develop permanent neurotic traits, or become mediocrities, he seems to have coped with all his conflicts adequately, and to have thrived by doing so. Of course, there are some who will see in him not an exception, but a confirmation of the rule that greatness comes only to the profoundly alienated, and they will justify this by denying his greatness, arguing that his happiness was that of a mediocre person. There might be some who will suggest that the optimistic ideology he fashioned for himself, with its religion of rationality and deliverance and its firm belief in the cunning of reason, was a neurotic way of coping with alienation, but that would reduce the concept of neurosis to an empty phrase.

POSTSCRIPT

WHAT ARE WE to make of a man's life? When we know how fleeting is our time on earth, and miss the presence of those who have made an impact on us, when we still feel the lingering influence of those who played outstanding roles in history, and seek to leave some mark ourselves, some legacy that will cause someone else in the future to be curious about our own life and take the time to read what we have left behind by way of clues as to what animated and inspired us, what are we to make of our own life, and the lives of those close to us, and the lives of those whom we never knew, yet who nevertheless touched us by their actions, their words, and their deeds?

What, specifically, are we to make of this biography? How can we explain the interest that my father, Alfred Meyer, had in this person, Friedrich Engels, born within a few months of one hundred years before his own birth? What drove him to read the voluminous correspondence of this man for the sake a rendering his portrait much like a studio artist, but in words instead of paint? A partial answer, for me, lies in the way that we form connections with other people. We do so based on similarities in our nature, on points of resonance and identification. We must see something of ourselves in others for there to be such a connection, and when this occurs, we can form bonds and even relationships with people whom we have never met and will never meet, except perhaps in the hereafter.

Anyone who knew my father, reading his biography of Engels, would be struck by the transparent self-portrait it renders of himself. When he characterized Engel's contribution to his partnership with Marx as consisting of "an orderly mind, a quick intelligence, a fabulous memory for detail and a remarkably journalistic talent for writing clear, forthright, informative, and stimulating pieces on the shortest possible notice," he was succinctly describing his own manifest abilities. When he mentioned Engels's good humor, his qualities as a host and entertainer, his talent for telling jokes and stories, his dilettantism, and his encyclopedic knowledge, he could not have more effectively summed up the principal characteristics of his own personality. When he dwelled on Engels's émigré status, it must be remembered that he was himself an émigré, and by coincidence that his elder brother was a British citizen who made his lifelong home in Manchester.

When he wrote that Engels sent Christmas cards to his friends and went to hear performances of Handel's "Messiah," it is as if he was talking about himself. Deeply uncomfortable with the Christian religion, whose history he viewed mainly as a bloody succession of inquisitions, colonization, and forced conversions, he was nevertheless an ardent lover of choral music, and sent out homemade greeting cards during the holiday season with as much Christmas spirit as Bob Cratchit. When he described Engels as in many ways a private person, in money matters careful to the point of finickiness, whose "favorite trait in men was to mind their own business, and in women not to mislay things," he also came close to self-portraiture. His description of Marx's painful home life and his regret at having married at all is poignant, since my father was often uncomfortable with his married life, frequently felt henpecked, and at such times sought to escape into solitude with his work.

My father did not excuse Engels's bourgeois attitudes and prejudices, yet his delight in uncovering and poking fun at these notably ironic frailties in his subject was equaled by his recognition and occasional struggle with similar tendencies in himself. He was often contemptuous American middle class attitudes and values, even while he was grateful to this country for having given him a home and conscious of his privileged position as a member of an intellectual elite. Moreover, he enjoyed life. He loved nothing more than relaxing at his summer home in Maine, entertaining guests, picking wild mushrooms or blueberries, cooking an occasional gourmet meal, and drinking a good wine with it.

The fact that Engels was a bohemian who took a two- or three-month vacation from the revolution in Burgundy appealed as much to him as did Engels's political idealism and his attempt to identify with the working class.

When he noted in his introduction to the biography (offered here as the conclusion), that Engels had written, *"Wir haben nicht umsonst gelebt!"* (We have not lived in vain) at a high point in his life, he commented additionally that Engels "had just visited a brother whom he had not seen for many years. He had then been feted in grand style at an international workers' congress, and had been elated to observe the strength and confidence of the movement. He had just fallen in love with a young woman, and was accompanied on his travels by another young woman he loved. Wherever he had gone during his trip, dear and adoring friends had surrounded him." Here he wrote as if he was dreaming of such a moment for himself, in which the abundance of life would in one portion be heaped on his plate, giving him the reassurance of having pursued a course of meaning and purpose.

When he wrote that "Engels subjected the world of his parents and peers to serious questions, again and again, and in that process defined his own role very differently from the wishes of his parents," perhaps only I, as his son, can know how deeply ambivalent he was in the role of a father. Fatherhood was often an intensely uncomfortable position for him, perhaps because he had secretly chafed at his own father's Victorian and Prussian attitudes. Thus, throughout his tenure as a parent, he encouraged his children to rebel, yet was equally aggrieved when they in fact did so. The way that Engels bargained with his parents to retain his privileged status was clearly amusing to him because he himself was just such a parent, bankrolling his children so that they could afford to protest the war and still go bumming around Europe the next summer.

When he wrote about "the Hegelian left, and its rather directionless activism so reminiscent of the American New Left in the 1960s," the ambivalence he felt toward the student counterculture of the 60s is manifest. On the one hand, he cheered the student protests, seeing them as evidence of a heartening passion and budding political awareness. On the other hand, he was skeptical of their naïveté, with the heightened historical perspective that his experience as a scholar of the communist movement gave him. He was more affected by the 60s than his children, wore a peace ring up to his dying day, and would have been dismayed to see how thoroughly forgotten those activist days are now, and how timid and conservative our present-day political culture has become.

In a chapter of his memoir not included here, he laid out the basis for his philosophy of 'male feminism,' yet this did not preclude him from enjoying 'special' relationships with his female students. He took particular joy in his relationship with Susan Fair, a former prisoner to whom he became an academic advisor and later something of a father figure. He was particularly fascinated by the insights she gave him into the prison system, and he entitled his memoir "My Life as a Fish," using a prison term he learned from her for a newly incarcerated prisoner. His relationship with her to some extent mirrors that which Engels carried on his whole life with proletarian women.

When my father wrote with undisguised irony about Engels's hypocrisy in championing the cause of the working class while allowing himself the privilege of the unequal relationships with women that his lower class associations afforded him, he may or may not have been aware that the same was true of him, who wished to see himself as a male feminist, yet nevertheless doted on the attentions of female undergraduates that were hardly his intellectual equals. In the description of his relationship with Susan Fair, we get a sense that he was secretly stimulated by the very 'proletarian' nature of her background and prison experiences, an intellectual indulgence that he patently shared with Engels.

His biography also offers us the chance to look at the lives and work of Karl Marx and Friedrich Engels at a time when they are perhaps regarded as less relevant than at any period in the past century. When he depicts Engels's Manchester writings as attacking the "humanist inversion of both theology and the bourgeois state leading to the 'materialist' conviction that the real life of a society goes on in its productive activities," one gets a sense not only of the idealism, indeed the intense Romanticism, that gave birth to the communist movement, but also of the continuing validity of that critique in the face of the rampant consumer society of today. In quoting Engels on the slogan of contemporary political leaders such as Bismarck and Napoleon III, *Ne soyons pas larrons* (We are not crooks), he cannot help writing in a footnote, "How familiar the ring of this," hearkening back, of course, to Richard Nixon. In describing Engels's contempt for the *Spiessbürger* and Philistines he could just as easily be referring to Middle Americans or George W. Bush, confirming that these cultural divisions are with us today just as much as they were prominent in Engels's time.

It is clear from the biography that what really set Engels against the bourgeoisie was not so much the unequal distribution of wealth in the society, but the *consciousness* of the members of this class, the fact that they could not go beyond the narrow limits of their ingrained thinking. Moreover, he and Marx did not necessarily believe that to participate in the revolution meant that one had to be in a state of constant rebellion. On the contrary, as my father quotes Engels in a letter to Marx, they conceived of the revolution as an inevitable maelstrom that would engulf everyone, and believed the best that one could do was simply "stay out as long as possible, maintain one's independence, and be 'in substance' more revolutionary than anyone else." In other words, to be a revolutionary was not necessarily a matter of action, but of attitude.

What are we to make of the downfall, indeed the disgrace, of the communist movement? How prescient were Engels's comments that it would all come to naught if it came into the hands of the wrong people! How impractical, idealistic, and indeed Romantic, their ideas seem to us now! All we have to note, in order to negate Marx and Engels's arguments, is that in this world individuals are *not* equal. They do not have the same capacities, the same talents, or the same power. For this reason, the weak must be protected, and the essential question is how to ensure such protection without destroying the dynamic qualities of the society.

Yet, at the same time, how continually valid is their essential critique of capitalism! For what are we to make of the increasing cultural polarization of American society, in which a liberal, urban intelligentsia is pitted against the rural working class and suburban petit-bourgeoisie preoccupied with 'family values' and Christian morality and exploited by a ruthless neo-conservative clique whose only interest seems to be in extending their own power and wealth? What are we to make of the control exerted over our political and economic life by the very military-industrial complex about which Dwight Eisenhower warned in his farewell Radio and TV speech to the country in 1951? When Engels wrote about the conflict between barbarism and civilization, how could he have foreseen that 150 years later, the same issues would still be seen as at stake in a world caught in a powerful clash of opposing cultures?

To some extent, the powerful interest that my father had in Engels's life was fueled by differences as well as commonalities. There were qualities about Engels's life that my father admired and even envied, because in possessing them Engels had been richer than he. The undisguised delight that my father took in exercising his intellectual prowess was something that he perhaps shared equally with Engels, but the intimate intellectual collaboration that Engels forged with Marx was almost unique in history, and was not something that my father could possibly have experienced in equal measure. His admiration for the close communication between the two men, and his wonderment at the way they were on each other's 'wavelength,' comes close to that which one might expect from an observer of a great romance.

My father shared Engels's need for friendships and yet was equally skeptical toward this need, for his trust in people had at times been misplaced and hardly anything caused him more upset in his life. Thus, he wrote, "If there was anything in the personality of Engels that strikes me as not entirely 'normal' or 'mature,' it would be his remarkable need for friends, especially older ones to whom he could look up and for whom he could play second fiddle, and his unshakeable loyalty to friends (indeed, to the friends and families of friends) even when everyone else knew they were scoundrels."

My father also clearly envied the prescience, or luck, that enabled Marx and Engels to find a place within the very center of the historical maelstrom. When we compare this sense of destiny that the two men shared with the academic life that my father led, far from the field of political engagement, we can understand why the feelings of contempt her harbored for Henry Kissinger, once a fellow graduate student with him at Harvard, were tinged with envy. He once noted that political scientists were people who could not succeed at being politicians, thus acknowledging his role as someone who looked at history from the sidelines. Engels, throughout his life, was in rebellion against his own bourgeois values, and my father identified with his predicament because on some level he probably regretted the largely conventional life that he had shaped for himself.

Most of all, I think that my father admired Marx and Engels's energy above all else. In every instance in this biography, we are aware of the drive of these two individuals, who felt that they saw clearer and farther than the mass of people, and who burned with a desire to pass on their self-consciousness and awareness to those same masses. The fact that they were dedicated to a cause that was completely impractical only made them work harder. In this sense, they had the temperament of artists, and indeed my father notes that Marx thought of his writings as an artistic whole. Who today thinks of Marx as an artist? Yet, precisely when the political relevance of Marx and Engels's work is in greatest doubt, its artistic and spiritual significance can perhaps be appreciated.

We tend to put historical figures into categories, to accord them a particular place or role in history, and then to think of them only in those terms. Marx and Engels had the misfortune to be elevated to the status of deities when their long hoped-for revolution occurred—not in Western Europe, as they expected—but in Russia in 1917. They are now caricatured because of the ultimate failure and collapse of that revolution and others that followed it. They are seen as ideologists, political and economic theoreticians, rabble-rousers, and amateur political strategists, and so identified in the public mind with historical events that occurred long after their time (and at which they would probably have been shocked and horrified) that they are judged today as irrelevant. A human life, however, is never irrelevant, and my father was interested in the lives

Marx and Engels in a fundamentally humanistic and even spiritual sense that can only be appreciated by reading his narrative of Engels's life.

While my father would not have used the term 'spiritual' to describe his subjects, the meaning of the word is worth considering. It is a loaded word that today generally causes people to stare blankly or react in some mechanical or knee-jerk fashion. Few people can offer a definition of it. In trying to define it myself, I would maintain first and foremost, that it has nothing whatsoever to do with religious belief or political persuasion. Atheists can be as spiritual as believers and communists as spiritual as capitalists. Spirituality properly denotes the sum and substance, even the essence of a man's life. It refers to the purpose for which a person lived, and thus has nothing whatsoever to do with one's belief system or the lack of it. To express this sum, this substance, this essence of Engels's life, was my father's aim in writing this biography.

My father's narrative clearly demonstrates that Engels lived a nuanced life that cannot be reduced to his role as one of the founders of communism. He was a complex individual with many different sides to his nature—an idealistic dreamer and a ruthless political operator, a rebel in relation to his family, who nevertheless compromised in order to retain his family connections, a dogmatic ideologist who nonetheless was capable of admitting his errors. The connecting thread between these diverse qualities was his sense of purpose. If such dedication to something beyond one's personal interest is not among the greatest of spiritual characteristics, then I don't know what is.

Something done with a spiritual purpose is anything that has the aim of raising, expanding, heightening, or broadening the consciousness or awareness of others. Marx and Engels did that. They, more than any other individuals in history gave the world an awareness of class divisions, class conflict, and the class struggle that was then, and is still, a major factor in the reality of our world. Through their work, major efforts have been periodically taken and are still ongoing in every corner of the globe to reduce, control, manage, alleviate, and eliminate class differences and conflicts. While communism failed as a political system, its constituent concepts nevertheless remain a potent ideological force in the world today.

Thus, more than anything, what my father appears to have been fascinated with was the energy, purpose, and sense of mission that Marx and Engels possessed. A question that my father left unasked, but which is under the surface of the entire biography is "Why did these men work so tirelessly and sacrifice themselves so utterly for what appears in the hindsight of history to have been such a chimeral purpose?" It is difficult for us to understand, perhaps, because class conflict has been reduced in our age, or obscured by religious and ethnic conflicts that have overshadowed them. We do not see as much of the egregious exploitation of workers that was so prevalent in the Victorian Age, nor are the differences between bourgeois and proletarian as pronounced. But exploitation and oppression of the powerful over the powerless continues today in many forms and in many places.

From a spiritual viewpoint, this is perhaps inevitable, since in the physical world individuals are not truly equal in their capacities and power, or at least not in their conscious awareness of them. Conflict and exploitation of man by man is thus unavoidable, perhaps, in this world, and yet what a powerful spiritual urge it is for man to dream otherwise, and even more, to work and sacrifice their very lives for such a dream!

ENDNOTES

THE STANDARD SOURCE for the writings of Engels and Marx that my father used was the edition published in Berlin, German Democratic Republic, in the 1950s and 1960s. It is cited as MEW, which stands for *Marx und Engels, Werke*. The volume and page numbers follow any reference to MEW. In MEW, the last volumes contain the correspondence of Engels and Marx, i.e. the letters they wrote to each other and to third parties. These are cited beginning with the sender, with addressee and date following (e.g. M to Bebel, January 15, 1878). Since the letters are arranged chronologically, this is a sufficient guide to anyone who wishes to check the accuracy of his citations or translations. He refers to Marx and Engels in his citations by their initials, M and E.

In citing works other than their letters, he was careful always to indicate the specific book, essay, article, draft, etc., that was cited, since he detested the habit of some authors to cite Marx and Engels as if they were scripture, simply by reference to the volume and page of their collected works, leaving it to the reader to find out when and under what circumstances the words were written.

[1] Prof. Helmut Hirsch, in a personal note, called my attention to a family legend according to which the name originally was d'Ange. See also Wolfgang Köllman, *Sozialgeschichte der Stadt Barmen im 19. Jahrhundert*, Tübingen, 1960, and Helmut Hirsch, *Friedrich Engels*, Rowohlt Verlag, 1968.
[2] See W. O. Henderson, *The Life of Friedrich Engels*, vol. 1, p. 3, London, 1976.
[3] E to Mohrhenn, October 9, 1890
[4] E to M, March 17, 1845
[5] Origins of the Family, MEW 21, pp. 72-3
[6] See his letter to Kautsky, October 17, 1888

[7] See his remark about the bourgeoisie of his hometown in a letter to Theodor Cune, June 10, 1872. For the bourgeois of the Wupper Valley, the big metropolis was Düsseldorf, some twenty or thirty miles away, "a small Paris, where the pious gentlemen of Barmen and Elberfeld kept their mistresses, went to the theater, and amused themselves royally."

[8] E to M, March 17, 1845

[9] E to Ludwig Schorlemmer, July 28, 1892

[10] Gustav Mayer, *Friedrich Engels*, p. 14

[11] Henderson, op. cit., p. 6

[12] Steven Marcus, *Engels, Manchester, and the Working Class*, Random House, New York, 1972, pp. 72-4

[13] Ibid. pp. 69-72

[14] Ibid.

[15] MEW 1, pp. 413-32

[16] E to Hermann Engels, January 9, 1877

[17] E to Wilhelm Graeber, October 1839

[18] Siegfried's Heimat, MEW Ergänzungsband II, pp. 108-9

[19] E to Filippo Turati, June 6, 1893

[20] Lombardische Streifzüge, MEW Ergänzungsband II, p. 154

[21] E to Paul Lafargue, September 2, 1891. Another topic of interest to him in his youth, and to which he returned in old age, was the critical examination of the New Testament, especially the Book of Revelation. In the last ten years of his life, he treated this theme in three different articles, and his treatment was based on lectures he had heard in 1841 at the University of Berlin.

[22] Ernst Moritz Arndt, MEW Ergänzungsband II, p. 122. See also "German Conditions" *The Northern Star*, October 25, 1845, MEW 2, pp. 568-9

[23] MEW Ergänzungsband II, pp. 137-8

[24] See his report of a journey to Bremerhaven, Ibid. p. 85

[25] Ernst Moritz Arndt, Ibid. pp. 121-2

[26] E to Wilhelm Graeber, November 13-20, 1839

[27] E to Wilhelm Graeber, November 13-20, 1839. See also E to Friedrich Graeber, December 1839 to February 1840.

[28] From an essay published in *Telegraph für Deutschland*, February 1840 in MEW Ergänzungsband II, p. 28

[29] From an early essay in literary criticism, see Ergänzungsband II, p. 46. In literary style, Goethe represented Reason to him, Jean Paul Richter represented fantasy and sentiment, and Boerne and Heine were credited with having begun the reconciliation and synthesis, Boerne from the side of Reason, Heine from the side of Poetry.

[30] Ergänzungsband II, pp. 120-1

[31] E to Friedrich Graeber, July 12-27, 1839. See also E to Wilhelm Graeber, July 30, 1839.

[32] E to Friedrich Graeber, July 12-27, 1839

[33] *Neue Rheinische Zeitung*, June 17, 1848, MEW 5, p. 76

[34] From an article on Blanquism in *Der Volksstaat*, June 26, 1874, MEW 18, pp. 531-2

[35] Ibid. p. 532

[36] *Ullstein's Weltgeschichte*, vol. VI, pp. 236-8, Berlin, 1910

[37] Ibid. p. 208

[38] "Die Rolle der Gewalt in der Geschichte, MEW 21, pp. 409-10

[39] *Ullstein's Weltgeschichte*, vol. VI, p. 190

Endnotes

⁴⁰ Chapter II in *Germany—Revolution and Counterrevolution*, MEW 8, pp. 14-19

⁴¹ E to Friedrich Graeber, April 8-9, 1839

⁴² Friedrich Engels, *Cola di Rienzi*, Peter Hammer Verlag, Wuppertal, 1974

⁴³ MEW Ergänzungsband II, p. 151

⁴⁴ Ibid. p. 153

⁴⁵ *Der Triumph des Glaubens*, MEW Ergänzungsband II, pp. 300-1

⁴⁶ E to Conrad Schmidt, November 26, 1887

⁴⁷ Ludwig Feuerbach, MEW 21, p. 272

⁴⁸ "Schelling über Hegel." MEW Ergänzungsband II, p. 164

⁴⁹ *Dialectics of Nature*, MEW 20, p. 312. The men Engels named in this connection as exemplar Renaissance men included Leonardo, Dürer, Machiavelli, and Luther.

⁵⁰ *Schelling und die Offenbarung*, MEW Ergänzungsband II, pp. 219-21

⁵¹ E to M September 28-30, 1847

⁵² MEW Ergänzungsband I, p. 594

⁵³ E to Mehring, April 1895

⁵⁴ Gustav Mayer, op. cit., vol. I, p. 108

⁵⁵ E to Ruge, June 15, 1842

⁵⁶ E to Ruge, July 26, 1842

⁵⁷ E to Max Hildebrand, October 22, 1889

⁵⁸ "Zur Geschichte des Bundes der Kommunisten," MEW 8, p. 582

⁵⁹ See his lengthy review of Thomas Carlyle's *Past and Present*, January 1844, MEW 1, p. 527.

⁶⁰ "Briefe aus London," in *Schweizerischer Republikaner*, May 16, 1843, MEW 1, p. 468. See also his vivid description of the process of political mobilization of urbanized Irish peasants, " Briefe aus London," *Schweizerischer Republikaner*, June 27, 1843, pp. 478-9.

⁶¹ "Die innern Krisen," *Rheinische Zeitung*, December 9, 1842, MEW 1, pp. 456-60

⁶² "Fortschritte der Sozialreform auf dem Kontinent," *The New Moral World*, November 4, 1843, MEW 1, p. 483

⁶³ Ibid. p. 480ff.

⁶⁴ Ibid. p. 480-1

⁶⁵ Walter Victor, *General und die Frauen*

⁶⁶ Georg Weerth, *Sämtiliche Werke*, vol. I, Aufbau Verlag, Berlin, 1956, pp. 209-10

⁶⁷ Ludwig Feuerbach, MEW 21, p. 289

⁶⁸ Ibid. p. 285

⁶⁹ "Fortschritte der Sozialreform auf dem Kontinent," MEW 1, p. 481

⁷⁰ Review of Carlyle, *Past and Present*, MEW 1, p. 544

⁷¹ Ibid. p. 545

⁷² Karl Marx, Preface to *Zur Kritik der politische Ökonomie*, MEW 13, p. 10

⁷³ M to E, January 8, 1868

⁷⁴ E to Evgenia Eduardovna Paprits, June 26, 1884

⁷⁵ Friedrich Hebbel, letter to Elise Lensing, April 2, 1844, in *Sämtliche Werke*, vol. III, Richard Maria Werner, ed., B. Behr's Verlag, Berlin, 1905, pp. 73-4

⁷⁶ "Umrisse," MEW 1, p. 502

⁷⁷ Ibid. p. 503

⁷⁸ Ibid. p. 510. See also p. 514. The word 'self-externalization' is a translation of the German *Selbstveräusserung*, which means at the same time the *sale* of the self. It is a major failing of Bertell Ollman's otherwise excellent book not to have pointed this out. His consistent translation of the

term as 'self-alienation' comes close to mystification. See Bertell Ollman, *Alienation: Marx's Conception of Man in Capitalist Society*, Cambridge University Press, 1973

[79] Ibid. p. 520

[80] Ibid. pp. 513-14

[81] Ibid. pp. 515-16

[82] Ibid. p. 517ff.

[83] George Lukács, *Lenin: A Study on the Unity of His Thought*, MIT Press, Cambridge, 1971, p. 10

[84] See, for example, his preface to the first German edition of Karl Marx, *The Poverty of Philosophy*, MEW 4, p. 559

[85] "Die Lage Englands," MEW 1, pp. 550-92

[86] E to M, November 19, 1844

[87] Ibid.

[88] Steven Marcus, op. cit., p. 184

[89] *Die Lage der artbeitenden Klasse*, MEW 2, p. 504

[90] Ibid. pp. 238-9

[91] "A slum in Salford described by Engels in his 'Condition of the Working Class in England in 1844' is still standing, still inhabited, and perhaps in almost as bad a condition as it was in his day." From an article by Polly Toynbee, "If Engels Could See It Now," *The Observer*, London, February 3, 1974

[92] Op. cit. pp. 404-5, 431

[93] M to E, April 9, 1863. See also *Das Kapital*, vol. I, MEW 23, pp. 254-5, no. 48

[94] Henderson, op. cit., pp. 62ff

[95] M to Feuerbach, August 11, 1844

[96] MEW 21, pp. 211-12

[97] E to M, October 1844

[98] *Die Lage der arbeitenden Klasse*, MEW 2, p. 230. For other expressions of his opinions of the workers, see Ibid. pp. 454-5, 526-8

[99] From a review written for the *Rheinische Zeitung*, in MEW 16, p. 213. Engels was aware, however, that Marx had contributed one additional and crucial element, i.e., the theory of surplus value and its underlying theory of labor as a special kind of commodity. See *Anti-Dühring*, MEW 20, pp. 189-90; also M to E, August 24, 1867

[100] E to Becker, October 15, 1884

[101] Moses Hess, *Briefwechsel*, pp. 79-80

[102] Ibid.

[103] Ludwig Feuerbach, MEW 21, pp. 291-2

[104] Preface to the 1890 German edition of the *Manifesto*, MEW 4, p. 577

[105] *Zur Geschichte des Bundes der Kommunisten*, MEW 8, p. 582

[106] E to M, May 6, 1868

[107] *Zur Geschichte des Bundes der Kommunisten*, MEW 8, p. 583

[108] E to M, October 1844

[109] E to M, November 19, 1844

[110] Elberfeld Lectures, MEW 2, pp. 537-8, 555-7

[111] *Die Heilige Familie*, MEW 2, p. 85

[112] MEW 8, p. 278

[113] E to M, March 17, 1845

[114] Ibid.

[115] E to M, February-March 1845

[116] E to M, January 20, 1845

[117] See, for instance, E to M, December 1846

[118] E to M, March 9, 1847

[119] Here Engels ironically wrote in the stilted jargon of a business letter.

[120] E to M, January 14, 1848

[121] Stefan Born, *Erinnerungen eines Achtundvierzigers*

[122] *Die Deutsche Ideologie*, MEW 3, p. 27

[123] Ibid. p. 38

[124] Ibid. p. 179

[125] Ibid. p. 523

[126] Ibid. p. 459

[127] Ibid. p. 20

[128] "Deutscher Sozialismus in Versen und Prosa," MEW 4, p. 232

[129] *Die Deutsche Ideologie*, MEW 3, p. 18

[130] Ibid. p. 21

[131] Ibid. p. 22

[132] Ibid. p. 32

[133] Ibid. pp. 22-6

[134] Ibid. p. 424

[135] Ibid. p. 37

[136] Ibid. pp. 417-8

[137] Ibid. p. 239

[138] E to M, May 15, 1870

[139] E to Bernstein, June 12-13, 1883

[140] E to M, March 9, 1847

[141] *Zur Geschichte des Bundes der Kommunisten*, MEW 8, p. 578; MEW 21, p. 211

[142] Ibid. MEW 21, p. 219

[143] Ibid. MEW 8, p. 579

[144] "Grundsätze des Kommunismus," MEW 21, p. 219

[145] MEW 4, p. 40ff

[146] MEW 4, pp. 309-24

[147] E to M, September 28-30, 1847, October 25-6, 1847, November 14-15, 1847

[148] M to E, March 16, 1848

[149] E to M, November 19, 1844

[150] MEW 4, p. 530

[151] E to M, April 25, 1848. See also E to Emil Blank, April 15, 1848.

[152] "The Prussian Constitution," MEW 4, p. 33

[153] MEW 5, pp. 64-5

[154] E to Bernstein, January 18, 1883

[155] MEW 5, p. 64. See also his article on the Ten Hour Bill, written two years later, in MEW, p. 226. In the same spirit, he waxed enthusiastically about the first signs of a Red Terror in Hungary and hailed Lajos Kossuth as a new Danton and Carnot wrapped in one.

[156] See, for instance, his report on the June uprising, MEW 5, p. 127.

[157] Hess to Berthold Auerbach, December 13, 1841, in Moses Hess, *Briefwechsel*, p. 85.

[158] *The Conditions of the Working Class in England*, MEW 2, p. 505

[159] See, for instance, an article in the *New York Daily Tribune*, September 16, 1857, MEW 12, pp. 285-7.

[160] *Revolution und Konterrevolution in Deutschland*, MEW 8, p. 42

[161] "Marx und die *Neue Rheinische Zeitung*, 1848-1849," *Der Sozialdemokrat*, March 13, 1884, MEW 21, pp. 16-24

[162] Introduction to Karl Marx, *The Class Struggles in France*, MEW 22, pp. 514-5ff

[163] For a masterful treatment of a line taken by the paper on the nationalities problem, see Roman Rosdolsky, "Friedrich Engels und das Problem der 'geschichtslosen' Völker (Die Nationalitätenfrage in der Revolution 1848-1849 im Lichte der *Neuen Rheinische Zeitung*)," in *Archiv für Sozialgeschichte*, vol. IV, 1964, pp. 87-282. For his opinions about Jews at this time, see E to M, August 19, 1846.

[164] MEW 8, p. 81

[165] "Von Paris nach Bern," MEW 5, p. 471

[166] See his comments, written jointly with Marx, in the *Neue Rheinische Zeitung*, May-October 1850, MEW 7, p. 440; also his column on the Hungarian Revolution, *Neue Rheinische Zeitung*, January 13, 1849, MEW 6, p. 167.

[167] "Die Polendebatte in Frankfurt," *Neue Rheinische Zeitung*, August 20, 1848, MEW 5, p. 333

[168] Ibid. p. 479

[169] Introduction to Sigismund Borkheim, "Zur Erinnerung für die Deutschen Mordspatrioten, 1806-1807," MEW 21, p. 347

[170] M to E, November 1848

[171] E to M, December 28, 1848

[172] E to M, January 7-8, 1849

[173] MEW 4, pp. 391-8

[174] "German Conditions," *The Northern Star*, November 8, 1845, MEW 2, p. 577

[175] For accounts Engels gave of this episode, see MEW 6, pp. 500-2, and MEW 7, pp. 128-31.

[176] Article on the revolutionary movement in the Palatinate and Baden, June 3, 1849, MEW 6, pp. 525-6

[177] E to Weydemeyer, August 25, 1849

[178] E to Jakob Schabelitz, August 24, 1849

[179] E to Jenny Marx, July 25, 1849

[180] M to E, August 1, 1849

[181] "Die deutsche Reichsverfassungskampagne," MEW 7, pp. 137-8

[182] M to E, August 17, 1849

[183] M to E, August 23, 1849

[184] E to Wilhelm Wolff, May 1, 1851

[185] In a book review published in the *Neue Rheinische Zeitung*, Number II, MEW 7, p. 201

[186] "Die deutsche Reichverfassungskampagne," MEW 7, p. 196

[187] Ibid. p. 138

[188] MEW 7, p. 202

[189] E to George William Lamplugh, April 11, 1893

[190] "Die deutsche Reichverfassungskampagne," MEW 7, p. 112

[191] Ibid. p. 196

[192] 1870 Preface to "The German Peasant War," MEW 7, p. 536

[193] "The German Peasant War," MEW 7, p. 338

[194] In the *Neue Rheinische Zeitung*, 1850, MEW 7, p. 443

195 "Die deutsche Reichsverfassungskampagne," MEW 7, p. 126

196 MEW 5, p. 131

197 "Die deutsche Reichsverfassungskampagne," MEW 7, p. 129

198 "The 18th Brumaire of Louis Bonaparte," MEW 8, p. 142

199 "Die deutsche Reichsverfassungskampagne," MEW 7, pp. 126-8

200 "Circular to the League of Communists," MEW 7, pp. 246-54. I am in wholehearted agreement with Richard N. Hunt, *The Political Ideas of Marx and Engels*, vol. 1, (University of Pittsburgh Press, 1974), which argues at considerable length that even in their most "Bolshevik phase, Marx and Engels were extremely careful to curb their own and the workers' vengeful and destructive urges.

201 MEW 7, p. 446

202 Introduction to Karl Marx, *The Class Struggles in France*, MEW 7, pp. 514-7

203 See his article in *The New Moral World*, November 18, 1843, MEW 1, pp. 488-9.

204 *Neue Rheinische Zeitung*, MEW 7, p. 440

205 E to M, February 13, 1851; "Germany: Revolution and Counterrevolution," MEW 8, p. 5

206 "Zur Geschichte des Bundes der Kommunisten," MEW 21, p. 220

207 E to M, August 1, 1851

208 M to E, June 26, 1855

209 Elise Engels to E, December 2, 1849, and April 11, 1850

210 E to M, January 8, 1851

211 E to M, July 6, 1851

212 E to Conrad Schmidt, December 12, 1892

213 E to Pasquale Martignetti, January 26, 1887

214 E to M, July 6, 1851

215 Mayer, vol. 2, p. 61

216 Lester Shaw, "Through the Eye of the Needle," published on the 50th anniversary of The English Sewing Cotton Company, Manchester, 1947, p. 11

217 E to M, December 17, 1850

218 E to Emil Blank, December 3, 1850

219 Lester Shaw, op. cit.

220 E to Charlotte Engels, December 1, 1884. See also E to Emil Engels, April 11, 1860.

221 E to M, May 11, 1860; E to Elise Engels, February 13, 1861, February 27, 1861

222 E to Elise Engels, June 16, 1871

223 E to Jenny Marx, January 14, 1852

224 E to M, September 19, 1851

225 E to M, March 17, 1851

226 E to Ernst Dronke, July 9, 1851

227 E to Marie Blank, December 15, 1851

228 Ibid.

229 E to Weydemeyer, June 19, 1851

230 E to M, October 19, 1857

231 E to M, January 22, 1852; E to M, February 17, 1852; E to M, March 18, 1852; E to M, April 21, 1854

232 E to M, July 30, 1862

233 E to Marie Blank, November 22, 1852

234 E to M, February 12, 1851

[235] E to M, July 31, 1870

[236] From an article about Blanquism in *Der Volksstaat*, June 26, 1874, MEW 18, pp. 528-9. For yet another comment on the same topic, see E to Isaak Adolfovich Gurvich, May 27, 1894.

[237] E to M, February 12, 1851

[238] E to M, January 8, 1851

[239] E to M, July 20, 1851

[240] *Zur Geschichte des Bundes der Kommunisten*, MEW 21, p. 221

[241] MEW 27, p. 563; also E to Weydemeyer, April 12, 1853

[242] E to M, May 9, 1851; E to M, February 13, 1851

[243] M to E, March 10, 1853; E to M, March 11, 1853; E to M, April 20, 1854

[244] E to M, April 10, 1853; M to E, September 28, 1852

[245] M to E, February 9, 1860

[246] E to M, May 1, 1852

[247] E to M, October 10, 1852; E to M, October 31, 1852

[248] Jenny Marx to E, December 2, 1850

[249] In a questionnaire submitted to him by Marx's daughter Jenny, MEW 32, p. 695

[250] E to M, December 28, 1848

[251] E to M, January 20, 1845

[252] Ibid.

[253] E to Bernstein, February 27, 1881; March 1, 1881

[254] From a review of *Das Kapital*, vol. 1, placed in *Demokratisches Wochenblatt*, March 28, 1868, MEW 16, p. 239

[255] E to M, May 1, 1854

[256] E to Emil Blank, April 1846

[257] Lizzy's living with Mary is mentioned as early as M to E, January 22, 1851.

[258] M to E, December 27, 1863

[259] E to M, February 13, 1851; E to M, October 27, 1852

[260] E to M, October 19, 1857

[261] E to M, August 12, 1868

[262] E to Natalie Liebknecht, September 17, 1878

[263] M to Jenny Marx, September 17, 1878

[264] E to M, July 6, 1869

[265] E to Elisabeth Engels, April 20, 1859. See also E to M, February 5, 1865.

[266] M to E, April 19, 1864; also M to E, December 10, 1869

[267] E to Bebel, February 2, 1892

[268] E to M, February 17, 1870; July 7, 1870; E to Jenny Marx, January 3, 1868

[269] E to Elisabeth Engels, October 21, 1871

[270] E to Jenny Marx, November 5, 1859

[271] E to M, November 17, 1859

[272] E to Carl Siebel, June 4, 1862

[273] E to M, February 7, 1865

[274] E to Kugelmann, November 8-20, 1867

[275] E to M, April 26, 1868

[276] E to M, December 31, 1857; see also his description of a hare hunt, E to M, February 11, 1858

[277] "Socialism, Utopian and Scientific..." MEW 19, p. 219E

278 E to Elisabeth Engels, April 20, 1859
279 From Jenny Marx's questionnaire to him, August 1868, MEW 32, p. 695
280 E to M, November 5-6, 1852; E to M, January 11, 1853; E to M, June 10, 1854; E to M, July 20, 1854
281 M to E, February 27, 1861
282 E to Ludwig Schorlemmer, July 1, 1892
283 E to Emil Engels, Jr., December 22, 1868
284 See, for instance, E to M, April 12, 1865
285 Karl Marx, "Die britische Konstitution," *Neue Oder-Zeitung*, March 6, 1855, MEW 11, pp. 96-7
286 E to M, September 27, 1856
287 E to M, November 15, 1857; E to M, December 31, 1857. For Marx's agreement with this diagnosis, see M to Lassalle, May 31, 1858.
288 E to M, July 22, 1870
289 M to E, February 13, 1863
290 M to E, September 11, 1867
291 M to E, April 13, 1867
292 MEW 32, p. 695
293 Ibid.
294 E to Philipp Pauli, December 16, 1876
295 Paul Lafargue to Danielson, December 14, 1889
296 MEW 32, p. 695
297 E to M, November 19, 1844
298 E to M, April 24, 1870
299 E to Jenny Longuet, April 11, 1881
300 E to Elisabeth Engels, April 20, 1859
301 "Dialectics of Nature," MEW 20, p. 312
302 E to Berstein, May 22, 1886
303 E to M, July 19, 1877
304 E to Emil Engels, Jr., August 20, 1882
305 E to Rudolf Engels, March 10, 1871
306 E to Carl Klein and Friedrich Moll, February 8, 1870
307 E to Bebel, May 10-11, 1883
308 E to M, April 27, 1867
309 "Die Abdankung der Bourgeoisie," MEW 21, pp. 383-7
310 "Die Rolle der Gewalt in der Geschichte," MEW 21, p. 458; see also *Anti-Dühring*, MEW 20, p. 105, and E to Bebel, April 12, 1886.
311 MEW 7, p. 434
312 "Die grossen Männer des Exils, MEW 8, p. 276
313 How familiar the sound of this!
314 E to M, April 27, 1867
315 See his article on the Ten Hour Bill, *The Democratic Review*, March 1850, MEW 7, p. 226.
316 E to M, May 1, 1866
317 E to Bebel, August 25, 1881. For other expressions of hope for vengeance, see E to M, December 14, 1866, E to M, April 14, 1856, E to Becker, April 2, 1885, and E to Rudolf Schramm, May 6, 1858
318 E to Laura Lafarge, September 13, 1886

[319] E to M, September 5, 1874

[320] MEW 21, p. 350

[321] Reply to Paul Ernst, MEW 22, pp. 81-3; E to F. H. Nestler & Melle, Publishers, September 11, 1886; E to Directors of the Schiller Institute, May 3, 1851

[322] Preface to the English edition of *Socialism, Utopian and Scientific*, MEW 22, p. 298

[323] E to Laura Lafargue, July 23, 1888

[324] In early 1845, both Marx and Engels independently of each other had similar ideas about publications they might want to issue, including a series of translations of major socialist literature and a critique of the economic ideas of Friedrich List, E to M, March 17, 1845. In one of his last letters to Engels, Marx notes with amazement how his response to a letter from his daughter Eleanor is identical, almost word for word, with that given by Engels, M to E, August 3, 1882.

[325] M to E, July 4, 1864

[326] M to Kugelmann, December 28, 1862

[327] M to E, July 15, 1858

[328] M to E, November 8, 1866

[329] "I hope the money will drive your carbuncles away," Engels wrote to him on October 22, 1867. See also M to Kugelmann, April 6, 1866.

[330] Jenny Marx to Kugelmann, January 30, 1869

[331] M to Kugelmann, October 13, 1866

[332] Jenny Marx to E, December 23 or 24, 1859

[333] M to E, October 3, 1866; E to M, October 5, 1866

[334] See M to E, November 24, 1851

[335] M to Lion Philips, June 25, 1864

[336] E to M, August 3, 1870; M to E, August 4, 1870

[337] M to E, September 11, 1855

[338] M to E, February 27, 1852

[339] M to E, July 15, 1858

[340] See her letter to Engels, April 27, 1853

[341] M to E, December 11, 1858

[342] M to E, February 22, 1858

[343] M to E, July 31, 1865

[344] M to E, July 22, 1869

[345] E to M, September 12, 1882; M to E, September 16, 1882

[346] E to M, March 9, 1853

[347] M to E, June 27, 1868

[348] E to M, December 3, 1860

[349] E to M, January 22, 1857

[350] E to M, October 11, 1867, October 15, 1867, October 18, 1867

[351] E to M, May 1, 1851, January 26, 1863; M to E, May 15, 1847

[352] E to M, April 8, 1863

[353] For example, E to M, November 12-15, 1847

[354] M to Jenny Marx, June 21, 1856

[355] See, for instance, M to Jenny Longuet, August 19, 1879

[356] M to E, August 8, 1851

[357] E to M, August 10, 1851

[358] M to Weydemeyer, January 25, 1852

[359] In a Marx biography, *Handwörterbuch der Staatswissenschaften*, MEW 22, p. 340

[360] E to M, January 22, 1852

[361] For instance, the article on the Crimean War published January 2, 1855, MEW 10, p. 588ff

[362] E to M, September 25, 1851, April 1, 1852

[363] M to E, January 25, 1854

[364] E to M, April 22, 1857

[365] E to Hermann Schlüter, January 29, 1891

[366] E to M, June 6, 1853

[367] M to Lassale, January 16, 1861

[368] E to M, December 3, 1851, December 10, 1851, December 11, 1851

[369] M to E, August 17, 1870. See also Engels's reply, September 4, 1870

[370] Preface to the 1885 edition of Karl Marx, *The Poverty of Philosophy*, MEW 21, p. 176

[371] *Anti-Dühring*, MEW 20, pp. 189-90

[372] "The best part of my book is (1)—and *all* understanding of the facts is based on this—the *double character of labor* emphasized right away in the first chapter, depending on whether it expresses itself as use value or exchange value; and (2) the treatment of *surplus value independently* of its special form as profit, interest, ground rent, etc.," M to E, August 24, 1867

[373] E to M, early October 1844, January 20, 1845

[374] E to M, April 3, 1851

[375] M to E, July 31, 1851

[376] M to Weydemeyer, June 26, 1851

[377] M to E, November 24, 1851

[378] E to M, November 27, 1851

[379] M to E, December 8, 1857, December 18, 1857

[380] M to Lassalle, February 22, 1858

[381] E to M, April 9, 1858

[382] M to E, February 13, 1866

[383] E to M, May 19, 1851

[384] M to Laura and Paul Lafargue, April 11, 1868

[385] See, for instance, Wilhelm Pieper's letter to Engels, January 27, 1851, MEW 27, p. 169

[386] M to Sigfrid Meyer, April 30, 1867

[387] M to E, July 31, 1865

[388] M to E, February 20, 1866

[389] E to M, August 7, 1865

[390] E to M, April 4, 1867

[391] M to E, August 16, 1867

[392] M to E, May 7, 1868; E to M, May 10, 1868; M to E, May 16, 1868

[393] E to M, April 15, 1870

[394] M to E, June 7, 1859

[395] Marx followed his advice carefully. See E to M, June 16, 1867 and M to E, June 17, 1867

[396] E to M, February 25, 1851

[397] M to E, January 7, 1851; E to M, January 29, 1851

[398] E to M, November 19, 1869. Marx replied with a long letter, November 26, 1869.

[399] M to E, April 22, 1868; E to M, April 26, 1868; M to E, April 30, 1868

[400] E to M, September 9, 1862

[401] MEW 16, pp. 243-87

[402] M to E, June 22, 1867

[403] E to M, June 23, 1867. Anyone who has struggled through *Das Kapital* will be grateful to Engels for this confession.

[404] E to M, June 24, 1867

[405] E to M, September 11, 1867

[406] M to E, September 12, 1867

[407] E to Kugelmann, November 8, 1867, November 20, 1867

[408] E to M, November 5, 1867

[409] E to Kugelmann, November 20, 1867

[410] M to Bartalan Szemere, November 22, 1860; M to Kugelmann, October 25, 1866; M to Laura and Paul Lafargue, March 5, 1870; M to E, January 20, 1864; M to Jenny Marx, August 8, 1856

[411] M to E, February 20, 1866

[412] M to Jenny Marx, June 21, 1856

[413] H. M. Hyndman, *The Record of an Adventurous Life*, 1911, p. 279

[414] M to Jenny Longuet, March 16, 1882, March 27, 1882

[415] M to E, December 12, 1853, December 14, 1853

[416] M to Kugelmann, July 13, 1867; M to Lassalle, February 25, 1859

[417] Engels's speech at Marx's grave, MEW 19, pp. 335-6; "Karl Marx," biographical sketch for a people's calendar, 1878, MEW 19, pp. 102-4; review of Karl Marx, *Zur Kritik der politischen Ökonomie*, published in *Das Volk*, August 6, 1859, MEW 13, pp. 470-1

[418] E to M, March 9, 1847

[419] E to M, June 28, 1860; E to Jenny Marx, August 15, 1860

[420] E to Weydemeyer, August 7, 1851

[421] I would hesitate to go along with Steven Marcus, who suggests that Engels's attachment to the Burns sisters must be understood in light of the fact that his mother's name was Elizabeth and his favorite sister's Marie. I do agree with him that one can see something exploitative and thoroughly bourgeois in his relationship with proletarian and peasant women, including not only the Burns sisters but also his many liaisons in Brussels, Paris, and rural Paris, i.e. in his bohemian period. See Steven Marcus, op. cit., pp. 99-100, especially the footnotes.

[422] M to E, January 8, 1863

[423] M to Kugelmann, August 10, 1868

[424] M to Danielson, October 7, 1868

[425] M to Kugelmann, March 3, 1869

[426] Jenny Marx to E, January 17, 1870

[427] M to Danielson, December 12, 1872

[428] E to M, November 17, 1869, January 19, 1870

[429] E to Kugelmann, April 28, 1871

[430] M to Danielson, June 13, 1871

[431] M to Kugelmann, May 18, 1874

[432] M to E, May 21, 1873

[433] M to Sorge, November 5, 1880

[434] M to Sorge, June 21, 1872

[435] M to Danielson, April 10, 1879

[436] For instance, in his Marx biography for the 1878 people's calendar, MEW 19, p. 106

[437] E to Bebel, April 31, 1883

[438] E to Lavrov, January 28, 1884. See also E to Danielson, March 5, 1895

439 E to Laura Lafargue, May 22, 1883
440 E to Bebel, August 30, 1883
441 E to Laura Lafargue, March 8, 1885
442 E to Danielson, November 13, 1885
443 E to Bebel, August 30, 1883. See Engels, Preface to *Das Kapital*, vol. 2, MEW 24, p. 12
444 Steven Marcus, op. cit., p. 248
445 Hegel, *Philosophy of Right*, pp. 12-13, quoted ibid
446 M to E, February 13, 1863
447 E to Adolph Sorge, June 29, 1883
448 Cited in Mark Twain, *On the Damned Human Race*, Janet Smith, ed., Hill and Wang, New York, 1962, p.111
449 Marx and Engels, *Die grossen Männer des Exile*, MEW 8, p.236
450 Apparently Carl G. Jung did not always agree with this. "The pathological is never valuable," he wrote in a letter. "It does, however, cause us the greatest difficulties and for this reason we learn the most from it... The normal person is infinitely more interesting and valuable." Cited in Rosemary Dinnage, "Jung and God," *The New York Review of Books*, XXIII/6, April 15, 1976, p.27

G. Meyer Books welcomes submissions in the genres of
history, biography & autobiography, and contemporary social issues. Send
inquiries via the G. Meyer Books web site at http://www.gmeyerbooks.com.

 G.MeyerBooks